Successful Management in the Digital Age

Successful Management in the Digital Age

John Harte

Transaction Publishers
New Brunswick (U.S.A.) and London (U.K.)

Library of Congress Catalog Number: 2015047585
ISBN: 978-1-4128-6277-6 (hardcover); 978-1-4128-6324-7 (paperback)
eBook: 978-1-4128-6227-1
Printed in the United States of America

Library of Congress Cataloging-in-Publication Data

Names: Harte, John, 1925- author.
Title: Successful management in the digital age / by John Harte.
Description: New Brunswick : Transaction Publishers, 2016. | Includes
    bibliographical references and index.
Identifiers: LCCN 2015047585 (print) | LCCN 2016008778 (ebook) |
    ISBN 9781412862776 (hardcover) | ISBN 9781412863247 (pbk.) |
    ISBN 9781412862271 (ebook) | ISBN 9781412862271
Subjects: LCSH: Industrial management--Technological innovations.|
    Leadership. | Advertising. | Selling.
Classification: LCC HD45 .H337 2016 (print) | LCC HD45 (ebook) |
    DDC 658--dc23 LC record available at http://lccn.loc.gov/
                                                        2015047585

For my daughter, Genevieve Harte,
whose initiatives with challenges and problem solving
have always made her a superior manager.

Contents

1

Introduction

Professional managers and industry leaders want knowledge to understand their particular spheres of interest and their own lives, in order to control their future. They want to be able to predict events, instead of allowing them to unfold against their best interests. They want to know what will happen if they select one course of action in preference to any others. This book shows how it can be achieved with different skills that are essential for any business to survive by penetrating the market, achieving a suitable market share, showing a profit, and remaining constantly vigilant for new trends and also possibilities of discontinuous change. It is about how to take control and overcome obstacles.

Bill Gates described the new algorithmic technology as a digital nervous system that enables a company "to perceive and react to its environment, to sense competitor challenges and customer needs and to organize timely responses." Although it is an elegant definition, it might lead entrepreneurs and corporate executives to suppose that the new electronic hardware and software makes inputs and outputs by managers unnecessary, as if we have achieved a society and an economy in which everything can be done by algorithms. Economist and Nobel prizewinner Wassily Leontief, who conceived a basic idea for input-output economics, "dreamed of creating a tool that societies could use to achieve a better life for all, an instrument that would give humanity greater control over its destiny," long before the recent invention of programmed electronic devices.[1] So it would not be unreasonable to ask why global economies are in the doldrums after the introduction of all the wonderful new technological inventions and innovations.

One answer might be that it has already bred complacency, which is possibly the biggest drawback in any type of business enterprise. Complacency can erode the initiative and momentum required of business managers, entrepreneurs, and marketing managers, who should rather be motivated to aspire to market leadership in their operational

1

sphere. The complacency of a chief executive of any large established organization, for example, is likely to result from historic successes that blind him or her to warning signals that may point to sudden failure. In short, past success can create an illusion of wisdom and invulnerability. On the other hand, there is the typical complacency of small business entrepreneurs who acquire investment capital without a comprehensive business plan and pay no attention to time. They become easily distracted by minor activities and time-consuming technological devices, at the expense of their primary objective, because they fail to establish goals and prioritize. Past success at obtaining investors leads them to believe they can borrow more capital when the initial funds are exhausted. But time typically runs out and is irreplaceable, so that any temporary success can turn into failure if they don't perfect a prototype on time.

Whereas the English Industrial Revolution led to expansion and modernization and the second industrial revolution in the United States to electrification, business bustle, and a rise in Western living standards, the new electronics revolution appears to have run its course, in much the same way that the dotcom revolution did before it collapsed. In the excitement of all the novel electronic devices, media, and games, we seem to have lost sight of the fact that management and marketing require the inputs and outputs of perceptive and analytical managers and marketers who take personal control by recognizing that new technologies are simply useful tools they need to know how to use effectively, and not executive toys that waste our time by misdirecting our attention and thinking from quality content to hardware devices.

Ironically, what Bill Gates pointed out when extolling the virtues of the new digital technologies was "The year 2000 and beyond will be marked by the word *speed*." What he failed to also mention were distractions, misdirection, and delusions.

The Law of Unintended Consequences

Despite the twenty-first century probably being tagged by historians as the digital age, business success depends more on marketing, creativity, and management than on technology. It is true we produced automation and robotics to replace many of the dull and repetitive laboring jobs in industry and do them quicker and, ironically, reduced our consumer base, as part of the law of unintended consequences. And it is not beyond our abilities to develop interactive technologies that make even more intelligent judgments for us in future with quantum computers.

We may yet produce a jobless society in which the rich 20 percent of the population provide goods and services electronically and pay a higher level of taxes to support the unemployed 80 percent in leisure, so that they can afford to buy what robots produce. But it is not here yet.[2] And perhaps it is just as well, since the concept resembles the type of purposeless totalitarian society we have been trying so desperately to avoid. But, unfortunately, "The major advances in civilization are processes that all but wreck the societies in which they occur."[3] *Disruptive* is the word most often used to describe it. So, having mastered the new technologies, it is time to get back to using the human skills that created a trading, manufacturing, and merchandising economy and a consumer society, in the first place.

Marketing is the essence of the civilized society we aspire to in a modern era, since it replaces war, violence, and plunder, with manufacturing, artistry, artisanship, new inventions, and trade.

Management guru Peter Drucker located the core of the situation when he wrote, "In every business the manager is the dynamic, life-giving element. Without his leadership, the resources of production remain resources and never become production."[4]

But as total quality control expert W. Edwards Deming famously proclaimed in frustration, "The problem is where to find good management."[5] So, just as robots replaced troublesome labor, there seems to be a premise (but not a promise) that inferior management can be replaced by more intelligent robots, like computers with artificial intelligence that are capable of performing logical operations, but only when aided by human intelligence.[6]

Many people have unrealistic expectations of the new electronic technologies. And although it is often claimed that about half the people who are fortunate to have a job don't like their work, there is an ever-present fear factor—just as there was with labor in the Industrial Revolution. So the purpose of this book is to remind managers, entrepreneurs, and business leaders how to produce a product or service that people want, and give it to them at the right price, in order to make a suitable profit and create more jobs, without imagining for even a moment that it can all be done by algorithms—as software designers would have us believe.

After writing his previous book on management and marketing, the author was invited by McGill University in Montreal to give a talk to their marketing association, consisting of the most recent batch of MBA graduates. The subject they chose for him to elaborate on was

"Marketing in the 21st century." Instead of theorizing by offering them a futuristic science-fiction scenario, like H. G. Wells did in *The Shape of Things to Come*, the author decided to demonstrate how marketing, management, sales, and advertising had declined after peaking in the mid-1960s, and ask them why they thought it had happened. He displayed a chart, blown up from the final chapter of his previous book, which illustrates the dynamics of change.[7] A breakdown of global market shares between each major economy revealed that management and marketing in every Western nation for the period from 1972 to 1992 had been dysfunctional, despite global growth. Trade in the United States shrank marginally by the end of that period or remained much the same. So did Germany's, France's, Britain's, and Italy's market shares. Most of the growth in those two decades went to Japan and emerging markets like Hong Kong, Singapore, South Korea, and Taiwan—still sometimes referred to as "Asian Tigers." The second question the author asked was "What did Asia do right during those twenty years while the West had apparently been unaware of an abundance of opportunities, since evidently it wasn't obtaining any of the global growth?" They had no answers, because they had not been taught about the dynamics of discontinuous change in the classroom or the gritty problems of the human condition that have a habit of stifling progress with complacency and creating inertia.

The Illusion of Literacy

It is perhaps significant that English school leavers "are among the least literate and numerate in the developed world."[8] They "have lower levels of basic skills than their grandparents . . . It is the only country in the world where adults aged 55 to 76 performed better than 16 to 24 year-olds who lag close to the bottom level in the world."[9] Moreover, "Policymakers and politicians who wring their hands about the mediocre performance of US students on international math and reading tests have another worry: the nation's grown-ups aren't doing much better. A first-ever comparison of adults in the United States and those in other democracies found that Americans were below average when it comes to skills needed to compete in the global economy."[10]

Similar research in Canada showed that 60 percent of students are intellectually disengaged from the public education system or simply not focused on their education.[11] Worse still are statistics that show 82 percent of Canadian students who were engaged in Grade 5 lost interest by the time they reached Grade 11, when interest declined to only 41 percent. The 50 percent falloff was due very largely to boredom. They blame the educational system and point out that whereas the social technology they use daily is state of the arts, the education system is old-fashioned. They feel frustrated with an angry authoritarian institution that insists students fit into their outdated concept of teaching and learning. Educational authorities claim they are aware that change is necessary as a consequence of the technological revolution but don't yet know what works. Meanwhile, teachers too are angry with the curriculum-based system. But bureaucracies are slow to change and always find reasons to resist it.

Said Marshall McLuhan of the technological revolution, "Now man is beginning to wear his brains outside his skull and his nerves outside his skin; new technology breeds new men."[12] Evidently the prophet of the electronics revolution considered electronic technologies would improve the human condition. But that is in question sixty years later, when it seems we have a problem in our eagerness to adopt the playful parts of the novelty, by disregarding the fact that it took millions of years to develop our plastic brains whenever we required more brain cells to confront evolutionary challenges.

Studies of the human brain are accelerating at least as fast as technological changes, as a result of fMRI machines that enable us to examine every level of a person's brain. As Dr. Norman Doidge informs us, "Freud anticipated what we are discovering today that there is mental activity outside of our awareness." For example, "Before we make a decision, the brain has already performed some of the operations unconsciously."[13]

As for McLuhan's comment that new technology breeds new men, there is plenty of evidence to show that the twenty-first century is more likely to be the century of new women. Statistics demonstrate women's astonishing progress in a business world formerly dominated by men. And their successes have nothing to do with the advance of new technologies, but with human attributes that software designers plan to replace with artificial ones.

This book is a celebration of the creativity of the human mind. But it is not a diatribe against technology. On the contrary; a new book poses the question, "What makes economies grow?"[14] Its answer is investment in science. "If you want to have a great economy, with jobs and prosperity for all, then you must spend money on basic science."

But being distracted and mesmerized by digital media and TV for eleven hours a day distracts us from the quiet contemplation required for study and creativity.[15] We need to look at the real workplace and the real marketplace in the real world—not a theoretical or virtual one that relies on algorithms. "A culture that cannot distinguish between reality and illusion dies," warns Pulitzer prize-winning author Chris Hedges. "And we are dying now."[16]

The examples that follow demonstrate how management, marketing, and manufacturing reached a pinnacle close to perfection from the 1960s to the 1980s, before digital technologies disrupted the cycle of consumer growth. Our economy has floundered ever since. Companies that continue to treat artificial intelligence, or cheap labor, as a substitute for human state-of-the-arts skills are likely to continue floundering, since too few working consumers are left to buy too many goods and services. The result is market inertia.

2

Taking Stock:
A Reality Check

Before we can even hope to consider all the skills required to initiate and maintain economic growth, entrepreneurs and business executives need to confront the fact that 90 percent of all businesses are now either start-up companies or new and growing small business enterprises that produce goods and services.[1] Start-up companies, by definition, are not the same as either one or two-person businesses: they generally emerge as a means to monetize new inventions or innovations which may or may not work. And even if a prototype does work, it may or may not find a demand in the marketplace when manufactured in quantity. It is even more likely that funding may be exhausted in the first four years without producing a workable prototype.

Most small business enterprises are me-too services or products where an entrepreneur has decided to exploit his or her skills in a market where he or she perceives there is enough demand for another source of supply. But they are generally categorized in statistics as small and medium-size enterprises. And in both cases, success is very often stalled by trial and error, through lack of experience and knowledge, or training. Necessary skills that are normally developed by informed knowledge and on-the-job experience frequently become misdirected, leading to loss of time, which is the most valuable of all resources, and may make the difference between profit and loss. The net result is that the failure rate of new small companies remains at approximately 90 percent, with most failing in those first critical four years when capitalization becomes eroded until exhausted.

Another statistic that should concentrate the mind is that, on average, 30,000 new products are launched every year, and 95 percent fail. We have to ask ourselves *why* before we sink money and time into any enterprise that is far more likely to fail than succeed.

The enormous ratio of business failures compared with successes is likely to have its equal in science and the arts, particularly now with jobless writers of books abandoned as a consequence of the chaos in the newspaper and book publishing industry and the book trade. Not only are millions of unemployed people thrown onto the job market by thousands of badly managed national and global business organizations, but many former employees have long since given up looking for a rewarding job. As a matter of self-respect, they now describe themselves as self-employed consultants or are classified in statistics as one-person SMEs, often reshaped as self-publishing business enterprises without any revenues. Viewed in a more positive light, it means the marketplace of ideas is filled with millions of creative people whose skills are unutilized. They are untapped potential waiting hopefully for someone or something to energize the economy.

To place the ratio between big and small businesses in its proper context, neither the United States nor any other Western economy is dominated by giant corporations anymore: 99 percent employ fewer than five hundred people, small enterprises in the United States account for 52 percent of all US workers. But it depends on how we define *small*. 19.6 million Americans work for companies that employ less than 20 workers; 18.4 million work in firms that employ 20–99 workers; 14.6 million work with 100–499 workers. Perhaps most importantly, small businesses provided three-quarters of America's new jobs in 1990–95.[2] More recently in Canada, small businesses accounted for 98 percent of all firms and created 77.7 percent of all new jobs.[3]

Women's Place

SMEs account for 60–70 percent of jobs in most OECD countries, "with a particularly large share in Italy and Japan, and a relatively smaller share in the United States." That share has grown in the past two decades. And "women-owned SMEs are growing at a faster rate than the economy as a whole in several OECD countries." The number of firms created and managed by women in the United States "has grown twice as fast as those set up and managed by men."[4] In Japan, 23.3 percent of private firms were set up by women (2.56 million out of 11 million).[5] Women in Germany were responsible for creating one-third of new firms since 1990. In the United Kingdom and France, a quarter of firms are headed by women. In Canada, women own and/or operate 30.3 percent of all firms, and the number of women-led firms is increasing at twice the national average. A similar trend exists in Australia, the Netherlands, and Denmark.

For greater clarification of this trend in the United Kingdom, "In 1968 only 19.2 percent of firms employed less than 200 people, but by 1975 the proportion of small to big rose by 20 percent. By the end of the 1980s it had climbed to 32 percent. And by 1991 it had leapt to 99.7 percent."[6]

The growth, shrinkage, and demise of companies, while they attempt to compete with each other for survival and cope with harsh macroeconomic conditions, is remarkably similar to the ways that all animal life compete for limited resources in harsh conditions and the ways that the fittest of some animals, insects, and plants survive because they are fortunate to be selected by Nature. Charles Darwin, who discovered and explained the evolutionary process in the mid to late nineteenth century, was well aware that a very similar situation applied to business enterprises, since he was acutely conscious of the English Industrial Revolution taking place around him. He was married to a Wedgewood, whose father was one of its initiators in the potteries. And he understood the ways that armies battle to win in wartime, because of the impact of the Napoleonic Wars in the same century. Whether natural life, military affairs, or business enterprises, the situation was famously summed up by Herbert Spencer, as "The survival of the fittest."

Most wildlife (animals, insects, and plants) survive by taking possession of territory and its resources, as armies do, while the territory that business enterprises aspire to possess is a share of the marketplace. So it should come as no surprise that the strategies and tactics used in business are closely similar, if not sometimes identical, to those used by animals, and even plants.

Does Size Matter?

To obtain market share, an entrepreneur or a corporate manager has three distinct types of models of business enterprises to follow. Entrepreneurs can choose to remain one of the 99.7 percent of SMEs in the West or follow the traditional path of market leaders like GE, Unilever, Matsushita, Walmart, or Toyota, for example – blue chip companies on the stock exchange. Or, if they possess an original new technological idea, they may become innovative high-tech companies like Apple Inc., Google, PayPal, Twitter, or Facebook—NASDAQ companies that produced fourteen billionaires in 1999 alone. Each type of company has its own distinctive advantages and disadvantages and also its own distinct attributes in order to succeed.

The reason why 57 to 99.7 percent of firms in the West are SMEs is that so many of the giant corporations that once dominated the economy were obliged by losses of revenues and profits to unload millions of employees from time to time. Most recent examples of former market leaders that failed to compete are Eastman Kodak, Sears, and Blackberry—the former seeking bankruptcy protection, the second unable to compete with discount companies and big box stores like Walmart and Target, the third unable to compete with Apple and Samsung's smartphones which offer more desirable apps and know how to get them to market on time. All three are prime examples of management or leadership failure to keep up with the times, and weakness in consumer research, market research, and marketing. But since management and marketing involve advertising, branding, public relations, selling, and sales management, it becomes a matter of conjecture as to where the real weakness lies, other than in poor leadership, since the total responsibility is the CEO's. Therein lies the crucial matter of human frailty with its subjective biases and prejudices, and irrationalities.

Nevertheless, well-led and well-managed global market leaders and national conglomerate do still exist, and some are extraordinarily successful, in particular, the winners in the financial sector and Silicon Valley, where talent is not only acknowledged as the cause of their remarkable successes, but is highly rewarded by turning imaginative people with brainpower into billionaires. Conversely, one result of working in a properly structured and sophisticated establishment company with well-trained and motivated top managers was complacency. Their executives tended to look down on small and medium-size companies, like the aristocracy once regarded the masses, believing that managers and staff of such small and unstructured enterprises were not fit to be employed by successful market leaders like themselves—even referring to them as *rats* and *mice*. Founders and entrepreneurs who managed them were considered to have "bought themselves a job," since evidently no one else would employ them. But their attitude was forced to change in economic recessions when giant corporations were in trouble and obliged to offload thousands of employees. Meanwhile, SMEs continue to compete and grow in number at their expense. Rats and mice are survivors because they are shrewd, quick-witted, flexible, and more nimble than dinosaurs. And it is hard to beat their street-smarts.

Most Successful Predators

In fact, Nature prefers the minimalist economies of small over big by producing more microbes than any other life-form. And 80 percent of animals are insects. So Nature is most successful in miniature. And the latest technologies enable SMEs to be even more competitive than before. Some say technology is the equalizer.

We have only to look over our shoulder at the situation when IBM launched its personal computer in 1981 and rats and mice nibbled at its heels for over a decade. Some, like Compaq, Apple, NEC, Dell, and HP, came out of nowhere to steal market shares and become market leaders in PCs, while a considerable number of other clones took smaller shares that combined in total to as much as 60.5 percent of the entire global PC market. They obliged IBM, with its massive budgets and its muscle power, to use a strategy of total force against Apple to prevent it from becoming the market leader in PCs. But no amount of money could compete against imagination, ingenuity, an instinctive knowledge of consumer needs from being closer to the market, innovation, superior product design, enthusiasm, teamwork, and drive.

Each small business enterprise must make a choice, at the most suitable time, whether to remain "a small fish in a big pond" or decide if they possess competitive advantages or resources to challenge established market leaders—as Apple did with IBM, and as those other new start-up companies, like Dell, did.

We should remember that the industrial sector in the United States comprised only 22.2 percent of GDP in 2010, whereas the service sector had already grown to 76.7 percent of GDP. Agriculture represented only 1.2 percent. Whether the shrinking of manufacturing in the West is one of the causes of our present economic stagnation is addressed more fully elsewhere with deindustrialization and offshoring.[7]

Meanwhile, if we examine the advantages and disadvantages of remaining small, we find that SMEs have the benefit of low payroll and other overhead costs, flexibility to turn on a dime because of fewer lines of command, and the speed and audacity to do so of a London taxi. Such companies are often started because of invention or innovation, initiative, and personal service. Two other major advantages are work ethic and persistence. Fifteen years ago there was still some hesitation in SMEs acquiring and mastering new technologies, but that is no longer the case, particularly with technologies that replace staff and increase output to enable them to

11

compete with the economies of volume and mass markets of bigger and more established organizations.

But remaining small has disadvantages, too. It may induce entrepreneurs to think too small. Inexperience of personnel is almost inevitable if bigger companies can offer greater incentives and then train staff on the job. And a start-up company, or two-person enterprise, will not have accumulated corporate knowledge, skills, or the type of business scheming linked to power and bullying that develops in bigger and more established companies over time. There are likely to be financial limitations with the entrepreneur living out of his back pocket. That may mean limitations on installing more expensive new technologies for R&D that in turn, may limit the production of enough new products for the pipeline. Lack of experience may also limit strategic planning. And a small new enterprise will not have enough time to establish a desirable brand and develop consumer loyalty to it. With limited staff comes distraction from burdening them with several different types of jobs, and lack of focus or unclear objectives through failure to prioritize the fundamentals.

With bigger companies, on the other hand, should come more sophisticated management and marketing skills, continuity that leads to a buildup of momentum and brand loyalty. There is easier access to finance and government aids because of a measurable history of successes. But bigger companies can easily become dinosaurs with corporate cultures of bureaucratic conservatism, and controls intended to minimize risks and stifle initiative. High overhead costs may result in too-careful budget controls that limit the creative and productive marketing side of the business. And a particular disadvantage of bigger companies is that executives tend to distance themselves further from the marketplace where all the action takes place, as they are drawn into endless meetings and all the debilitating effects of a bureaucracy that prevent managers from managing effectively and marketers from marketing their products and services as they should.

"There is something about the way decisions get made in successful organizations that sows the seeds of eventual failure," says Harvard Business School's Professor Clayton Christensen in *The Innovator's Dilemma*, which is about the effects of disruptive change.

Part of a reality check is a situational analysis that makes us aware that the global economy was in disarray in 2013, when the United States dropped to fourth place in competitiveness.[8] The EU teetered closer to collapse through debts. China's economy became questionable and dropped by 1 percent of GDP to 7.6 percent. It was foreseen as the beginning of a slide down even further. And China's national debt was estimated at 45 to 50 percent.[9] Wealthy Chinese were thought to be moving their capital overseas in anticipation of a sagging economy and a real estate bubble set to burst from overinvestment and overdevelopment.

India's economy too is not coming up to expectations and may worsen as a result of extreme weather conditions from the Greenhouse Effect. And the United States was still close to inertia at the end of 2014, because of unprecedented debts and the gridlock from Congress.

In the final analysis, there are really only two kinds of business enterprises—winners and losers. So the most important question that needs answering is, how do some firms manage to succeed whereas most others fail?

When British economist John Kay wrote *Why Firms Succeed*, in 1995, he found that measuring success presented him with a paradox.[10] "Some people emphasized size and market share, and others stressed profitability and returns to shareholders. Some people looked to technical efficiency and innovative capability. Others stressed the reputation that companies enjoyed among their customers and employees and in the wider business community." But there is no argument about which companies are successful.

Kay is visiting professor of Economics at the London School of Economics and was hailed as "the best management theorist in Britain."[11] That is what separates his book—written two decades ago, before the impact of the Internet and other digital technologies—and this one. Whereas he views the business world through the eyes of an economist, this one is written with state-of-the-arts marketing clearly in mind. While he prepared his theories for academics, this book is based very largely on its author's practical experience as a hands-on business manager facing typical problems and challenges daily in the marketplace and the workplace for much of his life. And the author had the deep insights and prescience of the marketing-oriented business guru, Peter Drucker, to guide him from the outset.

One link between the two different worldviews of business manager and economist is "the match between the capabilities of the organization and the challenges it faced." Another is his profitability objective: "to create an output that is worth more than the cost of the inputs that it uses." *Added Value* became a catchword by the twenty-first century, as a consequence of his book. This book places more emphasis on achieving and maintaining a comfortably profitable market share.

What we want to know is not so much *why* businesses succeed, but *how* we can achieve success in the digital era. As for those businesses that failed, we need to know *why*, so that we can avoid their faulty judgments and choices. What we find mostly are the same ingredients that contribute to most failures and a different group of ingredients that continue to contribute to most success.

3

Untapped Potential

Frank Stronach was a machine worker who arrived in Canada in 1954 with only a few dollars in his pocket. He found that there was a shortage of manufacturers and that Canada is not, and never has been, a manufacturing economy. Canadians have still not developed the knowhow to add value to primary resources in order to manufacture and market successful products competitively. Stronach immediately saw that the few manufacturers trying to make a go of it were stalled for reliable supplies of components. So he started a tool and die shop in a garage. His Magna International is now one of the biggest auto parts makers, employing 115,000 in 6 countries. The back cover of his recent biography, *The Magna Man*, features his vision. It could also be the vision of this book[1]:

"I am the son of working class parents, a tradesman who came to these shores with rudimentary English and barely any business knowhow. If I could accomplish all I have done with my life with a very limited education and modest means, I believe many others could do the same."

"The human mind has an incredible capacity for ingenuity and creativity, and I'm a firm believer that we all possess enormous untapped potential. If you walk in my footsteps and follow the simple formula for success I've spelled out in this book, then I'm confident your business could be among the very best in its industry and that you could be a more effective business leader."

Other advice from this global auto parts maker before he retired in 2012, after sharing millions with his employees, who became his partners, includes, "Avoid becoming centralized!"

1. Decentralization avoids the stumbling blocks of bureaucracy. 2. Small operating units as cost and profit centers are transparent, so that winners stand out from losers who can't drag others down with them. 3. It keeps the operational focus on customers, instead of multiplying unproductive executives in an anonymous head office. 4. Each operational manager is a stakeholder sharing profits as a motivation for initiative and work ethic.

Frank Stronach exemplifies the old-fashioned virtues of hard work, common sense, fairness, clear-mindedness, attention to quality, and helpfulness. Although they are barely enough in a competitive environment, he discovered a niche in which there was more demand than competition and where automakers were eager to buy his components because of his high quality and attention to customers' needs.

If it sounds too simple to be true, we need only study the revival of two national economies after World War Two that were based on the same concept and the same virtues and spirit—Germany with its small *Mittelstand* and Japan with its small *machikoba*. They are small family businesses which became the backbone of the industrial success of those two nations because their quality, control, and supplies were dependable for bigger industrialists to be able to order special products from.

Recent headlines in *The Guardian* claimed, "Germany's smaller firms emerge intact from the recession." And, "Skills make the difference in manufacturing. State aid helped firms keep workers in the slump—now the sector is taking off." Anyone might imagine the news media had only just discovered the source of Germany's postwar economic revival. If so, it took them about seventy years.[2] According to the press, "the mood among the country's small and medium-sized firms has improved dramatically since 2009. Recaro, one of the world's three biggest manufacturers of aircraft seats, was hosting visitors from British Airways—one of its roster of clients from around the world—on Tuesday and showing off its latest lightweight designs. Axel Kahsnitz, chief executive of the family-owned business in the small town of Schwäbisch Hall, said that unlike many of the other companies in the south-western state of Baden-Württemberg, Recaro had seen revenues dip only slightly during the crisis. 'We picked up market share in the Middle East and Asia, and also benefited from some airlines adding more economy class seats at the expense of business and first class.'"

"Like many German family-owned businesses, Recaro has a long history—founded by a saddle-maker in Stuttgart in 1906, who branched out into making car bodies for Porsche and other pioneers of the early automobile motor industry."

Theirs is a solidly established foundation with a history of quality and dependability that has been sustained into the twenty-first century.

Japanese Management

Japan was plagued by devastation from earthquakes and a tsunami in 2011, on one hand, and a nuclear plant meltdown on the other. Tremendous damage was caused across a wide area of Eastern Japan. Nevertheless, Japanese spirit and determination is at least as powerful as Germany's. And it is the human spirit that creates courage, leading to a positive outlook that motivates determination and persistence, resulting in success. So, despite their horrific tragedies, their mini *machikoba* factories managed to make a big economic breakthrough with their artisan and apprenticeship systems.

"A complex to accommodate small factories opened in Tokyo's Ota Ward in March, overcoming difficulties caused by financial consequences of last year's earthquake. Proponents found a way to work around the problems in order to support the growth of neighborhood-based industry. With 33 rooms, the facility provides space for the development of both traditional and modern technology. The close proximity of the companies to one another facilitates collaboration, creating an environment where they can take on new challenges and find solutions."[3]

Machikoba are small business enterprises that developed from artisan forebears to which bigger companies outsource the manufacturing of components in which they specialize and have made themselves dependable, if not indispensable. So, small and big businesses support each other. *Machikoba* are described as the underpinnings of Japan's economy.

Finding a Competitive Advantage

Whether billionaire Frank Stronach had such high ambitions in mind when he started up his own business in tiny premises in Canada or not, he achieved considerable success before he sold his company. One of the characteristics that undoubtedly set him on his path to success is a personality that genuinely wants to share his knowledge and help people. But first, he had to find the competitive advantage. And, as common knowledge has it, you simply produce the *right product*, market it at the *right price*, and at the *right time*. But, in order to do so, you must know the market, know your competitors, match organizational abilities to market challenges, motivate personnel, demand high standards from suppliers and distributors, and manage strategically.

Those are three different types of entrepreneurial companies: Frank Stronach's new startup that grew as a consequence of the founder's drive and skills and initiatives, like networking, the artisan-type of *machikoba* in Japan, and *Mittelstand* in Germany, which are growing medium-size enterprises. They follow a simple and successful formula based on apprenticeships, learning on the job, an appreciation and management of sound artisan skills, product R&D, and practical marketing practices. They often involve supplying components to each other and to much larger capitalized organizations.

All were successful before the advent of new digital technologies. But that does not mean they don't benefit from the digital revolution. It made them even more competitive against bigger established companies by increasing productivity and cutting labor and unit costs. Nevertheless, their future success is still likely to be based firmly on competing with the types of skills their founder brought to the market in the first place and avoiding being distracted from the primary purpose of their company by the new digital technologies, in order to exploit the strengths of the company's own special skills.

4

Strategic Management

Business strategies and tactics emerged almost instinctively out of two death-defying situations. They are the way that all life competes for limited resources in order to survive, and the traditional ways and means that armies use to train and plan in order to win battles and wars. Industrialists and businesses choose similar skills, weapons, strategies, and tactics to compete with others for a share of the market. So, at the very core of any thoughtful entrepreneurial endeavor or marketing plan are the same profound fact and goals that motivate all life. And, as Charles Darwin began to realize when he studied the terrain and animal life in Patagonia, competition favors individuals with characteristics which are a competitive advantage. It applies equally to business enterprises.

In order for a business to build up a competitive advantage to fight for market share, an effective corporate culture is required at the outset. It involves hiring creative people, instead of merely extra hands. An entrepreneur, or a business' human resource manager, has to ensure that every employee provides added value. And, as soon as financial equilibrium is assured, there is a need to accumulate organizational knowledge in its chosen sphere of operation. That requires sharing information, instead of embracing it selfishly or keeping it at the top, or isolated in a single department. Staff, from a receptionist to the most skilled machine operator or financial officer, need ongoing training and monitoring to keep them abreast of events and at the cutting edge of new skills and technologies. In short, leadership of the enterprise has to be constantly aware that take-off arises from motivated personnel who cooperate—like the small *machikoba* and *Mittelstand* cooperate with bigger manufacturers, instead of competing with them.

Knowing what is going on and seeking to exploit opportunities enabled another winner, Peter Thiel, to found PayPal and sell it for $1.5 billion to eBay in 2002. He succeeded by recognizing that consumers who buy goods and services online, and suppliers who sell them, needed a secure and confidential way to pay for them online. By overcoming consumer hesitation, he increased the number of online buyers, and indirectly created employment for people making goods and providing services.

When we jump from what one individual, like Frank Stronach or Peter Thiel, can do to what a global marketing organization can succeed in doing, we cannot help but admire the sheer effrontery and street-smarts of a company that can turn tap water or well water into an illusion of romantic encounters with boy–girl relationships. It is marketing magic. We can learn from Coca-Cola's strategic concept which involves fulfilling teenage wishful thinking. All it required was water, sweetener, and coloring, and a bottling or canning plant to put it all together. But that is only the tangible part of the enterprise, whereas it is the *intangible* component that mesmerizes consumers to buy and assure Coke's global success.

Coca-Cola was ranked as the most valuable brand in the world by the end of 2012. It came as no surprise, since it has repeatedly taken first place, although occasionally shuffled into second or third place on occasions when another brilliantly managed company like Apple or GE increased its revenues and profits in a particular year. GE, for example, owes its own global success to very similar reasons as other market leaders although, instead of beverages, it manufactures a diversity of industrial products like major and smaller domestic appliances, gas turbine aero engines, specialized financial services, health-care technologies, and wind-power technology.

GE is featured here because its successful manufacturing is based on "building customer and market appeal into the product from the design stage on," as its 1952 annual financial report spelled out.[1] It is what dedicated marketing companies do. Unilever is a prime example of this. Its global success is based on branding and marketing a large range of fast-moving packaged consumer goods which are targeted to the needs of consumers by building consumer benefits into each product from the design stage on. And, significantly, despite its factories in which it manufactures its own products, it has structured its enterprise and staffed it as a marketing organization, since marketing comes first, before manufacturing, as well as afterward, and everywhere in the middle.

The Legendary Steve Jobs

Steve Jobs of Apple is inevitably another winner in this marketing narrative, which is intended to deflect managers from a narrow bureaucratic mindset, or insular factory orientation, by describing how the real world works outside those narrow confines of office workshops and assembly lines—leading to the main reasons for success or failure of an enterprise, so that we can learn something from all those superior companies.

For example, Steve Jobs of Apple claimed, "What I'm best at doing is finding a group of talented people and making things happen with them."

What he recognized in himself was so insightful that it could have been carved on his tombstone as his epitaph. Whether he failed to recognize that he is a prime example of what is required in twenty-first century marketing is questionable. It is an ability to see things differently and do things differently. Because, if we look at the economics of industry and commerce over the past thirty or more years, it is clearly evident that industry leaders and managers in the West performed poorly, often by doing what they had been wrongfully taught were the right things to do. That was partly because human resource people chose the types of managers and staff that CEOs thought would be dependable and fit in to the established conservative culture of their organization and do what they were told.

That is why economist Theodore Levitt famously said, "The problem is at the top."[2] If a CEO has the wrong mindset and attitudes and values to lead a company, all the failings of his limited worldview will permeate every department and every layer of personnel and every one of their judgments and decisions. It will most likely include his guidance to the Human Resource person about the types of managers and staff they should hire. And so it turned out that the unimaginative but dependable worthies, with their apparently suitable academic qualifications, who probably belonged to the right clubs, failed us again and again, either because they were the wrong personality in the first place or because they were not taught the virtues of diversity, creativity, flexibility, or taking risks.

Say what you will about Steve Jobs, although he rubbed a lot of people the wrong way, he came into the marketing arena as a breath of fresh air, despite his idiosyncrasies, or rather because of them. He and all the other winners whose virtues are extolled here possessed an ability to turn tangibles into intangibles that appeal to customers' emotions first, and their reasoning afterward. Winners like Jobs understood what motivates people to want and buy things. They also know how to communicate their selected consumer benefits to their targeted markets.

What Motivates People?

It leads us to ask for a clear and brief answer as to what motivates people to buy things.

The short answer to that question has been provided by philosophers and psychologists. Karl Popper suggested that the Three Great Hidden Motives of Human Nature are hunger, love, and lust for power.[3] But time and the consumer society have changed social mores in the West and provided a better materialistic lifestyle, so that now the battle for market dominance is waged by fulfilling somewhat different consumer needs. They are (1) Sex, (2) Hunger to buy things, and (3) Money, which is so closely related to power and prestige, or celebrity, that they are virtually interchangeable for our purposes.

There is a fourth motivation that works for the right products and services, although it is a negative one: life insurance, savings, a tiny plot of hallowed ground, frail-care, retirement homes, and the like attract consumers of a certain age to some kind of imagined insurance against anxiety and fear.

Before the invention of the consumer society as we know it today, persuasive advertisements were regarded by some as vulgar exploitation of weak-minded people to buy things they might *want* but didn't need. No such inhibitions to buy exist in today's consumer society. And advertisers still regard their exhortations as a legitimate way to inform the public about new products that could make life easier or more enjoyable. But, of course, a consumer society had already existed for a very long time. "Buyer Beware!" said official signs that had to be placed outside the entry of retail stores in the Roman Empire. And there is the story often told of the oriental carpet business in the Middle East. "Fetch me my yardstick!" says the owner of the business. "Yes, master," says his assistant; "Do you want the one we use for buying or the one we use for selling?"

"*Consumption*," wrote the famous economist John Maynard Keynes, "*is the sole end and object of all economic activity.*" So the objective of all businesses is to serve the needs of consumers and continue to provide them with what they, and new customers, want. The profit motive that underlines the reasons for going into business is all about fulfilling other people's needs and wants. Or, as used so often to be said by advertising agencies in a more patriarchal society, "the customer is king." Today, with more women working and owning business enterprises and wealth, she is more likely to be a queen. And often, after resorting to a health diet, and even indulging in a detox, the customer may feel like she is a goddess. So it pays to treat her like one. Stores in Japan know this and engage a hostess to bow low to each customer who enters, never forgetting for a moment that their livelihood depends on sales, and more sales. They want customers to return and buy again and again.

There is more than sound material common sense behind that wish, since it may even be that our consumer society could result in fending off a third world war. Who would want to go to war if they can indulge in all the appealing benefits of being spoilt by endless and exciting shopping sprees! It is expressed somewhat more somberly by the World Economic Forum's statement that "Short of military conquest, economic growth is the only viable means for a country to sustain increases in national wealth and living standards."[4]

The Consumer Revolution

The smokestacks and squalor of the English Industrial Revolution left a bad image, with Marx and Engels wrangling about whether the working classes were better or worse off to leave the countryside for factory jobs in the industrial cities. They warned that it would lead to revolution, like in France. In fact, it resulted in a consumer revolution instead. Perhaps, if Marx had possessed the *joie de vivre* of today's shoppers with their hunger to buy things, the Russian Revolution would never have happened and a more peaceful evolutionary process might have taken place, allaying fears of a similar revolution happening in England, which haunted the middle classes.

As it turned out, manufacturers improved our lifestyles by mass producing things to make them affordable and created employment so that most of us could afford to buy them. And not only the small consumer segment known as the carriage trade. So successful was supply and demand in Britain that the local market became saturated and it soon needed an empire to export its surplus goods. Even so, salesmen had to be hired to clear slow-moving inventories out of the warehouses before they became damaged or out-of-date. But even salesmen were not enough, despite all the motivational books that extolled the virtues and financial rewards of *Bond Salesmanship*[5] and *How to Win Friends and Influence People*.[6] Or *Think and Grow Rich*.[7] And *The Power of Positive Thinking*,[8] to name only a few of the runaway bestsellers that were bought eagerly by millions of aspiring individuals with ambition.

But even professional salesmanship wasn't enough to move goods from factories and warehouses, and off the shelves of retail family stores. It required advertising to reach millions more of the public on a far broader scale and convince them to buy inventories displayed on their shelves, or store owners wouldn't be able to reorder. Repeat orders were essential, since factory machinery was being improved to produce larger quantities of goods, and the so-called scientific management of the factory floor created greater efficiencies that enabled suppliers to produce even more goods more economically.

Comedy movies made in France and Hollywood, and later on with Lucille Ball on TV, caught the mood of overproduction by exaggerating the speed of goods continuously being moved by conveyor belts and on assembly lines. Traders importing resources to be turned into packaged consumer goods were having them transported across the oceans on faster and faster ships. And with risks being reduced by insurance, confidence of rewards increased the exploration for even more resources, spices, tea, and rubber. The introduction of supermarkets in the twentieth century kept the goods flowing out to consumers.

It took a postwar period to clear inventories and manufacture new electric household goods and automobiles to meet a pent-up demand after wartime restrictions. But even with the demand for new goods, like an all-electric kitchen, some means had to be found to pay for it. It was a government scheme called Hire-Purchase, commonly known as "the never-never system." It was an innovation to encourage consumers to buy goods on credit. It speeded up sales even further, since it had been unheard of before, when work ethic demanded a scrupulous culture of doing without inessential items until you could afford to buy them. Hire-Purchase was the forerunner of credit cards that work electronically to speed things up. And, just as with plastic money today, the Hire-Purchase scheme oiled the wheels of commerce and industry and created new jobs.

Only when the pent-up demand was met did it became necessary to market goods and services in more professional ways. We can see it reflected in books about more sophisticated and persuasive and cost-effective, targeted advertising that was directed at making even more sales. Scientific or marketing-oriented advertising became more sales driven than ever before.[9]

The period between 1947 and the late 1960s was a major period when marketing and advertising became refined by experts and reached a point of perfection in selling many millions of new goods from the moment they were launched on the market. Marketing was the fifth out of six significant stages in creating the consumer society we know today. It was the heyday of packaged consumer goods makers and distributors like Unilever, Colgate-Palmolive, and Procter & Gamble. It could even be claimed that advertising and marketing descended into mediocrity afterward, when advertising agencies were dismissed as history. But why did it happen?

The Wizards of Menlo Park

As background to high-tech firms mentioned in the following pages, Silicon Valley in Northern California is named for a high concentration of the world's biggest technology companies that began their lives as small startups, sometimes in someone's garage. Its population is now close to four million. Its most famous earlier resident was inventor Thomas Edison who produced a whole range of inventions and innovations there, around 1877, because he was the man who electrified the world. He is the original "Wizard of Menlo Park." But its hero is Stanford Research Institute, because of the significant leading role it played in the electronic revolution and in developing the area.

Stanford University established itself as a center of innovation in 1946 to support local economic development. Silicon Valley would soon house a considerable number of other wizards who performed their magic by producing one invention or innovation after another, like Hewlett-Packard which started in the Hewletts' garage attached to their home in 1938. The legendary partnership began in 1939. Then there was Steve Jobs' startup that he called Apple. It began in someone else's garage on April Fools Day in 1976.

Stanford encouraged graduates to launch their own startups, and Silicon Valley soon spread around its campus, where Jobs dropped out. Research and development at Stanford saw three waves of innovations made possible by support from Shockley Semiconductors, Fairchild, and Xerox. Silicon-based integrated circuits were developed there with transistors, microprocessors, and the microcomputer. It now employs around a quarter of a million information technology workers. One of its earliest successes was Hewlett-Packard. They moved into Stanford Research Park after 1953. So did Eastman Kodak, and General Electric in the mid-1990s.

Among its best known residents at present are Google, Facebook, eBay, Cisco Systems, Adobe, Apple Inc., Yahoo!, Atari, Dell, Fujitsu, Hitachi, IBM, LinkedIn, McAfee, Intel, Microsoft, Nokia, Siemens, NeXT Computers Inc., Olivetti, Palm, PayPal, Samsung, Sony, Sun Microsystems/Oracle, Tata Consultancy, Twitter, Veritas Software, and

25

YouTube/Google, It is the biggest center for high-tech manufacturing in the United States.

Growth was encouraged by venture capital firms. Semiconductors are still a major component, but innovations in software and Internet services have also had an influence. It was also the center of the 1990s dotcom bubble that burst at the close of the century. It is one of the top research and development centers in the world.

They are the people and companies who already changed our lives in the twentieth century through invention, discovery, and innovation, which is the sixth stage required by today's business enterprises to serve and, yes, exploit today's consumer society. It recognizes new consumer needs and wants and fulfills them innovatively to feed men's and women's almost infinite appetite for novelties and distractions, since the dominant age group that demands them is easily bored, motivated by reckless curiosity, and fickle.

5

Integrated Marketing and Its Enemies

Everyone in a business needs to know what marketing is and does, particularly those who come into direct contact with consumers: from receptionists to salespeople, from CEOs to sales managers and advertising agencies. It means we need to define the main virtues of marketing for them. The Chartered Institute of Marketing in the United Kingdom gave it considerable thought: "Marketing is the management process responsible for identifying, anticipating and satisfying customer requirements profitably." Since it is all about fulfilling customer wants and needs, a shorter version was proposed in a previous book on management; "Marketing is finding out what customers want and providing it profitably."[1]

The question now is whether digital hardware and software and the powerful influence of the Internet, search engines, and social media have made any modifications necessary to those definitions. Although management guru Peter Drucker died before the twenty-first century, he always managed to anticipate events and warned us not to forget that computers are only useful tools. So the very essence and philosophy of integrated marketing has not changed, only the tools have. They simply provide us with a more effective means to implement management and marketing strategies and tactics quicker, cheaper, and more effectively across a broader global market. So both definitions still seem to apply.

But there is another side to marketing and managing that requires our attention if we take the view that "History is only the results of unintended consequences."[2] It is why the introduction to this book opens with a statement that managers and leaders want to predict results in order to avoid making errors of judgment that may lead to unintended consequences. Charles St. Thomas evidently had that factor in mind when he proposed that "Marketing is a way of managing a business so that each critical business decision . . . is made with full and prior knowledge of the impact of that decision on the customer."[3] All three definitions apply even if their emphasis differs.

In fact, marketing is so holistic and ubiquitous that it is almost impossible to encapsulate it in a simple definition. Even an admirable 914-page textbook like *Marketing* cannot define it more clearly.[4] Nor can most other marketing books elaborate further than that by adding the most recent trends in communicating by mobiles and particularly smartphones, because any books that feature the latest fast-changing technologies are likely to be out-of-date before publication.

Continuous and discontinuous change is such an important part of the marketing process that we need to take a sharp look at it. Economist Joseph Schumpeter called it "creative destruction." And one way to describe the process is by studying what happened to the typewriter when it was invented and innovated and finally made obsolete by word processors.

Creative Destruction

One of the dilemmas of innovation is that competitors who attack have the advantage. And "Whenever technological discontinuities occur, companies' fortunes change drastically," wrote Richard N. Foster.[5] We need only be reminded of Eastman Kodak recently seeking bankruptcy protection, because they failed to predict the technological discontinuity of digital cameras, and then failed to keep up with Apple and Samsung and Fujitsu.

The only previous technology that manual typewriters replaced was handwriting. That makes its life cycle easier to describe. But we always need to be reminded that all technology comes at a cost and even simple technology can distract users from work. Of the first typewriter bought by Samuel Clemens, he wrote, "It's fascinating . . . and wastes my time like an old friend." Sales were slow because of its high price and poor performance. Remington sold only four hundred in the first six months. But after they made improvements, they sold four thousand machines in 1877. They introduced a new and improved machine the following year, called "the No. 2." It sold one hundred thousand units. Its unique selling proposition was that "It supersedes the pen." (And people can write with it when traveling by sea, when writing with a pen is impossible.)

It became a fixture in the workplace from 1877 and changed society by producing "a whole new class of clerical workers." The numbers of typists and stenographers in the United States increased from only 33,000 in 1890 to 786,000 by 1920. Sixty-four percent were women at the beginning, and 92 percent by 1920, because "Women are superior to men, their greater quickness of perception and motion gives them obvious advantages." Men were described as "more frequently absent because of their vices."[6]

It was not long before me-too products were made and marketed. There was a Sholes typewriter and a cheaper version by Yost Caligraph. Its No. 2 introduced upper and lower case lettering in 1881. The Crandall, the Hammond, and the Hall were introduced in 1885 with different designs for striking the paper with the type. Meanwhile, Remington was producing about 1,500 machines a month by adopting mass production methods.

Since the Remington was the best made and most functional, they put up a $1,000 challenge to Caligraph and their other competitors to a public contest. Caligraph and their typing champion were beaten. But it did not prevent other typewriter models from entering the market: there were now ten patented models and twenty suppliers. Franz X. Wagner, who had designed the Caligraph machine, brought out a new design featuring "visible type," by striking the paper front and center, so that a typist could see each mistake and correct it immediately. John T. Underwood saw the advantages of that innovation, bought Wagner's design, and began producing his typewriters in 1895. The Underwood No. 1 was an immediate success. And each innovation made all previous designs and inventories obsolete.

After the success of the Underwood Model No. 5, they needed a larger factory to meet the demand. L. C. Smith & Brothers followed Underwood's successful Monarch model with its own No. 8 in 1908. But by 1920, Underwood was "selling as many machines as all its rivals combined" (a fairly typical situation with a dominant market leader when it came to PCs and smartphones). The Royal Company entered the market in 1904.

Around eighty-nine different manufacturers had competed in the US market by 1909, but most were clones, small operators with lower overhead costs—marginal companies that came and went in a hurry. The manual market was ultimately dominated by Underwood, Remington, Royal, and Smith & Brothers (who merged later with Corona).

Electric Typewriters

Electric-powered typewriters were introduced in 1925 but proved to be disappointing, largely because of the Great Depression. Now typewriter manufacturers "were leaving the business at a high rate." IBM bought

Electrostatic Typewriters in 1933, a smaller operator on the fringe. IBM made record-accounting and tabulating machines, but the US War Department passed them many orders for typewriters, which were part of IBM's learning curve. And demand for IBM electrics took off. When they did, they quickly replaced manual office typewriters, so that IBM were market leaders with 60 percent of the high-end, full-featured electric market by 1967. SCM, Royal, and Olivetti-Underwood each possessed around 10 percent market share.

Another wave of innovations made all previous designs obsolete at a time when about 20 percent of the US working population (five million) worked in an office. They represented around half of all people employed in the United States. Word processors appeared by the early 1970s, made by Wang, Xerox, Exxon, ITT, AT&T, Olivetti, IBM, and nearly fifty others. About two hundred thousand word-processing machines were installed in offices by 1975 and over four billion were sold in the United States by 1986.

But electronic offices proved to be unappealing to typists and failed to generate the improvements in productivity that had been envisaged. Working in word-processing pools was like drudgery on factory assembly lines. Wang folded. Exxon sold out and returned to the oil patch. ITT and AT&T lost their enthusiasm. But, by now, the typewriter and its grandchildren had changed the way that people worked, and also changed their social habits. Meanwhile, they were looking for something better. It turned out to be a personal computer.

The Altair 8800 was the first commercial instrument that could be used as a personal computer in 1975. It was offered to the public for $395. Within two years there were about thirty companies making PCs, including Apple, Commodore, Tandi's Radio Shack, and Heathkit. The Apple II launch took place in that year. What happened in the marketing cycle that led up to Apple Inc. becoming the global market leader is described in the author's previous book.[7]

That description is sufficient to illustrate how one new innovation automatically replaces all previous ones to make them obsolete; how crowds of me-too products enter the market with exuberance and disappear just as quickly when they fail to compete with better designs or better marketed machines; how most major players lose money and interest when they discover they are unsuited to the product or service sector; and how product designs and ways and means of manufacturing, and equipment, and marketing them, need to be destroyed, from time to time, in order to improve features and costs, so as to compete and remain in business.

The marketing cycle of the typewriter industry is fairly typical of most inventions in the way it exemplifies what happens in other industries too, like major domestic appliances or the automobile industry. It is a continuous and unending process. Economist Schumpeter claimed that only an innovator makes a real profit. But the innovation is always under threat from competitors and short lived. Immediately after World War Two, manufacturers of major domestic appliances were often accused of creating "planned obsolescence," so that as soon as buyers paid for them on the extended payment plan of hire-purchase, they were obsolete, and consumers had to buy a new one. But obsolescence doesn't need to be planned, it is implicit in the traditional cycle of new innovations that make every previous model obsolete.[8]

"The problem is that we cannot judge or predict which of many threats will have such potency, but . . . even the strongest product and business strategy will eventually be overturned by technological change. The central issue is not when or how this will happen, but that it will happen for sure. In the final analysis only that understanding will allow a firm to bridge a discontinuity, because only a total commitment will win the day."[9]

Diversity

We can see from that continual process aimed at the profitable survival of a company that business managers must understand strategic planning and tactics to meet sales forecasts and marketing goals. In other words, managers—whether of departments, branches, regions, or general managers of a company—are not just administrators hired to maintain the *status quo*, as in government departments where staff act under instructions from a minister and are not expected to possess imagination or show initiative or profits. Instead, the private sector demands creativity, initiative, and productivity, and in a hurry. And they can only do so within the framework of a written job description that defines the parameters and limitations of their responsibilities, while also providing scope for imagination and initiative. Managers working for a properly structured organization know what they are expected to do before they even commence at an entry-level job. And part of the job specification of those who manage them will also be to act as mentor to their assistants. They will also know they will receive annual performance ratings before being invited to move upward on established career paths.

31

From a top-down perspective, it means hiring and managing diverse personalities and skills to produce new ideas that were not available previously, compared, for example, with prewar England, when new ideas were suspect and managers and companies were not prepared to take risks. Private clubs assured that members mixed only with their own kind of people. Anything new was considered *foreign*. And anything foreign could not be trusted. Chairmen and CEOs had their vacations scrupulously vetted to ensure they did not stay at the same hotels as their management or staff, or be booked on the same flights or trains. Exchanges of opinions were not encouraged.[10]

The opening up of trade borders and the tourist industry, antidiscrimination laws, and the Internet have broadened minds and changed that. But, even in a successful multicultural society like Canada, each culture tends to retain its own biases and prejudices and myths and stereotypes. They are still the main causes of friction all over the world, because people become self-righteous about their own idiosyncrasies. And yet, they have to adapt to a new culture of the workplace where employees work together with the same aims and goals planned to arrive at the same objective.

Hiring and managing a diversity of skills and personalities with different experience and attitudes also means inviting new ideas from everyone and being open minded and positive when receiving them. Regular meetings at a round table to which users of systems are openly invited each month, to suggest improvements, is one way of being receptive—known as "Q-Circles" in Japan, where they were found to improve productivity and profits and help to maintain a harmonious workplace.

Unfortunately, the twenty-first century has brought us into an age of anxiety with overpopulation and competition for dwindling resources that creates problems and pressures, the most obvious one being unemployment. Government statistics don't help because they are selective. Just as inflation statistics often exclude the very categories where prices have risen, so the unemployment rate excludes all the people who can't find a job and describe themselves as consultants or self-employed, or "no longer searching," rather than admit they can't find anyone to hire them, although it may not be their fault.

Corporations have lost sight of the fact that it is harder to market goods and services when there are less people who can afford to buy them. Recognition that employees are consumers, and that you lose one every time you let an employee go, or thousands of customers when you downsize a failing company, has still apparently not entered the minds of Western businesses. Japanese business leaders are more holistic, and more sensitive to the desired effects of social harmony on the economy. It means that marketing executives must use their art and skills to turn problems into commercial opportunities that not only yield profits but also create more jobs.

Destructive Organizational Behavior

Lack of foresight is only one of the human limitations we suffer from. To put such liabilities in context, it may be useful to list what amount to the seven deadly sins of management and leadership. In fact, they are a normal part of our typically negative organizational behavior and our social psychology. Psychiatrist Wilhelm Reich would in all probability have linked them to his own list of what he called infectious "emotional plagues."

First and foremost comes *complacency*. It generally results from a history of past successes. Once we accept the fact that such successes are possible, we tend to expect they will continue. In that regard, we are like a gambler who gets a lucky break and goes on betting on an assumption that his luck will continue, when it is purely random. In reality—as shown in the life cycle of the typewriter—no one can ever afford to be complacent in business or when speculating in a business by buying shares in a company they don't know.

Complacency is synonymous with arrogance, and both stem from ignorance. They are a coverall for procrastination, even for disregarding urgent priorities. Complacency results in failing to prioritize, or losing valuable time in frivolous pursuits or distractions, and not keeping abreast of new and relevant information or technologies or trends, or failure to react positively to relevant new information, and losing sight of the parameters of the job, or failure to follow through. Complacency causes inertia.

Perhaps the greatest example of complacency in Britain came after the initial success of the English Industrial Revolution and imperialism. The upper classes believed everything was going well for them, since they were rich. Once they had made their fortunes by investing in industrial inventions and innovations, like the railways, shipping, and the potteries, and in companies trading with the empire, they built their mansions in the countryside to display their conspicuous consumption to everyone else and were complacent enough to believe there was nothing more to be done. They had arrived, and nothing else mattered.

As a result, once America and Germany copied the industrial revolution in their own countries, Britain began losing markets to them and lagged behind by the middle of the complacent Victorian era. It was in a Great Depression by 1870, when Germany turned out to be more efficient and productive and America was full of bustle and get-up-and-go. But the English disdained trade and commerce. Complacency caused Britain to neglect planning its future or educating its people in science and technology, which was considered of lesser importance than theology, Latin, and Greek.

Complacency caused England's political leaders to continue to ignore what the foreigners on the other side of the channel were up to. Their ignorance of Europe or other foreign cultures must seem unbelievable to today's average teenagers with their fingers on the pulse of overseas tourism through television and the Internet. But, with few exceptions, the English upper classes who held the reins of power didn't believe in reading books or in new ideas. Even their speculation in businesses tended to be more like an extension of the social custom of gambling on the turn of a card. It was not only a matter of attention deficit, but an example of mindlessness.

To illustrate mindlessness in that type of context, award-winning author Kazuo Ishiguro wrote a book, which was made into a film, named *The Remains of the Day*. It features an English aristocrat who is ignorant of what is going on in the world, and his complaisant butler who mindlessly follows his master into disgrace.[11]

Complacency in business can cause the same types of reversals that occurred with Britain's decline as a major world power, because it means not recognizing or acting on opportunities that present themselves and allowing competitors to take the initiatives instead. It leads to procrastination, which means failing to solve minor problems before they erupt into major disasters.[12]

Lack of resolve in leaders comes a close second in importance as one of the frailties of human nature. If it stems from the top, everyone else will follow the example set by the president of the company, by losing their own initiative and seeking distractions.

Poor communications is perhaps the most common failing of CEOs and top managers. It is partly due to the bureaucratic influence of offices concealed behind closed doors. Bureaucracy can be defined, in a business context, as making it harder for people to work.

Traditional offices began to disappear with the influence of companies like Hewlett-Packard, and open-plan offices replaced them with tiny cubicles for executives and staff alike. But even cubicles can cause insularity behind the screens. "Management by walking around" can partly solve the problem of failing to keep in touch with what is going on. And the fact remains that all the business that *is* going on is taking place out there in the marketplace, and in customers' and suppliers' premises, and in retail stores—all the activities that managers should anticipate and react to.

Lack of communications from CEOs and executives who work at a fast pace and are constantly busy often causes an exasperated attitude leading to vain attempts to catch up on events by calling executive meetings and then having to cancel them. Hours and days are often lost in unnecessary meetings or unstructured ones for which no one is sent an agenda to prepare in advance. A bad early meeting can have a debilitating effect on the rest of the day's work. And the sight of executives hanging around waiting for the CEO to turn up is discouraging to staff. Because, if a CEO or owner of a company can afford to keep a highly paid top management team waiting around while he takes a phone call or attends to other business, then the meeting can't be so important. It suggests there is no urgency for them to perform efficiently or effectively. As well as reducing time to complete work, it is one of the prime causes of negativity resulting in stagnation.

Subjectivity

Perhaps the fourth executive sin in importance is halfhearted intelligence gathering. There is less excuse now that most information can be found at the tips of our fingers on the Internet. But the danger is misinformation, on one hand, and also distraction from all the other sites only a click or two away. Statistics point to addictive social sites as the most likely sinkholes to fall in to. An hour can easily go by watching a seductive YouTube video without being aware of the management of time. Then there are electronic games and financial sites. According to ABC News, Google's introduction of the addictive game of Pac-Man cost about 4.8 million hours of lost working time and was estimated to have lost $120 million in productivity.[13] But Facebook is described as "the Internet's largest time-sink."[14]

The problem of intelligence gathering is twofold. If a marketing manager is searching for a revealing study of the market, which was carefully researched by using a selected world of a thousand or more consumers, he or she may not be so thorough or persistent again when the president of the company gives an impression that he values a purely subjective single opinion by himself. Or more likely, his wife or son, or the chairman—or even a recent acquaintance whose views impressed him more than the serious and more scientific research findings of his marketing people. It is more typical than reason might suggest. As a brain specialist remarked on television, "We sabotage ourselves with irrationalities that are going on as mental activity in our unconscious minds."[15]

How often do we hear a leading figure remark in a television interview of one recent personal encounter to prove his point, rather than use more meaningful research of thousands of people who more accurately resemble the object of the discussion?

In fact, there are times when it is better to go out and undertake some of the research ourselves, assess our competitors' stores and merchandise and customers with our own eyes, so that we know what we're up against. Perhaps the most successful strategic manager was Frederick the Great of Prussia, who would not delegate such an import task to a junior officer, but would always choose the terrain for battle himself, to be sure he would dominate the field. But such is the demanding effect of a bureaucratic type of organization that managers are often pinned to their desk by daily priorities of lesser importance. Cubicles may have replaced trap-like offices, but executives still need to get out from under their desk.

Poor coordination in multitasking is commonplace if managers don't prioritize at the beginning of each day and keep a constantly updated running list with activity dates and completion deadlines. It requires an ability for simultaneous thinking along entirely separate lines, not the skill of a bureaucratic administrator with only one idea at a time.

Forgetting the real objective is also common. It can result from distractions and short-term memories. But it is also culture driven. As managers focus on daily activities aimed at date-scheduled goals and events, they fumble and can easily forget some while managing to attend to others. The only way to avoid confusion and errors is by keeping daily records of every major activity to meet agreed goals and superordinate objectives and update them as we go along. The demands on a manager's time are too great not to organize priorities, and to complete one cycle of activities before commencing another. In fact, our brains can be trained to improve their cognitive abilities. EG monitoring or fMRI neuro-feedback is now producing measurable results of better self-regulation of attention, focus, and emotions. But what those measurements really mean is still debatable; so, it is better to hire people who are already suited to the tasks.

Vanity or ego can result from a number of different causes, like the power of giving orders to suppliers or to lesser mortals in the management hierarchy. Whatever the reason, there is plenty of it about in business and institutions. Managers have to cope with it from day to day, whether from a CEO promoted beyond his competence or from another ambitious manager who believes he must compete with others for the CEO's attention, instead of cooperating. Those are some of the factors that cause stress, and superior managers have to learn to cope with it.

Stress in the workplace is not new: it has always been with us in the struggle to succeed and survive. We can understand the working environment better when we reflect on the relevant novels that were written at the time of the English Industrial Revolution, like Elizabeth Gaskells' *Mary Barton* and *North and South*, about workers' relations with industrialists; and Jane Austin's *Pride and Prejudice*. They cover a period when people were conscious of unemployment, mass production, militant trade unions, class antagonism, and sheer desperation— not only of workers coping with long hours and unsanitary conditions and poor pay, but also, as in *North and South*, with mill owners battling with risks in order to survive and thereby create employment.[16]

Elizabeth Gaskell wrote in *Mary Barton* of "misery and hatefulness caused by the love of pursuing wealth, as well as egoism, thoughtlessness and insensitivity of manufacturers." Friedrich Engels was aware of it too, and wrote the Communist Manifesto with Karl Marx in the same year that Gaskell wrote *Mary Barton*, since his father owned a cotton mill in Manchester, and Friedrich was moved by the appalling conditions of the working classes.

Anxiety and Fear

Conditions have improved greatly since those fourteen-hour days of drudgery. Business employees work from nine-to-five, after which they can rush home gleefully to enjoy an evening of leisure. Not so, the conscientious CEO of an established organization or the hard-working entrepreneur of a smaller family business. He or she is far more likely to be conscious of the bottom line of the company's balance sheet or the company's debt-load, while the entrepreneur will dwell on the daily takings and whether the end-of-month revenues will cover payroll costs.

Stress is the price that a business leader or owner pays, and has to cope with on a daily basis. There are five particular situations that intensify tensions. One is the question of *what to do when the markets are saturated with goods?* It may be PCs that have become commodities since the dominant electronic communications devices are now mobiles, or the surplus of nine million homes foreclosed by US banks, and still vacant at the end of 2013, with some falling into ruin.

In one case, warehouses were rented to store a surplus of GE's major domestic appliances, running a risk of damage by piling them on top of each other in layers. Another risk, just as real, was that the inventory would be obsolete when the economy changed and competitors redesigned theirs with more desirable innovations.[17] It resulted from failure to research consumer customs and trends before scheduling production lines of appliances that might soon become unacceptable and unsaleable.

Different Mindsets

It brings up the difference between the mindset of engineers who design electrical or electronic products and the possibly different preferences of users. Did consumers really want a heating element in the bottom drawer of stoves to heat the dinner plates? In fact, they couldn't be bothered anymore. Did they really want an eye-level grill? No, it was too awkward to use and potentially dangerous. Neither innovation lasted long. Today, it is apps and software programs. So, a marketing manager has to be an intermediary between suppliers and users by viewing products through the eyes of consumers, and researching to discover what customers really want, before providing them at a competitive price.

An example of how everything changes and yet manages to remain the same is a similar unhelpful attitude of computer software designers who speak their own invented language to users, in the same way that doctors, lawyers, bureaucrats, and technocrats did in the past. But electronics is a new industry which is supposed to be user friendly. Their inflexible mindset—like those electrical engineers who are more in love with the technology than in customers—is entirely different from users of word processors, even though they have been manufacturing them for over three decades. No one seems to have brought in marketing people in the software culture, to find out what users want and ensure that software programs are easier and quicker to use. It has still not struck them that coping with clumsy or hidden and time-consuming computer tools detracts users from doing work that the devices are supposed to do more easily and quicker. Being forced to focus on the technology instead of on the quality of the content is another example of the failure of suppliers to understand basic marketing principles. Whereas we might expect software designers to be ahead of us, they are often behind the times.

Then there is the entrepreneur's difficult choice of what to do and what *not* to do, *when competitors cut prices to unload excess inventories.* Managers are damned if they follow their lead, because lower profit margins may put the company out of business. Wouldn't it be better to allow price-cutting competitors to suffer that fate? Or is it better to risk losing everything—resources, labor, and production—if the poor economic cycle persists and the value of inventories erodes? It is those types of ambiguous conditions and paradoxical choices that plague a CEO in the hot seat.

In one case, in Canada, the merits of banking on land suddenly and unexpectedly turned into a liability when lending rates rose sharply to over 20 percent in 1980/81 and builders' debt-loads forced them to unload their land holdings all at the same time. Since no one wants to buy liabilities in a recession, they were forced to cut prices down to fire-sale levels. Several went out of business when banks foreclosed on their loans. But some speculators know how and when to turn problems into opportunities. One new builder happened to require raw land to establish his business and kept a cool head while others were panicking to get out of the market. Consequently, he managed to buy an entirely new subdivision cheap, then found a well-capitalized land developer who thought long term, and sold him half the land he had just acquired at a rock bottom price. By the time that the economic cycle rose again, the new home builder possessed a residential subdivision which had cost him nothing. It became the foundation that turned him into one of the top three builders in the region. As for the other shrewd developer, he now possessed a long-term investment which had already appreciated and would continue to be an increasingly valuable asset, even before he built a shopping center on it.

The third stressful situation is *attempting to survive in a financial crisis that causes high levels of unemployment.* It is a similar situation as described previously, in which short-term thinking can cause the unintended consequences of a shrinking number of consumers and shrinking tax revenues. Perhaps the best example of this, in our own time, is the way that large business organizations chose to have their manufacturing undertaken overseas because "the grass looked greener on the other side of the fence."

Seduced by claims of lower labor and overhead cost, and government assistance, those companies who offshored created considerable unemployment in Europe and North America, which resulted in a lengthy period of economic stagnation that still plagues our economies in 2015. No thought was given to jettisoning former employee, who were also regular consumers keeping the economy going. Fire a worker and you pauperize an entire family and prevent them from buying your products and services. That simple equation has been understood clearly for centuries by Japanese culture that looks to the future of its people and recognizes the law of unintended consequences. Western manufacturers and governments have lost what anthropologist Ruth Benedict called a "meticulously explicit map of behavior" that "guaranteed security as long as one followed the rules."[18] Breaking those rules resulted in today's insecurity.

Other historic examples which demonstrate the results of unintended consequences are the eager way in which banks and insurance companies and real estate assessors overloaded people with debts they could never pay off, which led to our present period of mass unemployment and economic stagnation. And what continues to occur in some countries that depend largely on natural resources, like Brazil, the United States, and Canada, is deforestation for immediate cash, without consideration of the future cost of land erosion and greenhouse warming or the extinction of threatened species and the loss of irreplaceable ecologies that support our lives. Short-termism is a dangerous human characteristic and a tempting strategy for business enterprises—particularly today when a traditional objective of staying in business for the long term is frequently discarded in favor of an endgame called a "get-out strategy." Research continually reveals a human failing not to look very far ahead of each step.

The fourth situation that creates anxiety and stress is company inertia. It is a collective disorder, most often caused by previous successes like, for example, a housing boom that takes place long enough for the entire staff of residential builders to begin to assume that this is the norm and they no longer have to manage strategically, or market effectively, or plan for the future, or even *attempt* to sell anything when excess consumer demand automatically results in profits without much effort to acquire them. Instead, builders resort to cutting corners to keep up with consumer demand and push their sub-trades to complete framing, dry-walling, plumbing, and electrics, so that the quality of design and construction deteriorates and quality control standards fall. The result is once-attractive streetscapes destroyed by inferior facades and sprawling new suburbs that soon become slums.

Another problem when an economic tide moves up and all vessels rise with it is the deterioration in organizational behavior. Expectations of rewards have been raised to a level of delusion that neither managers nor other employees have to work, since customers are eagerly lining up to buy. Housing booms raise a question of whether marketing is needed any longer, and professional marketing VPs are let go to reduce costs in a frenzy of greed. Other personnel can easily become deadweights. The question is what to do with them when the economic tide recedes and companies have to hire better-skilled managers and staff who enjoy the challenges of working hard to research and design, develop, market, and sell their products and services again?

When Japanese automakers first opened plants in Ireland, they discovered that trade unions had conditioned members to demand more pay for less work. Leading Japanese companies realized it was quicker and cheaper to train new workers who didn't suffer from those types of delusions. Otherwise, productivity falls and the cost to do business rises, making companies uncompetitive and vulnerable to competition from better managed companies, resulting in job losses.

The fifth problem has plagued us ever since the English Industrial Revolution in the eighteenth century. It is, *How can you provide employment when the trade unions are digging your grave?*

Trade Unions

Trade unions have had their ups and downs wherever workers attempted to improve their conditions and pay by the weight of group bargaining. Sometimes it worked, more often it didn't, for the same reasons why management fails—short-termism. When Elizabeth Gaskell wrote her two major novels about industrialization in England, she portrayed not only the injustices and squalor of workers' conditions but also the huge risks involved in struggling to cover the costs of running a textile mill. Her hardworking and honest mill owner in *North and South* is only saved from financial collapse by marrying the heroine after she receives a substantial bequest from a wealthy friend without any heirs. Most of the other mill owners appear as unscrupulous speculators, only out to make a quick and dishonest profit by exploiting cheap labor.

Cheap labor was what all property owners have always wanted in order to squeeze a profit from their investments. Britain's first Act to protect workers was in 1802. But they did not abolish slavery until 1833. It suggests that either British people would not tolerate the importation of black labor or the white workforce were little more than slaves themselves. But, in fact, black labor was used in mines and quarries in that generation.

Weavers and other cottage industries were forced out of working at home by competition from factories. Even before that, their cottage industries had seldom shown a profit unless supported by a small-holding for subsistence farming. When forced to the cities to find work, their conditions were worse than slavery, because they were not fed, clothed, or sheltered as on American plantations. If lucky, they survived in urban squalor. Labor demands for higher wages came at a time when crops failed all over Europe and the potato famine in Ireland created an excess of available workers, many of whom found refuge in England. So the threat by mill owners to break strikes by bringing in bog-Irish labor was enough to send laborers and machinists scuttling back to work.

That description of class antagonism illustrates the ironic parallel of joblessness today in North America and Europe. What ended the dilemma of constant strikes that cost companies money in lost production in the 1960s was the introduction of robotics. Although the United States pioneered the robotics industry, Japan overtook them and dominated the robotics industry. It maintained its lead in the 1980s, when it was estimated that 80 to 90 percent of its auto assembly lines were automated. And Japan upgraded its software skills to run entire production facilities.[19] But solving one problem always creates others—introducing robotics resulted in job losses. The more recent deindustrialization and offshoring of many US industries caused even more unemployment as part of the law of unintended consequences.

"Last Car Plant Brings Detroit Hope and Cash," claimed *The New York Times* at the end of 2013.[20] "More than 4,600 workers staff Chrysler's sprawling Jefferson North factory nearly around the clock, making one of the most profitable vehicles on the market, the Jeep Grand Cherokee. The plant, painted white and surrounded by a fence topped with barbed wire, generates about $2 billion in annual profits and is a huge contributor to the health of Chrysler, the nation's third-largest automaker, and Fiat, its Italian parent company . . ."

"Few could have envisioned the turnaround when Chrysler tumbled into bankruptcy in 2009 . . . The plant was aging, sales volumes were plummeting and its future was in question. But a government bailout, along with a two-tiered pay structure that cut wages for new employees by $12 an hour, saved the company and delivered it into the hands of Fiat, which now is the majority owner . . . "Fiat has long had its own ups and downs and been saved by the Italian government. Ironically, it was reported that Fiat gets $1.3 billion subsidy from taxpayers in the Chrysler deal.[21] "The infusion of lower-paid workers has bolstered the plant's profitability and competitiveness and provided desperately needed jobs for the community."

It was a similar two-tiered pay structure that brought General Electric back from Asia to Louisville, Kentucky. And one cannot avoid thinking that, if the unions had proposed a similar deal years ago, Chrysler would still be independent of foreign ownership and many of the companies that deindustrialized would not have been tipped to a point where friction with labor unions triggered their departures for what looked like greener pastures overseas. And, with hindsight, we can see that it was all a mirage.

Deindustrialization

Deindustrialization is open to different interpretations, as either reducing a workforce by installing the latest technologies that require fewer workers to run a plant, or transferring all or some manufacturing processes to other countries where large-scale unemployment provides cheaper labor and other incentives, like in China, Mexico, or Bangladesh. Dell Inc. of Texas transferred most of their manufacturing operations from the United States to Asia and Mexico in 2008 and 2009, and many other companies fled from the possibility of labor disputes in the past three decades.

Studies give several reasons for their flight overseas.[22] But they are only theories and appear to be trying to describe the effects rather than the causes. *The Economist* described it as "reshoring manufacturing" and reported that a growing number of American companies were now returning home.

It describes how ET Water Systems moved their manufacturing operations to China during the general exodus to Asia in search of lower costs. They immediately began to lose money, partly because of capital invested in large shipments taking weeks to cross the oceans. Then quality became problematical. Five years later a financial analysis revealed that the cost advantage between making their products in China instead of in the United States was only 10 percent. So it seems the labor unions would have served their members better by agreeing to a 10 percent cut to keep their jobs instead.

But that illusory 10 percent sounds more like wishful thinking after the event, since they are unlikely to have taken into consideration costs incurred in distracting them from what they do best, because it cannot be quantified. It may be far higher than the advantages they would like to think they gained by the upheaval to their company and the US economy. And when the lifestyles of the new middle classes rise in China, the cost of labor is bound to be greater. That is why Chinese manufacturing is declining and some US companies are returning home.

The number of companies coming back, so far, in 2013, was well under a hundred. General Electric's major domestic appliance division in Louisville was one of them. And Google will make its new Nexus Q in San Jose. But, "for many of the biggest firms the amount of work that they are still sending abroad outweighs the amount that they are bringing back onshore. Caterpillar, for example, is opening a new factory in Texas to make excavators, but has just announced that it will expand its research and development activities in China." Caterpillar acquired SEM, a low-end Chinese competitor.

Professors Michael Porter and Jan Rivkin of Harvard Business School argued in 2013 that "firms are now ready to reconsider offshoring. They . . . are discovering hidden costs in moving production a long way from home."[23] Later facts reveal that the honeymoon between the United States and China seems to be over by now.

History reveals moments when weaker minds become perplexed and confused in irrational situations, like the imminent world wars in 1914 and 1939, when they lacked the will to prevent them and let others control their destiny instead. In this case, CEOs were pushed into a corner by the confrontational attitude of self-destructive unions. Management chose deindustrialization to avoid further conflicts they viewed as blackmail. But, by taking a factory-directed approach instead of a marketing one, they allowed themselves to be seduced and deceived by false cost-analysis equations. Wishful thinking turned them back to the eighteenth century gamble on cheap labor—not starving Irish this time, but Asian. But there is a fatal flaw in taking persuasive numbers out of the air, like gamblers in Las Vegas who measure future risks and rewards according to historic numbers, when there is no connection between them. They act on delusions, like trade unions were doing when they chose to become a threat instead of cooperating to improve the economy and create new jobs for their members. There is always a choice between competing or cooperating.

Economist John Maynard Keynes' warned such speculators that they were only gambling on a whim, when he wrote, "We are merely reminding ourselves that human decisions affecting the future whether personal or political or economic, cannot depend on strict mathematical expectations, since the basis for making such calculations does not exist; and that it is our innate urge to activity which makes the wheels go round, our rational selves choosing between the alternatives as best we are able, calculating where we can, but often falling back for our motive on whim or sentiment or chance."[24] That could be the epitaph for offshoring.

The intellectual disciplines required of integrated marketing avoid sentiment or any other persuasive emotional traps from disrupting and misdirecting and sabotaging us. But the drive to earn more and more is so powerful that companies without self-discipline tend to get more excited by unfounded numbers than more scientific strategic marketing plans which might not even be read.

Decline of UK Shipyards

As for Britain, jobs began to be lost soon after World War Two ended. The fate of Scotland's shipyards on the River Clyde sums up the angst. If it was complacency that lost Britain's overseas markets to Germany and the United States as soon as they caught up with the English Industrial Revolution, it was arrogance that lost her markets after the end of the Second World War—an arrogant and unshakable belief in the benefits of an outdated socialist ideology, like nationalizing industries from 1946 to 1969.

"By the late 1950s foreign shipyards (as in Korea and Japan) were more competitive than Scottish shipyards, because of huge subsidies, new construction methods and modular designs. The mid-1960s was an era of poor industrial relations and frequent strikes, making many Clydeside yards increasingly uneconomic. Harland and Wolff's Linthouse yard closed, while Fairfield's of Govan faced bankruptcy."

"The government response was to create Upper Clyde Shipbuilders (UCS) in 1968 with around 8500 workers in five yards—Fairfield's and Stephens on the south bank, Connel's and Yarrow's on the north bank, and John Brown's at Clydebank."

"In 1971 UCS went into receivership and was refused a government loan. The unions, led by [shop stewards] Jimmy Reid and Jimmy Airlie, organized a work-in to complete the orders in place. There were mass demonstrations and world-wide support for the campaign."

"In February 1972, the Heath government caved in and retained two yards, currently run by BAE Systems; Yarrow at Scotstoun and Fairfield's at Govan. Both focus on technologically advanced warships. At the site of John Brown's yard the 800-tonne Titan crane still stands as a lasting memorial to the many great liners and warships it once helped to fit out."[25] Britain, which had been one of the pioneers in manufacturing automobiles, and once boasted of the perfection and craftsmanship of Rolls Royce, the Daimler, the Rover, the Riley, and the Wolseley, ceased making the once-popular Morris cars, too. The brand became defunct in 1984, by which time Japan and the Asian Tigers were taking the lead in the automobile industry.

We don't need to look far for the causes of the collapse of industries in the United Kingdom or the United States. There is a long history of economic pressures that move peoples to encroach on the territories of others, like the history of the Viking raiders and traders that comes to European minds. By the middle of the twentieth century, trade union movements were looked upon by vulnerable businesses as if they too were raiders, since many of the middle classes in England saw themselves caught between the pincers of predatory trade unions and 95 percent super-taxes and took their skills overseas to avoid them both.

Trade unions were vital to protect agricultural labor in nineteenth-century England. And the sentence of transportation for Dorset's "Tolpuddle Martyrs," who formed the first union, was revoked because of large-scale protests. Unions grew in strength because of public sympathy and popular demand to protect working classes from exploitation. But postwar union takeovers of huge industries yielded enormous union profits and gave power to union leaders. Corrupted during socialist years of government in England, they became a threat to Britain's postwar economic revival. Formerly victims, unions became victimizers and were protected by Socialist Prime Ministers like Harold Wilson as long as they swelled the votes for Labour governments. Conservative Prime Minister Edward Heath's meager attempts to quell the damage they caused to Britain's postwar economy was too little: it needed Prime Minister Margaret Thatcher to end their tyranny.

The British trade union power struggle took place when the incidence of violent crimes doubled in England in only one year and prison populations tripled. There was popular hero-worship of new American-style armed gangs in the so-called "permissive society" of the 1960s. Gray and black underground markets burgeoned in a free-for-all, in which trade union leaders elbowed their own way to power and wealth as mobsters.

That and the trade union ties to the socialist government caused the brain-drain of the middle classes out of England—to be replaced by the unemployed from the former industrial north. So that the movement of unemployed agricultural workers and weavers toward employment in northern cities during the industrial revolution was finally reversed when their descendants were drawn south to London for work and caused another social transformation in Britain in the mid-1960s.

Much has changed since then, but not trade unions. With the possible exception of Germany, they still appear to be as confrontational as ever.

Fixed Mindsets

But the biggest enemy of integrated marketing is a tendency that arises periodically to revert to the type of management that existed before marketing became established by successful national and global market leaders. It is a habit of turning companies into unprofitable institutions by hiring safer administrators who set up and follow strict rules and regulations aimed at avoiding risks instead of developing new business.

Bureaucracies thrive on entirely different mind-sets and sets of skills that have nothing to do with commercialization. Whereas marketing aims at making a profit by managing risks that offer new rewards, bureaucracies are strictly controlled to avoid them. But we often see bureaucratic administration creeping in through the back door—as, for example, with the rigid mind-set of software designers. Despite Bill Gates' promise of ease and speed, they can create a virtual nightmare in which users of word processor are tunneled into labyrinths of unnecessary turns and dead-ends and repetitions that make it harder and longer to work. They provide distractions and erect obstacles against creating quality content. Artificial intelligence designed as a substitute for human thought merely exchanges a software writer's judgments for a user's marketing-oriented considerations, without the programmer understanding the user's real purpose. Instead, the program may be designed with the designer's own foibles and biases and tidy bureaucratic mind. Consequently, many users complain they need a pilot's license to operate TVs, the old VCRs, computers, and new automobiles, because of that old-fashioned and misdirected bureaucratic attitude in designing software that makes work harder and discourages business.

That syndrome is similar to the fixedness of mind of some engineers and also their uncritical exuberance at discovering more applications. They are often unable to restrain themselves from incorporating what they themselves enjoy, whether consumers want them or not. That indiscriminating impetuosity was also formerly typical of manufacturers of electric domestic appliances, when their real objective should have been to make it easier for customers to buy and use products or services.

The comparison between manufacturers of small electrical appliances for the home and makers of electronic consumer devices is apt, since, once we have grown accustomed to novelties and overcome our initial awe and admiration and excitement, they become much like any other commodity. Postwar consumers were just as excited at the idea of possessing an all-electric kitchen, which is now commonplace. The introduction of mysterious countertop microwave ovens in 1967, that claimed to make cooking dinners much quicker and easier, has gravitated to our viewing them now as merely a metal box with a technical attachment on offer at Walmart for around fifty dollars. No doubt the same thing will happen one day with smartphones too. What is now still an exciting novelty will very likely be just another commodity.

Obviously, that does not refer to useful electronic devices designed for the medical and scientific professions, architects, and the trade; even for tracking parcel deliveries in transport companies; or taking inventories and restocking shelves in supermarkets. Scientific machines like the fMRI brain scanner have already banished outdated theories and superstitions and mysteries of the human mind with its old-fashioned delusions. The failure of keyhole surgery, on the other hand, is described at the end of this book.

New ideas always excite, until the next big idea comes along to replace them. The manufacture and marketing of personal electronic devices is simply another stage of what began with the first manual typewriter in 1808, followed by the Kodak box camera by Eastman in 1884, the first adding machine by Burroughs in 1885, the first gas-operated automobile by Ford in 1892, the first application for a wireless telegraph patent by Marconi in 1895, the introduction of the telephone by Bell in 1896, and the phonograph by Edison in 1897. Electronics companies have to figure out the next big fashion in order to remain ahead in business.

What those original innovators understood was the virtue of keeping scientific design simple—the art of minimalism that Steve Jobs recognized. While his competitors were showing off how much their devices could do, and adding all the applications and bells and whistles they could think of, he was more focused on removing unnecessary features, apps, and buttons, to make his products more user friendly. It was one of the keys to his success.

6

Managing, Leadership, and Entrepreneurship

The pressures against managing a business enterprise against all of those negative forces are so great that it requires new leaders and superior managers. It immediately brings up the question of leadership style, since a CEO has to orchestrate human resources to have plans executed. He or she also has to keep up with the times and recognize trends, with their possibilities of significant future changes, as well as keeping the chairman and shareholders happy. Perhaps most importantly, the CEO has to create a suitable working environment for integrated marketing at all levels. To do so, he or she has to hire superior managers and ensure they are always directed at corporate and marketing goals and a penultimate target, which may or may not be a specific share of market.

Until the legendary Steve Jobs founded Apple and propelled it into global leadership, the traditional commanding attributes of a business leader involved choosing from about seven different options. They were, loosely, (1) *Autocratic Leadership*, or what amounts to dictatorship; (2) *Benevolent Dictatorship*, perhaps more suited to a family firm that also employs nonfamily managers and staff; (3) *Consultative Leadership* that involves managers in making decisions, instead of just saying, "Do it!"; (4) *Participative Leadership*, which is more democratic and involves mutual consideration and help between the president and managers directly responsible to him or her; (5) *Democratic Leadership* poses the CEO as "first among equals"; (6) *Free-rein* allows and encourages creative ideas and innovations, however unpractical they may first appear, so that they flourish spontaneously with younger and less inhibited, or more impulsive, high-tech or other intelligence workers.[1]

Since Steve Jobs' management style was free-rein, we should question whether it has changed the way a CEO should lead. Jobs was interested in hiring only intellectually and creatively superior designers and software or hardware computer engineers. As we know, he ruthlessly considered any others were a waste of time and space. In today's highly competitive and innovative consumer society, which also requires an instinctive knowledge of new communications technologies and their social and commercial implications, an effective CEO has to be ruthless in the search for superior managers.

But what *is* a superior manager? And what do managers actually do? Much of the rest of this book seeks to find out.

Management guru Henry Mintzberg complained that when he took an MBA course, no one ever discussed what managers *do*.[2] But he did share four facts with us about how managers work. (1) Managers work at an unrelenting pace, with brevity, variety, and discontinuity, and prefer action to reflection. (2) As well as handling major exceptional or unique situations, managers also undertake a number of regular duties, like negotiating and processing soft information that connects the organization to its environment. Also ritual and ceremony. (3) Since top managers need information, a formal information system provides it. (4) Managers are wedded to scheduling time, processing information, and making decisions.

Wrote Mintzberg, "To describe those activities we use words like *judgment* and *intuition . . . but those are mere labels for our ignorance."* *The New York Times* summed up his book by saying that, in total, it suggests that managers deal with calculated chaos and controlled disorder. It may certainly sometimes seem like that to an outsider, because of what a former US Secretary of State called "the fog of war."[3]

If we wonder why Mintzberg admitted to ignorance about *judgment* and *intuition* when attempting to describe what managers do, it is fair to assume it was because he hesitated to pursue either of those two subtle, complex and important subjects, in case he became caught up in a maze of words that might carry him and his readers all over the place, and even trip him up while trying to define them more and more clearly. The reason they are subtle and complex is because big organizations find a contradiction between the "practical" aspects of managing a business and the imaginative and creative ones of discovery, innovation, and invention, which are difficult to describe because that whole sphere was ignored or misunderstood in the past era of administrative management. Despite that, successful inventors in the English and American industrial revolutions, like Edison, Henry Ford, Ben Franklin, Marconi, and Josiah Wedgwood, possessed both sets of skills—an ability to dream up fantastic new ideas and also an instinctive understanding of how to commercialize and market them.

That is why bigger and more hierarchical companies are unlikely to be best for judgment or intuition, both of which require a searching imagination. They are more likely to be imprisoned in past traditions, unbending corporate cultures, and dogmatic philosophies based on what has already been proved to be successful. Consequently, their mindset is closed to new ideas and anything unconventional. But modern companies, like Google, Apple, Facebook, and Microsoft, know that acts of intuition or gut-feel, and creation, are inhibited by conformity.

A Union of Opposites

What makes creativity and innovation even more complex are the almost surrealistic matrices of ideas that often couple themselves together in the imagination to form an extraordinary new idea leading to a successful new product or service. Also the types of people who dream them up. Contrary to a popular idea that they are unpractical and artsy individuals, they are more likely to be scientific inventors—like Marconi or Edison. Or brilliant mathematicians like the secret wartime code-breakers at Britain's Bletchley Park.

Other clear-thinking types were also known for their imaginative and original uprushes, like psychologist Otto Rank with his penetrating study of art and the artist. John Maynard Keynes enjoyed the advantage of creative insights and was the leading economist of the twentieth century. He believed that creativity arises from a dual nature that combines opposites, like the male-and-female characteristics he possessed himself. They are reason *and* intuition, conscious *and* unconscious thoughts, logic *and* feeling, reason *and* imagination.

No doubt the reason why Henry Mintzberg was so reluctant to elaborate on how we make judgments was because judgment is derived from complex conclusions that arise through comparisons, by trial and error, made by intuition *and* reason.[4]

Academic institutions and conservative corporations tend to be scornful of "hunches" and "gut-feel." But they were often all that previous marketing managers had to guide them, when a wealth of knowledge gained by experience formed those subliminal matrices in their unconscious minds. Now we know that the unconscious mind holds information that enables us to pay full attention to other things related to our survival. In addition, the spontaneous and automatic brain, or unconscious mind, is wired for our survival too. One example given of this is that we don't fall out of bed when we are asleep. And, "The unconscious has a greater capacity to hold information," said

Dr. Heather Berlin.[5] Neuroscientists are now able to unlock the brain's hidden potential with fMRI brain imaging that shows unconscious activity as well as conscious. It reveals that the unconscious mind processes ideas outside of our awareness. Freud told us all this a century ago, but didn't have scientific evidence to prove it.

Such was the case when Fuchsian Functions were discovered by mathematician Lazarus Fuchs and solved by Henri Poincaré. They involved several complex variables that only his instincts could find solutions for, since reason failed.[6] "New ideas are thrown up spontaneously like mutations," he wrote, ". . . the vast majority of them are useless . . . A new theoretical concept will live or die according to whether it can come to terms with this environment; its survival value depends on its capacity to yield results."[7]

Now biologists and psychologists understand the value of "flight-or-fight" reactions that arise from intuitions through nerve ends in the gut. This is the dual nature of business that entrepreneurs need to recognize and marketing managers need to embrace—strategic management *and* creativity. It enables managers to be prescient in designing marketing strategies and tactics and predict market trends successfully.

Superior Managers

Turning market forces into opportunities requires superior managers. But what *are* superior managers? Even as early as 1776 Adam Smith warned in his *The Wealth of Nations* that managers would be unlikely to be as vigilant in looking after other people's money as the founder or owner of an enterprise. And when America's economy matured, the more staid and steady British management style was considered too slow, even feeble in comparison with America's "vigorous and original scheming."[8] (Or, as George Gershwin put it, the "national pep" and the "metropolitan madness" of Manhattan.)

Superior managers are as self-driven as entrepreneurs. They have to know instinctively when to delegate and what functions are too important to be delegated. While perfection can never exist, a single-minded compulsion to excel is the best substitute. And an overdeveloped sense of responsibility is an even greater motivator.

To add more specifically to Mintzberg's list of what managers do, they monitor other managers, manage workers, manage time, and manage work. Marketing managers develop plans with short and long-term goals and manage the activities and events in those plans. They are forever seeking opportunities and finding solutions to daunting problems. They regularly analyze the effectiveness of activities and the value of goals, in order to improve the ways and means to achieve a superior performance. And they outsource specialized work where necessary.

If properly selected according to a company's objectives, their personalities, abilities, and attitudes, are likely to enable them to predict well, more often than not, since no one can accurately forecast the future. They measure results by using benchmarks and research to set new standards. They ensure superior content in all their brief and succinct communications. And they are always open minded and flexible in listening to alternative opinions and in the ways they achieve their objectives in uncertain and disorderly circumstances.

And that is by no means all. They anticipate change and use it skillfully and in good time to meet goals. They create and follow management controls, procedures, and systems designed to increase efficiencies, and avoid stumbling blocks and unintended consequences. Since they have the authority to meet agreed goals and final objectives for each product and service, they are willing to be held accountable for their actions. And since they are responsible for their own work, they must be entrepreneurial—which means being creatively original, rather than being trapped in past traditions that may cause inertia.

The self-disciplined and risk-free "man in the grey flannel suit" of twentieth-century Hollywood movies, who simply obeyed his superior's orders, was proven to be unimaginative and sterile instead of inventive. Managers should rather possess Admiral Nelson's ability to disobey superiors when necessary and not succumb to agreeing with them when they know they are wrong.

Research shows that money is not the main or sole stimulus for managers or workers to achieve: they are motivated more by social acceptance and respect. Only weak or insular leaders or tyrants hire yes-men; and they are the type of CEO to avoid working for. Superior managers are self-motivated because they owe much of their identity to what they do: it is who they are. In short, they manage their department, or division or regional branch, as if it were their own company, with a similarly responsible attitude toward payables and receivables, and are ambitious for their company's success.

Superior managers possess other assets as a result of their character and attitude, like a variety of interests; brevity that saves time and avoids possible misunderstandings through talking too much off-the-cuff; a sense of direction; self-development; the productive scheduling of time; persistence in processing information; fine judgments; and positive intuitions. But the most important is imaginative ideation.

Other managers may possess such liabilities as lack of resolution, poor communications skills, faulty intelligence gathering, poor coordination of multitasking, forgetting or bypassing the real objectives, complacency, a negative approach to anything new, lack of imagination, or an inflated ego.

In an environment in which some nineteen-year-old school dropouts come up with original new ideas that turn them into overnight billionaires and create employment for thousands, and even initiate social changes, most people who are not creative are stuck for an answer as to where those new ideas come from. So it may help them to study the wildly inconsistent genesis of Steve Jobs's new ideas that created Apple and launched it on a dizzying ascent to the top of global markets. The online marketing of Michael Dell's personal computers and Microsoft's software, Yahoo!'s search engine, and Google's online advertising, demonstrate that all were masters of unprecedented new inventions. Brainpower was obviously part of the equation that led, in every case, to a point at which each youthful and energetic entrepreneur recognized he was wasting time listening to lecturers talking about theory in the classrooms when they could be doing something more challenging with their intellects and skills—something more useful than having information tossed at them which they could read far more quickly in books on their own, and be productive instead. In short, some highly intelligent students become sharper by avoiding classrooms.

And yet, the teenage Steve Jobs showed little or no promise when he dropped out from Stanford. He was an undisciplined adolescent who seemed to have no sense of direction. He simply went wherever his instincts led him. He tried vegetarianism and length fasts. When they didn't seem to produce results, he tried rock music and LSD. His Hare Krishna singing and dancing led him to India, where a culture of intuition appealed to him more than intellect—perhaps because he was not naturally self-disciplined. His rambling life, that seemed aimless, suggests he would have been hopeless as an executive in a properly structured business enterprise. And there was the dividing line, the fork in the road, indicating that, on the other hand, he was ideal for a more innovative and entrepreneurial company that required intuition aimed at new inventions.

He founded Apple Computer Company in 1977 with venture capitalist Mike Markkula, who insisted that Steve Jobs wrote down a mission statement at the outset and advised him *"to make something he believed in and make a company that will last"*—rather than commence with the usual aim in mind of getting rich. His philosophy was threefold: (1) empathize with customers' feelings; (2) Focus only on the most important opportunities with core products; and (3) Brand an image.

By analyzing what happened over the following years, we can deduce that new ideas come first from *seeing things differently*. That, in turn, leads to thinking differently. And what follows is doing things differently. It arises from intuition, innovation, inspiration, invention, and very often—as with scientists and mathematicians—serendipity. Steve Jobs' fateful encounter at school with Steve Wozniak, and other dysfunctional high-tech nerds at a local club, resulted in the Macintosh Computer.

But, to choose a team to manage and lead, and launch and market the new PC, there was a guiding influence that was the most important ingredient of all. It was called *reality distortion*.

The positive and successful side of reality distortion is, perhaps, best exemplified by Professor Jacob Bronowski's analogy when he described physical and mental gifts.[9] He used as an example the effects on a pole-vaulter's mind when targeted directly ahead of him on the competitive athletic activity he intends to perform immediately. His mind is so fixed on the jump he has been training for that *"he vaults in his imagination into reality"* before he actually jumps. Steve Jobs was often accused of distorting the truth when his reality distortion was what made him take his leaps of imagination and turn them into reality in the future. fMRI brain imaging machines since show that "imagining an act engages the same motor and sensory programs [in the brain] that are involved in doing it."[10]

Divergent Thinking

Creativity is as hard to define at foretelling the future, because it depicts something new and unexpected that has never been done before; so how can we hope to explain it? Perhaps only by analogy and metaphor and examples, as the ancients did when they attempted to describe the unknown. For example, you can stretch the scope of your thinking by deliberately reflecting on happy times, happy thoughts and experiences: it opens a door to unusual possibilities. Happy thinking makes us smile. When we do so, our mind conjures up possibilities and opportunities we never considered before. It is something that women know instinctively while most men apparently do not, because women smile far more than men from the moment they are born. It is one of their ways of reaching out. Hence, the theory proposed by LA studies at University of California claims that women do not instinctively react with flight-or-fight tendencies when threatened, but rather "tend and befriend."[11] That is why women's social skills are useful in all kinds of social sciences and services, including business management. They not only smile more often than men, in order to engage with people, they also talk three times more.

According to psychologists, there are five distinct steps to creativity: Preparation, Incubation, Insight, Evaluation, and Elaboration.[12] There are also four characteristics of creative thinking: Flexibility with playful thinking; Inner motivation; Willingness to make mistakes; and Objective evaluation. It is the "willingness to make mistakes" that opens up the field to all sorts of possibilities—the very opposite of conventional or traditional and sterile management of the past which paid more attention to not taking unnecessary risks. Willingness to make mistakes involves risk-taking.

Creativity is an ability to think about things in new and unusual ways in order to arrive at unconventional and original solutions. "Divergent thinking" produces many answers to the same question, which makes it more likely to arrive at the best ones. People who are open to experience are more creative than others who are not, since creative thinking is based on "insight experience." Even so, some claim that innovative thinking can be learned through practice. But it needs a guru who understands it and can train executives how to use it. One factor that interferes with it is technology. Badly designed technology can be such a hurdle to innovative progress that some readers who have experienced it may wonder whether the digital revolution may result in more problems than solutions.

Three ingredients considered to contribute to success are curiosity, creativity, and intelligence. Every one of the boy-billionaires had it in abundance, including Steve Jobs, whose mind never stopped working compulsively. Silicon Valley is overflowing with those three ingredients. So it should come as no surprise that up to 75 percent of the value of US public companies is based on an intellectual property.[13]

It has become almost axiomatic that intelligence industries cannot be managed autocratically. Typical of that situation was one of the main causes for the birth of Fairchild Semiconductors and Intel. It was Nobel prizewinner William Shockley's unfortunate autocratic manner and insensitive management style at Shockley Semiconductor Laboratory in 1956 that resulted in eight of the engineers defecting. They founded Fairchild Semiconductor in a warehouse in the valley already inhabited by GE, IBM, and HP. Fairchild now has nine thousand employees in locations all over the world. A further defection led to Intel, who employed 104,700 in 2012.

The Macintosh Computer

Steve Jobs mesmerized his product team. As one of them reflected later on, "You did the impossible because you didn't realize it was impossible."[14] He was quick to assess people, and his assessment fell into only two classifications: they were either enlightened geniuses he wanted on his team or he was ruthless in rejecting them. He had no time for negativity, closed minds, or what he thought of as stupidity. He particularly wanted them if he respected their conceptual, engineering, or design skills.

He admitted candidly to stealing ideas that would otherwise have failed in the wrong hands. They succeeded only because he improved them. There's an old saying about composers of music: "amateurs borrow and professionals steal." Steve Jobs was a professional at what he did. But he was an awful manager. That wasn't where his talents lay: he was an impresario, like Diaghilev, who recognized talented people and put them together to make something more meaningful than they could do alone or with anyone else. A sign of his leadership was when his team made T-shirts that said "90 hours a week and loving it!"[15]

But it was one thing for Steve Jobs to innovate, quite another for many business organizations to do so. Even if they have the right creative people and are in a suitable product or service sphere, innovation is too costly and too risky for some companies. Nor is it easy to manage. It requires special attitudes and skills. And it is difficult to recover innovation costs. What's more, it is costly to defend your innovations from competitors. That is why superior managers are needed in the twenty-first century. For example, what came naturally to Steve Jobs was considered too daunting to commercialize by most other companies, like SmithKline's antiulcerant, EMI's CAT Scan, and Xerox's computer. They had to be sold to another company to improve and launch them successfully. It is worth repeating that hierarchical organizations do not encourage original thinking. It means new inventions require a different type of organization altogether.

The Drive to Perfection

Laudable though Steve Jobs' drive for perfection was, it was an obsession more than an asset to insist on design and material perfection in areas of hardware that couldn't even be seen. As a former chairman of Unilever remarked, quality alone cannot guarantee success. There must be a "willingness to modify designs, to adapt . . . this focus on consumer needs is what it is all about . . . How focused is it on the precise solution of customer problems?"[16]

Pained not to be appointed President of Apple Computers, Jobs left to found a new company in 1985, which he named NeXT Computer. Without the corporate restraints on his obsessions and irrationalities and eccentricities, he seemed to do everything wrong in a distracted drive for perfection. He failed to research consumer needs, created the wrong concept and design for the market, overpaid suppliers to get what he insisted he wanted, created an expensive new factory rather than focus all his attention on his product, the pricing, and an appropriate market. He really made this computer for a market of only one—himself. Then he inevitably painted himself into a corner where he had to make a judgment whether to abandon his product and company when funds evaporated or overprice his new computer. But there was no way he'd admit to failure. So he sweet-talked a billionaire into investing in his company and marketed his new product regardless—to end up in the graveyard of unfulfilled hopes. All because, like many other CEOs, he was on an ego trip.[17]

Evidently he also had a split personality. When he first worked on Apple's computers, he was inspired and inspiring. He was led by his own intuition and senses, all of which seemed to be imbued with curiosity that made him acutely analytical, discriminatory, and uncompromising. Impressed by his father's professionalism as a craftsman, he was purposefully driven by his instincts for fine design, and became a driver of others. His restless and free-spirited imagination made him a visionary. And he was consumer oriented in a consumer society in which he knew how to promote and market his products competitively and on time. Those were the powerful, positive, personal characteristics he brought to Apple Computers.

Jobs was already a multimillionaire when he founded NeXT Computers. Whether it was money or power that inflated his ego, he showed himself to others as the same quirky and cranky individual who was driven to have his own way. But a different personality emerged to manipulate and control all the new situations. His temperament was even more volatile than before, because there was no one to calm him down and restrain his impetuosity. He became even more manipulative and even more doggedly uncompromising. He was given to bizarre behavior. He was even ruder to people like suppliers who needed his business, and he bullied them because he could get away with it. He became self-indulgent and blind to market needs: not one bit consumer-oriented as he had been before. Without anyone to rein him in, he became rebellious and insular, an altogether superficial and obsessive-compulsive individual.

Yet, with all those contradictions and an odious personality (as his wife said, he thought he could get away with anything) he became something more than a mere celebrity. After he was invited to return to Apple Inc., as its CEO, and proceeded to lead it from decline to profitability by 1998, Steve Jobs was already a legend in his own lifetime, and a role model. He turned Apple into the most valuable global brand before he died at the end of 2011.

His example leaves us with numerous choices of what to do when managing a company, and what *not* to do. And with the extraordinary successes of other popular new brands in the twenty-first century, and the way they too are apparently loosely managed, his type of management style appears to have had a huge influence on how new and innovative companies are led and managed today.

Leadership by the Dominant Male

On the other hand, the following leadership profile is offered as one that has existed and endured since the beginning of the human race. It is the traditional image of the dominant alpha male that evolution designed to lead a band of apes, or other intelligent animals, and in a hominid society of hunters and food gatherers.[18] "Controlled, cunning, cooperative, attractive to the ladies, good with children, relaxed, tough, and eloquent. Skillful, knowledgeable and proficient in self-defense and hunting."

For an example of this in our own time, we might choose President Clinton or President Obama, either of whose likable personality gives some credence to the definition. But Republicans take a more belligerent attitude about leadership. So we should bear in mind a remark made by a political scientist: "Out of the warlike people arise civilization, while the peaceful collectors and hunters were driven to the ends of the earth."[19]

Of course, we are no longer hunters and gatherers, and business leaders and managers are not involved in military wars. To describe management even more succinctly than business guru Harold Mintzberg, an entrepreneur juggles continually with five balls, or business operations: (1) Customer Relations—through marketing, advertising, and selling; (2) Ways to perform, such as a company philosophy and culture, including its mission; (3) With the most suitable means or operations; (4) Dealer relations; and (5) Employee relations.

In the end, it all depends on choosing the most suitable people with the right temperament and skills and allowing everything else to fall into place.

That applies to virtually any size enterprise, providing a one- or two-person business outsources specialized skills that are only required from time to time. But if a bigger and more traditional organization requires a template for hiring its managers, they will be fortunate to find individuals who can live up to the standards considered desirable for selecting officers to manage departments of the US Navy.

1. *Intelligence:*   Comprehension and mental acuteness
2. *Judgment:*   Discriminating perception
3. *Initiative:*   Constructive thinking and resourcefulness
4. *Forcefulness:*   Moral power
5. *Leadership:*   Directing, controlling, and influencing others
6. *Moral courage:*   Fearless conviction
7. *Cooperation:*   Working harmoniously to achieve common duties
8. *Loyalty:*   Faithfulness, allegiance, constancy
9. *Perseverance:*   Maintaining purpose despite discouragement
10. *Reactions:*   Instinctively logical reactions in emergencies
11. *Endurance:*   Able to carry on under any conditions
12. *Industry:*   Energetic performance of duties
13. *Bearing:*   Correctness and dignity of demeanor

That is their ideal. But reality always differs from ideals. When a company grows beyond the size of a typical SME and becomes either a GSME or a big business—or even a smaller family business that has no management training or sophisticated experience of management from a properly structured company—a fairly common pattern emerges that can result in inertia. It is born largely out of complacency or faith in a bureaucratic style of management. That means, as Peter Drucker might have expressed it, creating a structure and ways and means that prevent a business from operating successfully and making a profit. It is a result of the functional fixedness of tidy administrators with tunnel vision, more intent on filing information away so that no one can use it. The inertia they cause tends to lead to the creation of a glass ceiling through which opportunities can be seen but never fulfilled.

The typical characteristics of six top managers who are exemplified here might have come straight out of one of social psychologist Edwards de Bono's books on behavior in the workplace.[20]

The cast of characters are (1) A president who is rarely seen because his management style is to remain aloof from the company and marketplace in his ivory tower, from which he communicates to top managers by memos with innuendoes intended to keep them off-balance. (2) He employs a cautious general manager whose main skill is criticizing other people's ideas or performance, so that new ideas for improvements cease and inertia takes over. (3) His assistant's sole responsibility, as "Control Center," is to refuse any sales that do not conform to the company's rules and regulations, such as when customers modify the confusing legalese of agreements of purchase and sale to add more consumer-friendly conditions of purchase, which have not been authorized by the general manager. (4) The marketing vice president is generally bursting with ideas and contacts and provides the cash flow that covers payroll costs and bills; but he can rarely obtain cooperation and constantly has hurdles placed in his way. (5) A CFO who is responsible for managing Payables and Receivables and is invariably genial, except when asked to approve budgets, when he has an opportunity to say no. (6) An irascible operations director who is committed to his work and impatient to cut short unnecessary meetings to return to it, by claiming he has no skills in any of the subjects raised.

"The main difficulty of thinking is confusion," wrote de Bono, which suggests that business executives were not doing much thinking in the 1980s or were confused and bemused. He was right, since most companies in the Europe and North America were evidently ignorant of the amount of global business that Japan and the emerging Asian Tigers were taking away from them. Wrote Robert Heller a decade earlier, "Any company that couldn't double its earnings in an inflationary era, in which all manner of juggles for the painless boosting of earnings per share were invented, has no claim to any managerial skills, even low cunning."[21]

Company Characteristics

Fortunately for the economy, not all businesses are like that. The following are more typical characteristics that contribute to successful and unsuccessful companies, from which we can easily see many different reasons for failure or success.

Successful companies have a long-term commitment to their staff, which results in stabilizing and controlling the management of the company and its market position. They plan for the future as well as setting short- and medium-range goals. They communicate through regular meetings of department heads by circulating structured agendas in advance, which give managers time to prepare to share information and set goals. Leadership is top-down so that the tail does not wag the dog, but responsibilities are shared, even though managers are accountable for their actions. Leadership involves creating a harmonious workplace where staff can enjoy their work and working relationships. Good relationships with suppliers result in preferential products and service, prices, discounts, or rebates.

In contrast, companies that hire the six types of top managers that de Bono depicted above have a high staff turnover that results in waste, discontinuity, and lost time and organizational knowledge. Their long-term survival is sacrificed for short-term gains, like bureaucratic neatness and tidiness from (metaphorically) taking everything off the table. Meetings are irregular and frequently postponed at the last moment when the CEO is distracted by other things, discouraging managers and leaving them waiting, resulting in disorganization and lost time. Communications breakdowns lead to costly errors and loss of direction. Lackluster leadership leaves managers and staff powerless to control events. Autocratic CEOs cause frustration, insecurity, anxiety, and even fear of failure, resulting in inertia.

Inertia is an emotional disease that can paralyze a company. Once it sets in, it is difficult to energize a team by warning executives or staff of the danger of failure. Executives with mortgages and other commitments are in denial, while staff are already deserting the company. Meanwhile, careless management leads to loss of controls, and adversarial attitudes result in loss of preferential treatment by suppliers.

Tensions lead to carelessness, demoralization, mishandling customers, loss of sales, faulty judgments, and mishandling debtors and suppliers. Careless budgeting and pricing begins to erode profits, causing apathy among unmotivated staff. Failure to follow up, due to apathy, causes indifference and neglect. Faulty quality controls result in losses from damaged goods. It becomes impossible to replace listless managers who leave, with superior ones, because superior managers will not join a company that is evidently expiring from fatigue and indifference.

Because of huge offers made to attractive companies during periods of mergers and acquisitions, we see two entirely different approaches that identify companies that plan to grow and last, compared with a purely speculative entrepreneur who plans to build an attractive parcel of investment benefits for a takeover bid by planning an end-strategy at the outset. In that case, the entrepreneur has to play his hand without the top management team being aware of his primary goal.

Top managers fall into three fundamental categories. There are those who are adept at climbing a career ladder and moving from company to company as more attractive opportunities present themselves elsewhere, to reach the top rung. They are driven by challenge. So the best will leave to join a more exciting company that rewards initiators, "and leave behind the less able."[22] And there are others who acquire more skills on the job until they reach a point at which they feel confident enough to start up a new company themselves. That type may well be found in intelligence and creative industries. Many others look for long-term security. They are the ones more likely to bring profitability to a company through new ideas and efficient implementation of their plans.

Motivated and organized management and staff enable a company to survive economic downturns with good morale that leads to growth. And a positive culture and working environment that establishes a reputation for being a "best company to work for" attracts superior managers and staff who will contribute new ideas and skills to a winning company because they see there are opportunities there.

Cycles of Change

But just when we think we have mastered the necessary worldview and skills and attitude and tools to meet the needs of the times, everything changes. For example, there was a time during the years of postwar austerity in England when you could drive through the countryside in the southern counties and find an abandoned water mill beside a torrential stream and wonder what happened to what was once a thriving business. Or you might visit an old family trading company in

London that was much reduced within its shabby premises. And you might discover a neighborhood department store that looked dusty and uncared for—not only in a London suburb but also in any other major city—indicating a further dip in a company's life cycle. All are signs that change took place while their owners were unaware of what was happening.

The same thing happens to brands that are not cared for by eager champions. The case of Lyons, which was once the biggest caterer in Europe, is an example of lack of interest by a new generation made wealthy and secure by founders who imagined and initiated and grew the company lovingly, and then passed on, leaving it in disinterested, less ambitious, and less skillful hands.

Jones & Higgins of Peckham was one example of a buy-out by Sir Isaac Wolfson, who was famous at that time as an asset-stripper who recognized the value of properties when others did not. He built up Great Universal stores by acquiring old family department stores that its new family members were disinterested in, even ashamed to admit they were in trade. Another example is the Sainsbury grocery store chain. It was founded in 1869 and became the biggest in Britain, until the brilliant and ambitious Lord Cohen of Tesco Stores displaced their leadership. Nevertheless, Sainsbury are the second biggest, and that is no small achievement in times of brutal competition, when every competitor eyes the pot of gold at the top and wants it for himself.

Change comes regardless of efficiencies or sensibilities, sometimes in generational cycles, sometimes in economic ones. And, more often than not, change comes with other peoples' ambitions and drive which can displace your own if you allow yourself to be complacent for a moment. There may also be family or social problems that distract from business, as the classic novel *Buddenbrooks* portrayed with the rise and fall of a family's fortunes.[23] Worst of all, and far more common, is that just when we need wisdom, it "immediately goes out the door when we are in crisis."[24]

Every business enterprise is vulnerable to dynamic competition from elsewhere, and not just from one energetic and imaginative competitor, but from everyone else in that business category—as we constantly see in statistical breakdowns of market share by companies in most industries, in which a whole horde of nameless "others" often constitute more than 50 percent of the share of business. Companies are also vulnerable to economic downturns.

If managers have a complacent belief in some kind of equilibrium, it is false thinking. Being in business means competing with others, which implies a perpetual state of change—a never-ending process.[25] And change always presents problems that need solving by managers, as well as new challenges to exploit new opportunities that emerge. It needs dynamic top management teams with the wits and skills to understand what is going on in the marketplace and compete, because competition is continuous and dynamic.

Fortunately, superior managers demand continual challenges, because they find purpose and meaning in establishing new goals and fulfilling them. To some, the journey is more important than the destination, whereas for others, the goal is more important than anything else in their lives. It is a substitute for the hunt and the chase. The following example of business dynamism features, in particular, the damaging effects of not being able to distinguish the difference between reality and illusion.

Ten Lessons from Failure

Bob Campeau was greatly admired in the province of Ontario, Canada, because he rose from obscurity to become a multibillionaire property developer. His Campeau Corporation was one of the most respected and successful local brands of tract home builders. Then it suddenly vanished. The lengthy headline of a book about Campeau's impetuous pursuit of power and fame describes what happened to the titan: *Going for Broke: How Robert Campeau Bankrupted the Retail Industry, Jolted the Junk Bond Market, and Bought the Booming 80s to a Crash.*[26]

Campeau's success began when he was demobilized from the armed forces and used his ex-serviceman's grant to obtain a mortgage and build an attractive home. When he received a tempting offer for it, he sold it at a profit and decided he was capable of becoming a professional builder of tract houses. He engaged a first-rate housing vice president and a creative marketing director. One reason he became a local market leader and a legend in the housing industry was because of his appealing designs and excellent construction. Consequently, the Campeau brand became a household name that represented charm, quality, and good value. And he prudently invested his profits in raw land for future construction, since a builder cannot succeed in the long term without serviced land to build on.

Such was the magic of Campeau's brand that, even when other builders were failing to make sales, it required him only to advertise his new residential subdivision, for buyers to arrive in their cars and half-trucks at his provisional sales center. They were prepared to sign agreements of purchase and sale even before he'd priced his new homes, because of his range of designs and location and consumer trust in his brand—a situation almost unknown before or afterward.

Campeau's problems began when he was already established and wealthy and ambitious to hunt bigger game and conquer bigger territories. It was the department store industry in the United States, which he knew nothing about, but was wealthy enough to become a raider. Then, almost on a whim, he liquidated his successful business to obtain shareholder control of Allied Stores Corp. in 1986 and Federated Department Stores in 1988. Campeau's wealth was estimated at $10 billion. He paid $3.5 billion for Allied and $6.6 billion for Federated, without investigating the industry or the marketplace. Otherwise, he would have known it was in deep trouble.

Campeau evidently imagined he could repay his debt-load from future profits, without having any idea of the retail trade or the values of store locations, or merchandizing, or local competition. Despite those omissions, he felt so successful that he built himself a thirty thousand square-foot mansion with thirteen bathrooms on Toronto's exclusive Bridle Path.

Paradoxically, he believed he could obtain a better return from his capital investment in department stores than from building residential and commercial properties. And yet his own experience had already shown him how huge profits could be made in real estate. The gap in his reasoning could only be explained by the adrenaline rush of a gambler that turns him away from reason to make him a victim of his own emotions, which appear to have been dominated by egotism.

Campeau Corp. was reeling under its debts by 1990, and Allied and Federated filed for bankruptcy protection. Bob Campeau was ousted from the company. He became locked in a legal battle for the remains of his family assets which were tied up, since he'd put everything in his wife's name. He was also being sued by his daughter. Even the land he planned to build on for a comeback in Ottawa was frozen by his wife; and his marriage was ended. Campeau was living out the results of the fable of the greedy dog in Aesop's story that drops the bone in its mouth for the bigger one it imagines it sees reflected in a puddle. It had all been a delusion. Now he was being treated for clinical depression.

Lesson number one is that it is safer to stick to what you know. Second, you have to recognize when to exit gracefully from a deal before it is too late. Campeau became mesmerized by the potential rewards without fully considering the extent of the risks. In that regard, he was neither an investor nor a speculator, but a gambler.

Ego becomes a very large component where money and power and property are concerned, and an inflated ego often makes people act stupidly. So the fifth lesson is that CEOs can act irrationally just like everyone else, but their risk is greater, because they gamble the entire company, as Bob Campeau did. And we all know the temptation when the grass looks greener on the other side of the fence.

The seventh lesson is, don't enter a market you don't know, without considerable research and time to accumulate enough knowledge to be able to either reduce the risks or walk away from them.

The eighth lesson is that discarding a real opportunity for an illusory one results from a personal delusion of grandeur. Lesson number nine is that it takes unusual foresight to anticipate the unexpected. It arises generally from considerable experience in an industry and market, from curiosity, sensitivity, intelligence, and flexibility in the uneasy choice of the instinctive fight-or-flight reaction.

The tenth lesson is one unfortunately learnt only from hindsight: it is that hubris is always punished by failure. Those who possess it are usually blinded by self-love. That is why Roman generals awarded a triumphant parade were obliged to have a slave with them in their chariot to whisper repeatedly in their ear, "Remember you are only human."

The Ancient Greeks Had a Word for It

Apple's Steve Jobs was only human too. Nevertheless, he was intolerant of the second rate and always strove for a competitive advantage. So, before he dropped out of Stanford, he may have been directed to read a particular book by the Greek philosopher Aristotle. Aristotle studied under Plato in Athens and opened his own Academy around 340 BC. He was invited by King Philip of Macedonia to tutor his thirteen-year-old son, who would become Alexander the Great. One of the many books Aristotle wrote that survived Christendom and the destruction of the library at Alexandria is called *Nicomachean Ethics*.

If Steve Jobs had read it, he would have learnt that Aristotle considered "professional pride in work" to be a prime virtue. Aristotle encapsulated that attribute in the most suitable Greek word. It is aretē. For example, the aretē of a shoemaker makes him produce good shoes. Aretē is the quality in a racehorse that makes it win. The aretē of a musical instrument makes it respond with perfection when correctly played. In other words, aretē is the quality that enables its possessor to excel.

Not everyone is driven to excel. Some think it excessive, others view it as compulsive. Nevertheless, it is a desirable quality in any business organization that aims to be a market leader. And Steve Jobs was driven by aretē.

But how can chief executive officers or human resource directors find superior executives with the same mind-set and goal as theirs? When it comes to sourcing superior managers and marketers, the big five personality traits, as psychologists describe them, are (1) Openness, (2) Conscientiousness, (3) Extroversion, (4) Agreeableness, and (5) Neuroticism.[27] Steve Jobs fell into the fifth category.

Human resource companies have continually tried to head-hunt executives with the first four personality characteristics in the past, and most companies that hired them generally produced only lukewarm results. Knowing the conservatism of many large business organizations and personnel departments, most recruitment companies took care to avoid the fifth important characteristic—important because many or most brilliant creative people are sometimes thought to be neurotic—although the label is often used loosely to describe nonconformists. But it is a quality that enables creative knowledge workers to stretch the boundaries of their imagination to produce original new ideas and solutions to complex problems—particularly in today's intelligence industries. But it was not viewed favorably before World War Two.

That crisis resulted in a deliberate search for brilliant people who think and act differently from most others. It began in 1939, when Britain was unprepared for war against Germany's bigger and better armed and better trained military forces. Britain needed a dominant competitive advantage in order to win. So brilliant cryptographers were required to crack Germany's military codes at England's "National Codes and Cipher Centre" at Bletchley Park in Surrey. It became a famously successful enterprise that included a number of outstanding mathematicians who were successful code-breakers. And all possessed that rare and much sought after quality that Aristotle called aretē.

The rainbow of personality characteristics also includes eight introverts with more stable personalities, which were once thought ideal for staffing more conservative Blue Chip companies. They are "Passive, Careful, Thoughtful, Peaceful, Controlled, Reliable, Even-tempered, and Calm." But it turns out that they are more suited to government employees manning defensive positions to keep risks at bay, rather than imaginative and motivated to take risky initiatives. Devoid of offensive tactics, they are unlikely to be competitive in today's age of anxiety.

Part of that anxiety arises because the whiz kids at Menlo Park created a market that became a willing herd to be harvested, or fleeced, like past nomadic cattle cultures. Laplanders survived by living off the milk, hides, and hair of reindeer herds—an imaginative survival strategy which endured for centuries. While the cattle simile may be unflattering and seem extreme, the Internet and social media tend to demonstrate that most people's lives are nothing more than food-gathering and sexual reflexes to be programmed and conditioned by pseudo-situations arranged by the masterly manipulators of Silicon Valley.

But those whiz kids must be asking how long their target market can last and how to perpetuate it in such a slack economy. The consumers they harvest are notoriously inquisitive and fickle, easily bored, and always searching for something new. And with the decline of industrial manufacturing, our economy is concentrated largely on those restless thirteen to twenty-three-year-old consumers. If software and hardware suppliers fail to provide suitable apps, or other bells and whistles, or new electronic devices, or confuse them, the services they offer may become even more complicated, instead of easier as originally promised. And the herd may lose interest in what were once novelties and be drawn to other, newer, fashions.

7

Advertising and Communications

It was difficult to find a manager who still knew how to write a persuasive business letter by 1975. Although they might have been out there somewhere among the Top 500 companies, other priorities appeared to be distracting them that prompted Robert Heller's dissatisfaction with management skills, including an inability to make profits by exploiting opportunities in the marketplace.[1] That was long before the smartphone era of texting brief messages.

Although some of the finest marketing companies still managed to coax cost-effective advertising out of major ad agencies that continued to sell their products and services, the quality of strategic creativity had declined. Then a new advertising agency was opened by two brothers in London in 1970. Hired by the Conservative Party at a run-up to the general election in Britain, it made an impact on the electorate with a simple poster that said "Labour isn't Working." It showed a very long lineup of unemployed people snaking its way across an empty horizontal space to an unemployment office in the far corner. Such was the immediate effect of the innuendo or double entendre that their message didn't need a "screamer" at the end of its statement, or another word of explanation. It obviously referred to the Labour Party.

Captivating ideas make more impact with minimalist execution—as French impressionist painters discovered when they saw seventeenth-century Japanese wood block prints. They very likely influenced the startling posters for the *Folies Bergere* by Toulouse Lautrec. The Lautrec effect was captured later on by Abraham Games, Ashley Havinden, and E. McKnight-Kauffer—even Fougasse's posters—in London's Underground stations in the 1940s. Perhaps they influenced the Saatchi brothers.

At any rate, Saatchi & Saatchi had arrived.[2] And their influence became palpable. The Labour Party sneered that the Conservatives were "selling politics like soap-powder."[3] Lord Thorneycroft claimed the poster won the election for the Conservative Party. And, before the twentieth century came to a close in 1999, *Campaign* voted it the "Best Poster of the Century."[4]

Despite the desirability of minimalism and economy of words, no one could have foreseen that writing persuasive business letters, or any letters at all, would become a lost art, derisively known as "snail-mail," and replaced by online emails and text messaging on mobiles and smartphones with a maximum of 160 characters.

The following time schedule outlines the way the digital communications revolution took place one step at a time.[5]

1950:   The Internet began as a Department of Defense communications network.

1971:   Emailing, or electronic messaging, was developed.[6]

1971:   eBooks began at the same time with Project Gutenberg.[7]

1975:   The first email program was developed.[8]

1977:   The PC modem was developed and sold to hobbyists when the Internet was designed as we know it today.[9]

1978:   The first advertising appeared on email, known as SPAM.

1984:   Domain names appeared.

1985:   Virtual communities appeared online.

1987:   The Internet grew significantly, popularized by AOL (America Online).

1989:   Considerable speculation was voiced about the coming World Wide Web.

1991:   The first web page was created.

1995:   The Internet became commercialized when Netscape developed a Secure Sockets Layer to conduct financial transactions safely online by credit card payments.

1995:   Amazon.com appeared online.

1995:   eBay started up on the Internet.

1996:   Hotmail, the first web-based email service started its operations.

1998:   Google's online search engine got going.

2000:   The dotcom bubble burst because websites failed to offer consumer benefits online that could be monetized; revealing a first glimpse that consumers were not prepared to pay for information online.

2001:   Wikipedia was launched.

2003:   Print On Demand (POD) technology enabled books to be printed only when sold, and led to self-publishing authors.

2004: Web 2.0 became a user-driven interactive website platform for software applications that exploits the connectivity of the Internet.

2004: Social media became a mainstream concept for creating and sharing content with users around the world.

2004: Facebook opened to college students.

2005: YouTube streamed online videos free to the public.

2006: Twitter was launched.

2007: Hulu enabled consumers to choose popular TV shows online.

2007: The iPhone became a successful innovation, renewing interest in mobile applications.

2008: The first Internet Presidential Election took place in the United States and Hillary Clinton was quick to make campaign videos on YouTube.

Cause and Effects

Several of those new technologies directly affected the publishing industry. There was good news and bad news. Some led to digital publishing that created more book readers through the conveniences and low prices of eBooks. But the Internet—which publishers once feared might replace the printed book trade—had a destructive effect on the newspaper industry. The introduction online of Amazon.com took sales away from retail book stores but, at the same time, became indispensable for self-publishing authors. Print On Demand technology (POD) reduced publishers' printing and inventory and warehousing costs to make smaller publishers more competitive. Social media, like Facebook, became flooded with authors' own public relations blogs for their crime and romance novels. And smartphones and other mobiles gave users access to all other online media and television.

In the past, print media could reassure advertisers by disclosing print runs and readership figures. Statistics certified by the Newspaper Press Union revealed readers' demographics. Media agencies used computers to calculate the cost per thousand to reach targeted audiences. And there were consumer studies by Nielsen Media Research. Now it is even more difficult for advertisers to know which medium to advertise in. Said Nielsen in 2014, "Today's viewers consume almost 62 hours of content each week across TV, radio, online and mobile, and are exposed to thousands of advertisements—in such a cluttered environment how can you create advertising that breaks through this noise, register with the consumer and ultimately drive sales for your brand or product?"

The cost to advertise in print had become far too great for most advertisers after newspapers continually increased their advertising rates as they became more confident that they were indispensable. And advertising rates for television became prohibitive for all advertisers except national and global market leaders. Magazines proliferated until it became too difficult to know with certainty which ones showed a return on investment and which were a waste of advertiser' dollars.

But it took a long time before the Internet became, for many, the only medium worth advertising in, because at first it was almost impossible to know how many viewers used it regularly. Usage steadily increased, with viewers becoming addicted to it at work during the day and at home at night. Two decades later, we know that regular users represent almost as much as 80 percent of the population in the West. Some countries are further ahead than others, with North America already habituated to it. Even so, it is uncertain what to advise advertisers to use, to maximize online sales, because there are so few hard facts available. Ones that are, like those released by the long-established Nielsen Media Research, tend to view the use of advertising media through the eyes of their major clients who have very large budgets to play with, which allow a margin for possible waste, whereas the average small or medium-size businesses do not, and can't afford to allow any waste at all.

At the other end of the scale from national and global market leaders, a custom home builder is more likely to advertise in a glossy homes magazine with beautifully photographed interiors of new houses, because of the fine reproduction and the relatively modest overall cost of the medium. The same applies to real estate agents. And it is unlikely that either of them estimate the cost per enquiry, or the even smaller number of enquiries they convert into sales. If they did, they would find it far too expensive. But what else is there for a small entrepreneur?

Real estate agents are more likely to be able to afford only local outdoor advertising at bus stops. And, since there is no accurate way to measure how many people even notice such displays, and how many who do are interested in selling their home or buying a new one, the odds mount up against that type of outdoor advertising being cost-effective.

National and global market leaders in the manufacturing industry, like Procter & Gamble, who sell packaged consumer goods, are likely to have among the biggest advertising budgets, since their products sell at low unit prices and have to be fast-moving in enormous volumes to produce profits. That requires a lot of brand advertising, and also promotional advertising when inventory levels are too high. Since those are the types of companies who use the expertise of sophisticated research companies, their studies and results are bound to relate more to their kind of production volumes and scale of distribution.

In short, it is still too early to advise advertisers where to place their messages in order to maximize sales and minimize budget wastage, except for national and global market leaders who can afford the cost of TV advertising. Advertising on social media is still in its infancy, with online media still looking for ways to monetize their websites.

The following is a summary of the main advertising media available, so far, in the twenty-first century and the characteristics of each one that make it desirable or undesirable for different industries or types of advertisers to use.

Outdoor Advertising Depends on Location

Advertising began outdoors. Stick up a poster to draw attention to your shop, or your products and services, and you instantly imagine all the people who will see it and buy your goods. But that is not what happens. In the first place, the advertiser is bound to be subjective and biased in his own favor, because he took time involving himself in his advertisement and has lived with his products or brand long enough to believe that everyone else is familiar with them. In reality, pedestrians are unlikely to notice a sign above their own eye-level, and vehicles pass too quickly for drivers or passengers to glance up at a sign from an even lower perspective. Even if they did, it would be unreadable at speed.

The question of whether an advertisement is structured properly in the first place, or its concept or design is good enough to actually sell the products, is answered in the following chapter.

In any case, we can assume that all the best locations for billboards that advertisers consider may have some merit have already been rented by those huge market leaders who use them as a support medium to their main advertising on TV. They may decide to fill in any possible demographic gaps in the market by using signs, since they can afford to risk their spare change. So billboards may become part of a marketing mix to keep their established brand continually at the forefront of consumers' minds for when they are ready to buy—like a gambler spreading his bets and hoping to keep his brand at the very top of all the other brands hovering in consumers' minds.

Outdoor advertising is generally placed in densely crowded downtown areas to catch the eye, and in heavy traffic suburbs, and it is impossible to measure their effect on sales with any accuracy. Smaller billboards identify local retail shops and local services, like beauty parlors and real estate brokers, or funeral directors. Since responses cannot be scientifically measured, other than having customers fill in cards asking what brought them to a store, there is inevitably an element of gambling, or recognition that there are few other alternatives, except for small online advertisements, which they are likely to use anyway. Consequently, the amount of ad budget allocated to outdoor billboards represented only 5 percent share of total US ad spend (according to Strategy Analytics).

Newspapers Take a Dive

The long-lasting communications and advertising medium of newspapers began mass market commercial advertising by renting out space in their pages to advertisers or agents. The space is still measured and charged for by column inches. Despite increased costs that already discouraged advertising even before the global economic crisis and the introduction of the Internet, newspapers still play an important role in the media mix to reach the mass market. But there are fewer readers than before and readership is still declining. Reduced revenues have even affected the content of most newspapers, because of cost-cutting in order to stay in business.

The introduction of the Internet changed reading customs, because online news is immediate and free. Reducing quality was one way to stay in business. And, in many cases, experienced reporters, journalists, and editors were replaced by bloggers. Since blogging is defined as writing anything, such writers can be uninformed amateurs. In general, bloggers are compulsive writers who like to see themselves in print and produce a variety of gossip and personal opinions, rather than the objective, responsible, and professional investigative journalism that readers were accustomed to.

In any case, police enquiries into the unsavory practices of the multi-billionaire newspaper tycoon, Rupert Murdoch, in the United Kingdom, demonstrated that more revenues could be derived from searching out and reporting gossip and scandals to a mass market, instead of more serious journalism. But experienced advertisers know that the image of an advertising medium can tarnish their own brands. And its lack of credibility can destroy confidence in their advertising message.

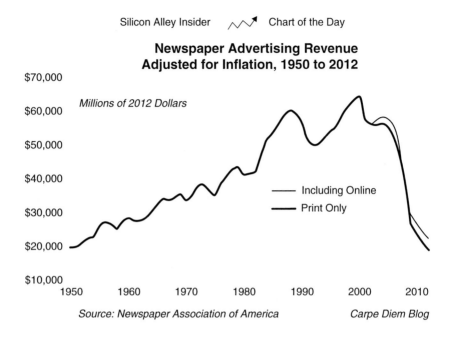

Silicon Alley Insider   Chart of the Day

**Newspaper Advertising Revenue
Adjusted for Inflation, 1950 to 2012**

Millions of 2012 Dollars

— Including Online
— Print Only

Source: Newspaper Association of America   Carpe Diem Blog

Newspapers attempted to join the Internet by publishing their news online rather than be beaten by online news media. But most attempts to charge the public for special informative articles failed, except for a small handful of leading newspapers whose strong brand image created trust and confidence in the minds of more intelligent readers.

The introduction of online news media led to a plunge in sales of newspapers, and advertising revenues shrank. No one can foretell the future of newspapers at this moment in time. Nevertheless, the share of advertising media budgeted for print, including magazines, in 2015 was 15 percent.[10]

Provincial, suburban, and country newspapers that provide local news are more stable because they selectively target local consumers and are, more or less, distributed to the entire local population, whereas the growth of ethnic newspapers in an immigrant language in multicultural societies is problematic. Although opportunities motivate entrepreneurs of a particular community to start up a newspaper in the local vernacular, most do not charge for copies and rely on advertising, which is also problematical; so the life of many of those print publications is short.

Magazines Take Time to Warm Up

Magazines come and go, too, depending on the whims and fashions of each new generation. Advertisers will use them only if the volume and demographics of readers are meaningful for their products and brands and marketing objectives.

Magazines and trade journals can target even narrower market segments by gender, age group, income, profession, or trade. But they take much more time to build up the momentum of a brand image or the impact of a selling message. It is often the subtle subliminal type of advertising that works in fashion and home magazines over the long term. Glossy magazines are aimed largely at creating a bigger mind-share for quality brands by featuring exceptional, and often startling, photographs of glamorous models using or demonstrating exclusive products like perfumes or toiletries. Magazines that appeal to young women readers in particular use all kinds of sex appeal, from dieting and detoxing that promise to transform them into goddesses, to plunging necklines and well-chosen legs of beautiful fashion and photographic models, all displayed glamorously as intended role models for readers.

There are clearly designated magazines for DIY men, bodybuilders, automobile fans, tourists, young mothers, and teenagers. But sex plays a particular role as a motivation for using cosmetics, toiletries, swimwear, lingerie, and fashionable clothing and accessories, with stylish imported labels. So the two key elements in women's magazines, and even glossy ones featuring fashionable homes, are brand momentum and sex appeal.

TV Is the Most Expensive Advertising Medium

TV became first choice for major market leaders to advertise on. It led to Lever Brother's successful soap operas, the "Colgate Comedy Hour" and "Kraft Television Theater," which drew large audiences. Such was the hypnotic power of television to entertain in the home that it competed successfully against cinemas and theaters, destroying the old Hollywood studio system and closing down many theaters in Europe and North America. It demonstrates that people prefer entertainment to come to them, rather than having to go out for it.

Advertisers who pay for TV commercials like to assume "on astonishingly weak evidence, that some meaningful percentage of viewers actually watch commercials. They have further agreed to believe, again without good evidence, that the sort of people who watch a particular program have more than an ordinary interest in the products advertised in the program."[11]

The average American now spends 20 percent of the day watching TV, and more than thirty-three hours a week watching videos across all their screens. So how do advertisers know if they caught their targeted audiences when viewers have several screens in different rooms and a multitude of different channels to choose from, plus the Internet? A measurement that includes the Internet is called "Cross Platform."

TV's great advantage was showing how dysfunctional lifestyles could be transformed into leisurely and glamorous ones after buying the advertised products and also in demonstrating how small and large appliances work. It became so addictive that many bought additional television sets for the bedroom and the kids' room, or the sunroom. And the rapid increase of TV viewers enabled the content distributors to increase their rates. The cost to advertise on prime time soared, leaving it largely to national and global mass marketers to use TV media.

Television is particularly successful for advertising at major sports events like "The Super Bowl Championship" in the United States. CBC and NBC networks charged $3 million for a thirty-second advertisement in 2009, making TV the most expensive advertising medium. In spite of that, TV advertisement spending was $18.4 billion at the last quarter of 2012.

The 2015 shares of US ad spend for TV amounts to 42 percent of the total advertising media budget. (*Cinema*: less than 1 percent).[12]

But, with over five hundred channels to choose from, the odds are loaded against a specifically targeted audience watching when the advertising aimed at them is screened. It would be understandable if advertisers consider they may be gambling rather than investing in the media to obtain a good return for their money. That might depend on Nielsen's numbers when they use Gross Ratings Points to measure the degree of "Engagement and Response."

Radio Can Draw Crowds

Radio offers far lower rates because continual research findings show that people's memories for audio messages fade quickly. So it currently represents only 6.9 percent of advertisers' media mix. Its advantage is that its low cost makes it available for small businesses, in particular, using local radio stations to promote special sales in local retail stores. It can draw crowds on weekends if done well, particularly as car radios and transistors and boom boxes are used more than ever today, partly as a consequence of longer traffic jams and more traveling on vacation. There is almost a captive family audience in an automobile or a caravan trailer. But even then, there is competition from DVDs or old-fashioned audio tapes, and squabbles between family members for favorite radio channels.

Research shows major listeners of radio in a wide age spread of eighteen to forty. Peak listening times are the best for advertising and promotions. But, due to other distractions and short memories, messages must be brief and focused on only one selling idea, message, or theme, and constantly repeated to make an impact on listeners who are easily distracted. Thirteen percent of the US population now listen to radio on the Internet.

Radio's share of total media budget in the United States in 2015 was 10 percent (Strategy Analytics).

Internet Users Are a Hybrid Audience

Online advertising is the fastest growing medium and considered to be the most cost effective. Eighty percent of consumers in North America and the United Kingdom used the Internet regularly in 2013. Measurement of Internet audiences also includes users of all devices, like mobiles, tablets, and secondary PCs—also of locations outside of homes and work stations. Revenues from online advertising amounted to $36.57 billion in the United States alone in 2012, which was 15.2 percent more than in the previous year. It was used by most industries. But much of the Internet is still controversial. Nevertheless, digital's share of total US advertising budgets in 2015 was 28 percent.

Specialized websites enable advertisers to target niche markets. And "interest-based" advertising provides individuals with advertisements that match their typical preferences which Google's algorithms analyze and pinpoint from the user's own regular online searches.

Nielsen describes online audiences as *hybrids*—defined as a cross between two or more different types. For example, one might be "a shopper, a car-pooling power mom, a TV watcher, a tweeter, *and* a texter."

User-friendliness of the Internet led to the success of online social media, like Twitter, which reported 236 million monthly active users worldwide in Q1 2015. Facebook claimed 1.44 billion monthly users in 2015. LinkedIn reported more than 364 million members worldwide in Q1 2015. YouTube claimed more than a billion viewers generated six billion views of videos a month in Q1 2015. Half of YouTube views were watched on mobile devices.[13]

Google still maintained its leadership of the search engine market with 66.9 percent, followed by Microsoft with 18 percent, Yahoo with 11.3 percent, Ask with 2.5 percent, and AOL with 1.3 percent.[14]

Mobile Is Now the Preferred Medium

Mobile has now been the preferred medium for communications since 2013, and growing faster in use than ever—probably because we like to have something with us, rather than have the hassle to go find it (just like TV replaced going out to cinemas and theaters for some audiences).

As the mobile smartphone became more than just a phone, with its digital camera, and its apps, it became addictive for its owners, then indispensable. Owners have become so dependent on it that it is often the last thing they talk to before sleeping at night and the first thing they greet in the morning. It would certainly appear to be the one digital device that won't ever be taken for granted, as new apps mirror new changes in the social scene. It has already become so personal that its users miss it if they happen to leave it behind.

The following information from 2011 to 2015 illustrates the trend from a useful portable phone to obsession with it as an entry into fantasy encounters in a twenty-first century *Arabian Nights*, for which you don't even have to say "Open Sesame!" to be transported to wherever you want to go.

Texting is now the most popular form of communicating in the United Kingdom. A new report showed that speaking on a mobile phone declined for the first time in 2011 in favor of sending messages by text. Brits sent two hundred texts per month, on average in 2011—more than double the number they texted four years previously. According to Nielsen Research, the average teen sent or received 3,339 text messages each month. And the behavior of the thirteen to twenty-three age group is key, since few people are seduced by new ideas after age twenty-four.

Smartphone penetration in the United States was 70 percent by the second quarter of 2014. And they quickly became addictive, so that US consumers spent seven more hours a month with their phones than in the previous year. Mobiles (said Nielsen) have already become an extension of the individual (echoing what electronic technology guru

Marshall McLuhan had predicted long before its mass introduction to the marketplace). They have become our alter ego.

The extent to which users have become emotionally connected to their smartphones, which frequently contain a considerable amount of personal information, is shown by one of the saddest cases of mobile ownership and its possessiveness. It involved a young Canadian man of eighteen, who accidentally left his phone in a taxicab in June 2015. As soon as Jeremy Cook discovered the loss, he tracked down its location by using his friend's digital apps and raced after it. Instead of tracing it to the taxi driver, it was already in the hands of three armed men in a car. They responded to his attempts to retrieve it by shooting him multiple times. He died from the gunshot wounds.[15] Police now advise owners who mislay their smartphones to call them immediately and not risk the unintended consequences of tracing it themselves.

"People expect a new experience with technology," said Nielsen in 2014. "Our phones are with us all day every day, giving recommendations, directions, information and more . . . People spend more than 38 hours per month on their phones." That was in 2014. And smartphone usage increased by 2015. Yet, Nielsen points out, advertisers spent only about 4 percent of their total ad budget on them.[16]

- Due to increased tablet and smartphone use, Canadian consumers reported listening to 20 percent more music than two years earlier, in the first quarter of 2015 (teens 40 percent more). And music was listened to twenty-four hours a week (thirty-one hours by teens). Most was in the background while performing other activities.
- In 2015, teens spent a third of their music time while playing video games, reading, and surfing the Internet.
- In a 2015 Canadian research study, 46 percent of consumers reported streaming music, with teens spending twice as much time as the others (56 percent of music festival attendees); 37 percent were also radio listeners.[17]

Mobile Communications (United Kingdom, Mid-2011):

	Average Use (Percent)	Age 16–24 (Percent)
Texting	58%	90%
Face-to-face	49%	63%
Mobile	47%	67%
Social Networks	33%	74%

By 2015, "Nearly two-thirds of Americans own a smartphone" (64 percent); 19 percent use them for "accessing online services and information and for staying connected to the world around them." The most recent consumer survey in 2015 revealed that using a smartphone created two different types of emotions that lingered—one a feeling of productivity and happiness, the other of distraction or frustration after mobile screen encounters.

IDC predicted that "87% of connected devices will be Tablets and Smartphones by 2017, and the trend to mobiles will very likely propel cellphone and tablet ownership past PCs in 2014."[18] It has.

Mobile and Tablets

Previous numbers don't necessarily apply to commercial communications or advertising, but 39 percent of adults in the United Kingdom own a smartphone which encourages bargain-hunting. Calls on landlines continue to decrease at a rate of 10 percent a year. And the behavior pattern formed by teenagers is likely to continue and even increase in volume.

Ownership of tablet devices, like Apple's iPad and Samsung's Galaxy Tab, rose to 11 percent of UK households by mid-2011; 10 percent have an e-reader; 37 percent of adults in the United Kingdom watch online catch-ups of TV programs on the Internet; 85 percent of tablet owners watch TV on their tablets.[19] The largest recent movers to the Internet were "diehards" aged sixty-five to seventy-four.

Social Networking Sites

- About 74 percent of online adults used social networking sites in 2014. Demographics of users varied little according to gender, age group, or education.
- By 2015, 24 percent of American teens (age 13–17) were constantly online using a smartphone; 92 percent of teenage users go online daily; 71 percent have access to a smartphone.
- Facebook is the most frequently used social media platform by teens. Half use Instagram and nearly half use Snapchat. Twitter, Google, Vine, Tumblr, and others follow in that order.[20]

Smartphones for Engagement and Response

Since the Internet has become movable, and so small you can carry it in a pocket, and the dominant device for accessing it is a smartphone, the following are the most up-to-date statistics on their use, which may also involve TV.

1. Video apps are by far the main method for viewing mobile video in 2015, a research of twenty-four countries showed.[21]
2. One in five (or 22 percent) of users regularly stream video on smartphones while watching traditional TV.[22]
3. In Canada by 2015, there was an overall decline in the number of apps on respondents' phones—twenty-six in 2014, down to less than nineteen in 2015.[23]
4. About 89 percent of owners use less than ten apps on a daily bases; 30 percent use a smartphone when shopping; 18 percent a tablet.[24]
5. About 48 percent now use a smartphone while watching TV; 54 percent a tablet.[25]

Typical of increased volumes, economies of scale reduced costs. And other new ways were found to cut them further, like less expensive materials or methods so that prices of leading smartphones and tablets were expected to be cut by at least $100 in 2014, bringing smartphones under $300 and tablets down to, or below, $400. The consumer electronics industry generated a little over a trillion dollars worldwide in 2014, with much of it coming from the sale of smartphones and tablets.[26]

The Law of Unintended Consequences

Unforeseen or unintended consequences in the social sciences are defined as undesired outcomes which are entirely different from the purposeful actions intended and undertaken.[27] Sometimes the outcomes are great social changes. They are often harmful. The concept is an old one. And the introduction of new technologies always has unintended consequences.

Print On Demand (or POD), for example, developed out of a new and faster printing technology that cost less than before. It allows new copies of books and documents to be printed one at a time, after they are already sold. It eliminated the publisher's nightmare of running off 100,000 copies of a new book with the risk of tying up capital in slow-moving inventories that required warehousing, and books being returned by the trade. Reducing risks and operational and capital costs now allows small publishers to compete with bigger ones, similar to other types of SMEs and GSMEs that adopt new technologies.

But there were unintended consequences. For one thing, it allows writers to publish their own books, instead of wasting time submitting manuscripts to numerous literary agents and publishers. Amazon.com, working as online brokers, have made it so easy and without up-front costs, that there is nothing to lose and everything to gain. Writers choose their own cover and do the marketing themselves.

Some publishers and literary agents used to claim they received about a thousand submissions every month that ended up on a "slush pile." That slush pile has now become the content of an industry of self-publishing writers, with established authors selling *them* books about how to write and market them. But established publishers have their own experienced marketing department and distribution channels, whereas authors are inexperienced in those spheres, which require objectivity, training, and knowledge acquired from a track record that most writers lack. It means they are in the very same situation as any other small start-up company—ones with a 90 percent failure rate.

Results of the self-publishing business are shown in a study of four categories of writers: Aspiring, Self-Published, Traditionally Published, and Hybrid.[28]

A Social Scientist Separates Fact from Fiction

Dana Beth Weinberg, the writer of the study, asks, "Is self-publishing an amateurish endeavour, a means of sharing stories, a strategic move in a writing career, or an entrepreneurial activity? To gain insight into this question, I have been analyzing the responses from the nearly five thousand authors who contributed to her 2013 Digital Book World and Writer's Digest Author Survey.

Some authors admit on social websites that they are happy to pay to see themselves in print, while others feel their writing has been overlooked by publishers and is bound to sell if only they can have their books printed. It might even be the first step to catching the eye of one of the big publishers who will take them up and pay the author a huge advance—as apparently happened with the so-called erotic novel *Fifty Shades of Grey*, with sales now allegedly running at ninety million copies.[29] Huge advances exist mostly in the past or in the mind. But for writers who are frustrated at repeated rejections, and feel unfulfilled at not seeing themselves in print, becoming an entrepreneurial self-publisher is challenging. However, the new study of the differences in income of self-publishing writers is likely to deflate their expectations.

"Most aspiring authors in the sample reported no income from their writing . . . While most of the survey respondents clustered at the lower end of the income distribution. Some authors did report earning $100,000 or more for their writing: less than one percent (0.6 percent) of self-published authors, 4.5 percent of traditionally published authors, and 6.7 percent of hybrid authors who reported their income."

In short, "Self-published authors earned a median income in the range of $1 to $4,999, while traditionally published authors had a median income of $5,000 to $9,999, and hybrid authors earned a median income of $15,000 to $19,999."

The consequence of POD and eBooks was to encourage millions of aspiring authors that fame and riches are theirs once they are in print. And authors have always complained that publishers prosper while writers starve. It is even suggested that there will no longer be any more professional full-time authors. But to be realistic, the odds differ little from the failure rate of other types of small entrepreneurial enterprises—90 percent, remember?

The new self-publishing trend seems to be more about creative fulfillment than money. Imaginative people enjoy the best of life by fulfilling creative challenges that lead to personal development. Hence, a passion for the arts, song, and literature.[30] Successful self-publishing requires the same skills and hard work as other businesses. And although a one-person enterprise, it creates employment for others. Nevertheless, it certainly matches the deceptive nature of other digital communications technologies, which are mere delusions, empty of any real meaning.

What Happened to the Publishing Conglomerates

That study would be incomplete without referring to what happened to the successful old publishing houses which were acquired and merged by the bigger conglomerates when their founders retired or died. Although they retained their original identities as imprints, their once-valuable brand images no longer have the same meaning. The latest merger was between two long-established giants of the industry, Penguin Books and Random House. Penguin began business in 1935 by selling cheap paperbacks in kiosks on railway platforms. The new Penguin Random House publishing company formed in 2013 will control a quarter of world book publishing. The merger was described by *The Guardian* as "one of the biggest events in publishing." And it has a lot of people worried that maybe this is the end of literature as we know it.

Michael Korda, an eminent former editor-in-chief for Simon & Schuster, warned us it was going to happen when he wrote his memoir on how publishing changed in the past forty years in New York.[31] Founders of successful publishing houses who were admired so much that they were eagerly bought out were first replaced by skilled editors like Korda, and became imprints. But the influence of editors was replaced, in turn, by the authority of accountants who asked why so many books failed to find enough readers to make bigger profits? (About 80 percent of published books are unprofitable.) Who chose new titles and on what basis? And why were distributors allowed to return books that didn't sell? The answer that the very essence of the publishing business was the intuitive skills that discovered new authors who became runaway bestsellers and investments for the future no longer satisfied a business interested only in short-term profits.

Instead of following the marketing approach that made publishers successful, conglomerates became convinced that the unreliable gut-feel of literary agents and their own editors for the literary merits of a manuscript was not bankable. They would filter out slow-moving authors, by instructing agents not to recommend writers without celebrity names or those who did not have a track record of a number of previous best sellers. Defensive cost-cutting and number-crunching replaced aggressive marketing.

Making a profit in the mass market was a realistic business strategy for companies no longer interested in literary merits or scholarship. That was how F. W. Woolworth and Universal Stores started. And Marks & Spencer, and Walmart. Why should they concern themselves with books aimed at modest niche markets beloved by readers who enjoy scintillating prose or scholarship about cultures, when the Internet reaches a massive global mass market with all its economies?

But, "bad books drive out good," argues literary critic Bloom.[32] Fortunately, there are thousands of other, smaller, imprints. And some, at least, are like the original dedicated publishers before mergers and acquisitions diluted their identities and tarnished their brand image. But, "independent presses," wrote *The Bookseller*'s editor in 2014, "have had a good run, thanks to strong eBook sales, and that is coming to an end. It's not business as normal, as the high street is more damaged now than it was three years ago. We are all waking up to a new reality, which has come more suddenly than many thought."

The new reality has enlarged and spread the imaginary world of fantasy in which best sellers are largely romances based on a formula with stereotypical heroes and heroines, and crime mysteries involving unbelievable private detectives who could never make a real living at it, and incredible events. Except for teenage fantasies and science fiction, they appear to be the only subjects that are selling in bulk to a mass market. There have never been so many. Perhaps that is what critic Harold Bloom meant when he claimed that bad books drive out good.

If the original dedicated publishers were alive today, they would see that the advent of selling online divided publishers between small and dedicated literary enterprises that still believe in building up brands, and big business more suited to trading in mass market commodities.

Platform versus Brand

The main difference between the original publishers and conglomerates that grew by mergers and acquisitions is the difference between *platform* and *branding*. Whereas publishers like André Deutsch or Scribner had a talent for discovering and developing brands, like George Orwell or Ernest Hemingway, conglomerates look for a celebrity with an existing "platform," which is an author's social reach. For example, the young topless woman who regularly paraded her boobs on page three of a high-circulation British tabloid developed an appreciative audience who were willing to buy a book with her name on the cover. So it seems that celebrity books sell on expectations rather than fulfillment.

Is selling all about make-believe? According to Peter Hildrick-Smith of Codex Group, brands sell books, not platforms. Codex is a book industry researcher which measures the value of author's brands. Jane Austin, for example, is a brand, not a platform. Daniel Defoe was a brand. So is Margaret Atwood. Stephen King is a brand. So are Salmon Rushdie and J. K. Rowling, because readers want to buy more of their books. Despite literary critic Harold Bloom's gloom that literary standards continue to decline, it seems that good books still find readers. Only half of adults read books, says Hildrick-Smith, but one-fifth are regular readers who read branded authors regularly. And they are happy to pay more for those brands.

In fact, publishers did not invent "platform." Many successful advertisers exploited the public's addiction to celebrities before them. One example is Unilever with its TV soap commercials featuring endorsements by Hollywood stars. Another was bodybuilder Charles Atlas with endorsements from famous boxers. Platforms and brands are both valid marketing strategies. But there is a third approach, which might explain the reason for the recent formation of Penguin Random House. It comes on the heels of the closure of Borders' remaining 399 bookstore outlets in the United States, laying off about eleven thousand employees in July 2011 and enabling its chief competitor Barnes & Noble to survive.

Borders were hurt by the recession in 2008–09 when they carried a huge debt-load from overextending themselves with too many outlets. Digital books began to outsell paperbacks at the same time. And latest sales figure show a consumer swing to buying more books online; 43.8 percent of books were sold online in the United States in 2012, compared with 31.6 percent sold in retail stores (37.7 percent online versus 44.0 percent in the United Kingdom). Since online book sales may be the future, it suggests that Penguin Random House's merger may have more to do with a strategy to compete with Amazon.com

Amazon.com

Amazon.com is the biggest online retailer in the world, reputed to sell 41 percent of books and dominating 65 percent of all online new printed and digital books in the world.[33] Jeff Bezos founded it in 1995 as an online bookseller but, on successful, diversified into all kinds of electronic devices, and then into clothing, furniture, toys, and food. It became a twenty-first century big box store for regular Internet users who prefer to shop online. The beauty of the Internet is that it enables viewers to imagine it as a giant warehouse, whereas it is really a broker. Instead of a chain of big box stores with overhead costs of huge warehouses and inventories and staff, it reaches everyone on the worldwide web through the skills of its reality distortion.

Bezos is quoted by the *New York Times* as "possessing a determination to do whatever is necessary to succeed." His disruptive approach to selecting and selling books was exactly what was needed to break the gridlock and power of the publishing conglomerates. It restored books to the marketplace, where they will succeed or fail according to their perceived value by readers, instead of being filtered through subjective literary agents and publishers who are self-appointed gatekeepers.

When self-publishing burgeoned, the best way for its authors to create visibility was to have Amazon.com advertise and sell their books online. The more successful authors probably owe most of their sales to Amazon.com, because the reading public would never have heard of them otherwise. And Amazon knows how to promote them. Now that once-famous publishing brands have lost their virtue and meaning as arbiters of good literature, it is evidently more realistic for an author's books to be sold online by Amazon.com and leave it for readers to decide, rather than bear one of the old lackluster imprint brands.

Founder Jeff Bezos began by making a list of everything he thought could be sold online. He finally decided on books because of the global demand for stories, the conveniently low price level of books—almost like fast-moving packaged consumer goods—and the enormous number and range of titles already in print. In effect, he could stock any number of titles because he didn't need a real warehouse, only a virtual one. Knowing that other innovators could easily copy his online enterprise, he took care to establish his own brand which now enjoys instant recognition and trust. The fact that his company went on growing past the bursting of the dotcom bubble shows the strength of his brand and the huge demand for his services. Amazon has become indispensable to publishers and authors alike. In April 2014, Amazon reported revenues grew by 23 percent in the previous quarter to approximately $20 billion. Its concept, development, and operations are so successful that it is bound to attract competitors.

There appears to be only one major problem—it is that there seem to be fewer and fewer readers of books. And those that do read are mostly young women in the thirteen to twenty-three age group who are known to be fickle in abandoning one novelty for another, like apps on digital mobiles.

eBooks

The invention of electronic books caused considerable anxiety among publishers at first. Despite the unlikelihood, they feared the era of printed books was on the way out. One strategy was to get into the eBook business for themselves and corner a large market share with their weight and power. But it gradually emerged that consumers buying electronic books were not traditional readers who had previously enjoyed printed books, but a different market segment who prefer the benefits of electronic readers—the portability of one device to display any number of different books, and easier to read in bed. And eBooks are much cheaper. They are becoming, in effect, a substitute for the five cent paperback that once launched Penguin Books—ideal for students and lower income readers like retirees. So instead of reducing book sales, eBooks became an add-on for publishers but a potential threat to book retailers.

At first count, it was estimated that eBooks created an additional 11 percent of new readers. They represented over 20 percent of the book industry in the United States in 2012, up from 15 percent in 2011.[34] Hardcover book sales in the United States grew by over 10 percent in the first eight months of 2013, quelling anxiety that printed books were history.[35] Adult fiction is by far the largest driver of eBook sales. But sales of children's and religious eBooks shrank. Since young adult books are gaining growing shelf space in retail book stores, those figures may be confirmation that reading print on paper is easier and more convenient than reading on a screen.

Interruption Marketing

Descriptions of some types of Internet advertising are as idiosyncratic as their advertisers appear to be in a catch-as-catch-can online cyber world, despite all the security software intended to protect users from digital scams and outright frauds. A summary of this fast-changing advertising medium includes display ads, banner, pop-ups and pop-unders, floating ads, and expanding ads. Trick banners described as "bait-and-switch" are designed to deceive viewers. Interstitial ads display while a user is searching for something else—known as "interruption marketing." Text ads are embedded and often delivered by email or text messages and are harder to block.

All suggests it is a game played for the benefit of eager online predators, with little consideration for advertisers or consumers. Payment for advertisements is based on CPM (cost per thousand displays or impressions), CPC (cost per click), CPA (cost per action), PPP (pay per performance), or fixed cost (usually over a specified period of time).

Online advertisers can collect data of the effectiveness of their advertisements, including audience size and response. Publishers can target narrow market segments as well as reach most global markets. But there is no measurement of when, where, and how often viewers ignore advertisement zones on any page—as most do with outdoor advertising hoardings. And there is potential for fraudulent charges. Anyone can click on any advertisement on a massive scale by automation, including competitors. Advertisers can be overcharged, too. Some users have learnt how to use technology to block out advertisements, because there are two basic types: pull digital marketing is where users look for advertisements to pull out marketing content that interests them and push digital marketing is when pushy advertisers send messages to viewers' sites without their consent.

It raises the question of the difference between good and bad advertising. The next chapters dig deeply and broadly enough to answer it. In general terms, it may be the same as the difference between good and bad literature. Literary critic Harold Bloom quotes Walter Pater on the subject of influence: "What is this song or picture, this engaging personality presented in life or in a book, to me? What effect does it really produce on me? Does it give me pleasure? And if so, what sort or degree of pleasure? How is my nature modified by its presence, and under its influence?"[36]

Pater was acutely aware that everything is changing at every single moment when, "some mood of passion or insight or intellectual excitement is irresistibly real and attractive for us,—for that moment only." The creative team in an advertising agency has the task of recognizing the moment and responding to it with swift and witty repartee.

The Phenomenon of Social Media

Online social media fills an emotional gap by turning reality into illusions to portray millions of pseudo-events in a continuous stream. Its main function being to keep viewers mesmerized by the site as long as possible. Its purpose, like TV, is to increase audience ratings in order to charge premium prices for advertising. It does so by deluding users that they have achieved recognition by their peers and created new friends. It is part of today's electronic make-believe world that fills the emptiness of our lives.[37]

Facebook's inventor, Mark Zuckerberg, may have just read *The Great Gatsby* at Harvard before coming up with the idea that solves Daisy's plaintive problem: "What'll we do with ourselves this afternoon," cried Daisy, "and the day after that, and the next thirty years?"[38] Apparently the answer is blog your friends, strangers, anyone, and everyone, to tell them all about your daily dramas, like a TV soap opera.

Reality TV shows are another distortion of reality. Thousands more apply to be on it than apply to enter Harvard. Although well devised and orchestrated with a keen eye on audience ratings and box office takings, the mass hypnosis or delusion comes in convincing audiences that everything is real and spontaneous, since their audiences *want* to believe it.

"Blind faith in illusion is our culture's secular version of being born again. Those illusions assure us that happiness and success is our birthright. They tell us that our catastrophic collapse is not permanent.

They promise that pain and suffering can always be overcome by tapping into our hidden, inner strengths. They encourage us to bow down before the cult of the self."[39] The same Pulitzer prize-winning author warns us of "the power of the senses to overthrow the mind, the power of emotion to obliterate reason."

As for the Internet as a whole, "although we're getting a lot more information via the Internet, we're also getting a lot more bad information. On the Internet, we constantly live in a twilight between fact and fiction."[40]

Part of the problem is uninformed blogging and mere gossip that shares false information which can lead to false rumors. Those rumors and character assassinations spread far more rapidly than before and remain online forever. Most blogs, it appears—and there is much confirmation from bloggers themselves—are impulsively triggered by the emotional needs of the blogger. Many resemble Freud's "talking cure" with their need to confess, but are written down for anyone to follow up like an online stalker. Young women, in particular, have no qualms about exposing themselves recklessly to online abuse. At the same time, there are endless pictures of pretty women to seduce men.

An acting edition of a famous play called *Love from a Stranger*—first produced and then filmed in 1937—is described by its publisher as, "A whirlwind romance with a handsome and charming stranger sweeping a traveller off her feet. Little does she know the ghastly truth about her new beau." The so-called "beau" turns out to be a psychopathic serial killer, after her money.[41] Despite the lurid cases of several *actual* murders, suicides, and rapes, caused by online stalkers seeking vulnerable women, men, and children, on the Internet, "nearly 60 percent of *Facebook* users said they weren't very concerned about privacy."[42] But, if you find it creepy that social networks are collecting everything you say online—and so is the government, sexual predators, and other control freaks who search for your vulnerabilities—then you would be wise to stop exposing them on the Internet. What may seem to be fun is a very serious business. And the power of emotion can be harnessed for good or evil, for love or money.

"We measure our lives by those we admire on the screen or in the ring. We seek to be like them. We emulate their look and behavior. We escape the chaos of real life through fantasy."

"Find love online," says one dating service, as if it wasn't already risky enough before the Internet. Another company warns, "The future carries a Colt."

A Cry for Help

Despite all the "oohs" and "ahs" expressed by excited teenagers at the sight of new mobile designs or electronic games in the stores, some of them are as deadly as leaving a loaded handgun on the bedside table for the kids to play with. Electronic games—whose main objective is to kill and kill again and again—could desensitize teenagers and condition them to target real victims for repeat murders, since the impulse can become addictive. We might want to ask ourselves if that is what the accelerated spates of violence, suicide, and even terrorism by confused teenagers are really all about. Is this one of the unintended consequences of the new culture of smartphones, video cameras, or the Internet and YouTube? And will it include more cries for help, like the harassed and abused fourteen-year-old girl named Amanda Todd?

The now-famous teenager was first bullied at school, humiliated on the Internet, and appealed for help on YouTube, before killing herself in a state of confusion, anxiety, and depression, because she couldn't handle the threats and derision and blackmail from a predator who stalked her online. Using a series of flash cards in a brilliant performance, she systematically unveiled her pleas before a video camera, like a striptease artist tantalizingly shedding each article of her clothes, while famously proclaiming on her display cards in writing, the words, "Cried every night,/ Lost all my friends,/ and respect."

Brought up in the digital revolution of her generation, which coincided with a powerful celebrity culture, the impressionable and credulous preteen Amanda sought fame. She achieved it after her death when seventeen million viewers watched her video on YouTube. But it is doubtful if that was her intention.

Self-absorbed teenagers and preteens, confused by their burgeoning hormones and deluded into believing they are at the stage-center of everybody's mind all the time—and even infants who are introduced to the novelty early on—can quickly become addicted to the artificial fantasy world into which the screens seduce them. There they become easy prey to predatory manipulators who get their kicks from persuading immature, inexperienced, and naïve young people to do what they say. They browse the web for vulnerable victims and persuade them to humiliate themselves as a first step leading to blackmail, or the hunt and the kill. Amanda naively posed for a picture of her immature boobs, cajoled into believing it would result in fame.

Shame and shaming have become part of the online bullying process. This online bully—a man aged thirty-five—was allegedly charged in the Netherlands for her suicide, together with extortion, Internet luring, criminal harassment, and child pornography. And there have been other similar cases. Google her name and you are automatically shown others who committed suicide or were killed, like Dawn-Marie Wesley, Molly Bush, Kelsey Smith, and Raul and Brisenia Flores.

It is a never-ending story, spread by the technology of online media, but which apparently began with the invention and use of television cameras. It became obvious soon afterward that whenever a TV cameraman attempts to capture a news incident on the street, anyone seeing the lens turning in their direction immediately begins to act unnaturally in front of it, hoping for a moment of exposure and instant fame on the screen, for which they obligingly overact.

Excited body language, like spastic head-shaking, or inane verbal expressions, and other impulsively ecstatic ejaculations, began to be repeated by copycat audiences, and at ball games with jumping high-fives or knuckle contacts between athletes in a mysterious jock culture. Mesmerized preteen and teenage audiences were manipulated into hysteria at rock concerts, where gazing at their favorite rock stars with idolatry brought them to a high pitch of unnatural sexual hysteria and masturbatory body-shaking—typified at concerts featuring the Beatles, the Rolling Stones, and The Animals.

Hysteria and suicide appear to be partners, not only for impressionable girls from about the age of eleven, but also for gullible teenage boys. They are characterized by the violent and irrational acts of suicide bombers and terrorists, some of whom take videos of themselves beforehand, or of their bloody hands, as they murder or execute their victims, knowing it will achieve their celebrity and turn them into media heroes.

In many cases their bizarre acts are accompanied by superstitious beliefs of escaping the material world for a better place, and even being martyred and rewarded in paradise or heaven. Such confused delusions characterize an unconscious shift from the real world into the virtual or illusory one which is typical of electronic games. The link between their violent criminal acts and the digital technology they use to disseminate propaganda videos is mysterious and unfathomable. "Just as you love life," says one bloodthirsty ISIS terrorist, jubilantly, onscreen, "we love death."

Assassinations of famous people were once known among anarchists as "the propaganda of the deed" and used to be reported in only a few lines in a newspaper, with no one paying much attention to their lunacy, since they were clearly out of control and irrelevant. But today's online technology posts their rampages to mass audiences all over the world. And once the sad, offensive, or repugnant pictures appear on the Internet, they are there for ever as a constant reminder of the flawed human condition—as are the pathetic stories of harassment, shame, and punishment of thoughtless teenagers on Facebook.

Obviously, those flaws in human nature can't all be attributed to social media or the digital technology revolution, which mirrors it in a looking-glass world. But it spreads them to a whole range of dysfunctional and emotionally disturbed copycats and influences our society with its zest for novelty and celebrity, as a way to get attention. Indeed, it is no secret that the Internet and social media are simply vehicles to provide exhibitionists with ways and means to get attention, in return for providing personal information and allowing themselves to be bombarded with advertising.

Manipulation or mind control, or reality distortion, has been practiced for a very long time. The following chapters demonstrate how well that power was harnessed by industry, trade, and commerce to sell more goods and services and keep the economy going by providing more jobs and creating more consumers before the digital age. Google and Facebook are not the only businesses that search for people's weaknesses and attitudes and lifestyle and desires, in order to target them with their advertisements. Many other successful businesses are eagerly waiting to exploit consumers by selling them more and more through what Vance Packard called "hidden persuaders."[43]

8

How Words Sell Billions of Goods and Services

Entrepreneurs need more than capital, cunning, and scheming to succeed in business. Having invented a new product or service or innovated one with more or better applications than existing competitors, they have to find ways to get out of the garage or backroom and get attention. But just creating visibility for their offering to the public and their company and brand is not enough—they must persuade consumers and distributors to buy it. To do that, they need to come up with appropriately persuasive words and illustrations that encapsulate a promise or guarantee to prospective buyers, which triggers their attention and turns it into interest that results in purchases and revenues.

Only established GSMEs and big businesses, like the Top 5000 companies, can afford to use a leading advertising agency like Saatchi & Saatchi or J. Walter Thompson to do it for them. Smaller companies are left to hope that their own creativity is good enough to direct a small studio of commercial artists and copywriters in producing advertising that will make an impact—not just any impact, but a suitable one that results in their goods moving from dealers' shelves or racks. For example, when Google advertised their new Google Maps, they created an interesting and atmospheric street scene to illustrate their message, which is, "Know before you go."

Conveying an almost magical atmosphere is important to achieve instant and singular attention and retain it for long enough for the message to be absorbed. Even though drawn to a two-dimensional picture, the visuals should influence viewers to imagine they are being swept into a three-dimensional scenario and can almost feel the textures and colors and peer through the shadows as if they were part of the cast in the illustration. They should be able to absorb the scene almost through the pores of their skin—as J. Walter Thompson's artistry managed to do when they made their own commercial films in their

TV production unit in London's Berkeley Square, so that their client's unique consumer benefit was absorbed by viewers without them being aware it was happening, or how. It seemed to impact *all* their senses, which stored the message for later recall, far more effectively than if it had just been baldly stated and instantly forgotten.[1]

Confucius famously said that a picture is worth a thousand words. It was certainly true when most people couldn't read. Today we have returned to a situation where pictures have become more important than narrative text, because of digital cameras and a passion to take and show everyone our pictures on online social media. Whether digital cameras and texting on mobiles will erode literacy is too early to know, but there are signs of it, like poor literacy examination scores and popular websites that contain only pictures.[2]

A Lust for More and More

The atmosphere of Google Street View is redolent of sex for good reason. The extraordinary photo engenders sex by showing two people gazing into a sex store, with a poster advertising thirty girls in a strip show next door, and an intimate hotel in between that somehow suggests it rents rooms by the hour. In short, "Know before you go" is an invitation that triggers a suitable response, because each word of that phrase was carefully thought out with that intention.

Every successful advertising agency knows that sex appeal is the biggest motivator for getting immediate attention and selling all sorts of products and services as a consequence. But—just as we learnt from Saatchi & Saatchi's award-winning poster for the Conservative Party in the United Kingdom, which said "Labour isn't working"—its most important attribute is that it is a double entendre. Its double meaning makes you pause to take it in. And doing so means it will be more memorable, partly because it is linked to the warning to know where you go to have sex. And Google's online maps and directions tell you exactly how to get to where you want to go. Dominating their picture is a streak of variegated reds and shades of pink that suggest, almost subliminally, stimulated erogenous zones of either sex.

A previous chapter referred to "The Three Great Hidden Motives," which used to be hunger, sex, and the will to power.[3] But in today's consumer society with our more comfortable lifestyles that give us an illusion of certainty and security and almost endless credit from banks, the battle for market domination is waged by effectively filling consumer needs for (1) Sex; (2) Hunger to buy things—which, nearly a century ago, the impulsive Zelda Fitzgerald called "a lust for more and more"; (3) and Money, Prestige, or Power, which are interchangeable. But a persistent question arises again. How can entrepreneurs manage their advertising if they cannot afford to employ an experienced advertising manager to ensure it is sales driven and cost-effective? The founder of a start-up company with something new to offer or the president of a medium size one who needs to differentiate his products from all the others on the market, needs to learn what is effective advertising and what is costly and useless. If she doesn't, she is likely to spend too much money on ineffective advertising that fails to find enough buyers.

Fortunately, a great deal of practical knowledge has already been accumulated over the years about what works and what does not, and which approaches sell goods and services most effectively. "Scientific advertising" began with copywriter John Caples in the 1920s and, arguably, reached its peak of perfection at some point in the mid-1960s. We can learn from those geniuses of the art and craft who created original advertising that sold billions of products and services during that period. And although the formats still being developed by trial and error online may differ somewhat from the most successful newspaper or magazine advertisements, the fundamental ingredients that create sales do not, because they are based on sound psychological principles that adapt easily to the Internet and social media sites.

In order for advertising to be meaningful to consumers who are invited to engage and interact with it, advertisements and public relations editorials have to be socially meaningful by reflecting contemporary society and its customs. Every one of the following six highly successful print advertisements was based on what was socially desirable at the time. And, step by step, they reflect the trend to the permissive society of the 1960s and the consumer society of the twenty-first century, by recognizing society's wants and needs and fulfilling its dreams.

Steve Jobs understood that you have to sell dreams, not products. But there was nothing new in that. Most advertising agencies understood over a century ago that you have to "sell the sizzle, not the steak."[4]

They Laughed When I Sat Down at the Piano

The headline for an advertisement for the US School of Music in New York made people sit up and take notice in 1926, when people had to create their own entertainment if they wanted a social life, and there were no dating services. So the headline that became an all-time classic had an additional line that promised success:

> "They laughed when I sat down
> At the piano
> But when I started to play!—"

It sold music lessons on a variety of different instruments, when relationships could be initiated by an outgoing individual who entertained girls romantically. It became as much a part of the social scene as taking dancing lessons after the suave Fred and Adele Astaire popularized dancing and initiated leisurely afternoons at social tea dances.

John Caples included a coupon at the bottom of his advertisements to ensure his targeted readers replied, and offered them all sorts of benefits to fill it in and mail it to him. He set his ads in a format like news in newspaper columns that created conviction that this offer was something new and exciting. Although he wrote an enormous amount of copy that we would be too impatient to read today, people read every word of it then, because it conveyed conviction. Some copywriters had learnt to introduce a *conviction* step at the bottom of their advertisements to reassure readers when invited to interact. Caples didn't hesitate to use several invitations to action. He probably did so on the basis that, if they haven't bought your pitch the first time, it doesn't mean they don't want your service, only that you haven't convinced them yet.

He also injected new ideas into the body copy of his advertisements to create excitement and encourage readers to carry on to the end of his story, like "Thousands of successful students never dreamed they possessed musical ability until it was revealed to them by a remarkable 'Musical Ability Test' which we send entirely without cost with our interesting free booklet."

He also knew that the word "free" arrests attention and can seduce people as if by magic. The following advertising copy shows how he went about inducing action with compelling copy that included one seductive offer after another. But he never included a word or a sentence that was not aimed at selling the service; every word had its proper place in a psychological structure designed to sell. And he focused on the underlying reasons for the attraction of the service—to achieve happiness and popularity.

"If you are in earnest about wanting to play your favorite instrument—if you really want to gain happiness and increase your popularity—send at once for the free booklet and Demonstration Lesson.

No cost—no obligation. Right now we are making a Special offer for a limited number of new students. Sign and send the convenient coupon now—before it's too late to gain the benefits of this offer. Instruments supplied when needed."

Today's general run of advertisers on the Internet would ask readers to click at suitable points online, instead of mailing a coupon. And in place of concise and meaningful copy, we are more likely to find empty words and sentences that ramble and meander and lose direction as they reveal the desperation of the seller. And yet, in those days almost a century ago, the return rate of newspaper coupons was impressively high. Coupons were one of the innovations of the times. But they only worked if the invitation appealed to the intended target market, and it was clearly an honest, believable, and convincing offer from a genuine company that offered reassurance that they could be trusted to fulfill their promises.

It is easy to see how advertising is a business of words. And John Caples knew how to appeal to shy people as well as outgoing ones. Reticent people needed prompting and reassuring to encourage them to make contact and initiate relationships with the opposite sex, without having to mention the three-letter word that might trigger their motivation. Consumers were generally more subtle about sex, which was still synonymous with romance and even linked to marriage, like most Hollywood movies that ended in a chaste kiss. Playing a piano was a metaphor for something more fundamental that might lead to romance—as Fred Astaire's dance routines with Ginger Rogers did in the movies. Effective advertising was full of symbols and metaphors and allegories that contributed to double meanings, because sex had to be implied subtly then, rather than boldly explicit as it is today.

Caples made it seem as if even those who considered themselves to be musically inept really possessed a hidden talent that the course would reveal. He created curiosity with a "Musical Ability Test." It was a challenge to find out! And he assured readers sincerely that they had nothing to lose by completing the coupon in the advertisement, since the test was free. The booklet he offered was free. They were not obligated to buy anything. In other words, he said everything possible to clear away any possible doubts, reservations, or suspicions, in a more cautious age than ours which recognized that interludes with strangers could be thrilling but dangerous.

To limit responses only from suitable people in the social and psychographic group he was targeting, Caples qualified respondents by

103

repeating that he only wanted replies from people who were serious enough to go a step further. And he urged those to reply by offering them popularity and happiness—just as Coca-Cola does to its target market today. Then, to spur them to immediate action, he warned them they had only a limited time to receive the "special offer"—as aggressive big box stores frequently do with special promotions today.

We would be briefer and far more direct in our advertising now, when people are more outspoken and don't shock so easily. But sex wasn't mentioned then, so it required a more gentle and indirect approach. Today's advertising would also encapsulate all those ingredients into shorter messages with less copy and a headline only a third as long.

Making People Happy

The 1920s and 1930s were times when seductive charmers and skilled wordsmiths were needed to write advertisements, sell goods and services, and write songs and film scripts for Hollywood, to make people happy. Men worked harder to entertain and interest women in ways that wouldn't scare them off. So, despite long headlines and voluminous body copy, John Caples' three newspaper columns full of words caught the reader's attention and created curiosity and interest in preparation for his pay-off line. In short, he laid the foundation for sales-driven ads that got attention and triggered immediate action, of the successful kind that other advertising geniuses built on in the even more competitive 1960s. It was more demanding because of much higher media costs. Market leaders were paying millions of dollars, or pounds, to global advertising agencies, and they demanded results.

Whereas that advertisement appealed to both sexes, the following offer was obviously aimed only at men:

In only 7 days I can make YOU a new man!

It was targeted at a particular psychographic group—young men who felt at a physical disadvantage when attempting to impress women. It was created by Charles Atlas, another advertising pioneer. His famous 1936 press ads made a claim that turned into a promise: "*Let Me Prove in 7 Days That I can Make You a New Man!*" It was hard to resist. And millions of applicants responded by feverishly filling in the coupon at the bottom of the ad.

Photos showed Charles Atlas as a muscleman in imitation leopard skin briefs, his magnificent torso expanded like a granite sculpture, with a noble and piercing look that would not have been amiss if carved in rock on Mount Rushmore. His real name was Angelo Siciliano, but he needed a more suitable image for his newly developed body-building program. Fortunately, it was the time of the popular *Tarzan* Hollywood movies featuring the handsome film star and Olympic gold medal swimming champion Johnny Weissmuller. The silent version of the film was screened earlier in 1918 with a different actor cast in the muscular role of Tarzan. And the novel *Tarzan of the Apes*, which was so popular that it was filmed several times, was published even earlier in 1914.

The fictional Tarzan legend was based on an Edgar Rice Burrough's story which had previously appeared even earlier in a pulp fiction magazine called *All-Story Magazine* in 1912. It featured Lord Greystoke, who is killed in the jungle. His infant son is adopted by a female ape. So Siciliano probably read the story as a kid and was able to cash in on all the momentum of seventeen years of publicity before he began to advertise. It was the type of exposure that breeds celebrity, which Penguin Random House and other publishing conglomerates now look for as a platform from which to launch a story into a runaway bestseller.

He formed a company in 1929 that transformed him into Charles Atlas—no doubt because the mythical Atlas carried the weight of the whole world on his shoulders. He advertised in what is described as "one of the longest and most memorable ad campaigns of all time." His most successful media were men's sports magazines and cartoon comics. He never forgot that *Tarzan of the Apes* began as a strip cartoon and never undervalued their impact on his particular market, to the extent of using cartoons in his own advertisements.

Three heavyweight boxing champions endorsed his bodybuilding courses by claiming to have taken them: Joe Louis, Rocky Marciano, and Max Baer. They were among the first advertised testimonials of a service.

Charles Atlas became a wealthy national hero and a household name by making a clear and direct promise—even guaranteeing it—and fulfilling every word he said. What's more, he knew that every new generation of teenage boys feel dysfunctional about girls and sex, particularly when confronted by bullies at school or in the army. One of his most famous strip cartoon advertisements shows a frail young man sitting on the beach in swimming trunks with his girlfriend. A muscular giant approaches them and provocatively kicks sand in his eyes to show off in front of the girl. The young man knows he will be tested all through life and must be ready to stand up for himself. Millions signed up for a bodybuilding course with Charles Atlas and were unlikely to regret it.

The Headline Represents Eighty Cents out of Your Dollar

Advertising agency genius David Ogilvy had to create a headline to sell the most expensive car in the world. It said "At 60 miles an hour the loudest noise in this new Rolls Royce comes from the electric clock."

That headline was another winner in 1959 with people who had surplus capital to spend on the best designed and technologically perfect automobile in the world.

"On the average," Ogilvy explained, "five times as many people read the headline as read the body copy."[5] It represents eighty cents out of your dollar. What is extraordinary about it is that it was another unusually long headline, whereas an ideal headline today generally consists of only about five to nine words. The lesson is that it takes whatever it needs to sell a product or a service, providing it is done with the self-confidence and panache of a brilliant wordsmith who knows when and how to break the rules and make a new mold by thinking differently and illustrating his idea differently.

Although as subtle as the previous two advertisements, both of which were aimed at creating sex appeal, this one was aimed at more sophisticated consumers who display their sex appeal through expensive symbols of success.

To impart conviction, Ogilvy used a subtitle that asked "What *makes* Rolls Royce the best car in the world?" It was answered by an expert: "There is really no magic about it—it is merely patient attention to detail," says an eminent Rolls Royce engineer.

Ogilvy researched every ingredient required of a selling advertisement. The following are a few of them:

1. Best-selling print ads consisted of a squared up half-tone photo occupying at least 60 percent of an advertisement, so that a reader's eyes are caught by an appealing picture.
2. Then the eyes drop down to read the headline beneath it (not above it).
3. Ogilvy considered Garamond in upper and lower case was the most readable typeface.
4. He deliberately placed his headline in the Rolls Royce ad in inverted commas to hint that he was quoting a spontaneous and delighted reaction from a real but unseen passenger.
5. To create conviction, he used a "blind testimonial" from an engineering expert.

6. He used three columns of body copy to replicate a news item in a newspaper, since it introduced something new to the public: the latest model of the most famous car in the world.

"A Diamond Is Forever"

The following advertisement is claimed to be the most effective and memorable headline of the twentieth century. "A Diamond Is Forever" was thought up for De Beers diamond mines by one of the oldest advertising agencies in the United States, N. W. Ayer & Son, when the price of diamonds was declining and De Beers wanted to expand sales to America.

Since Americans wanted to show that everything they have is bigger than anyone else's, Ayer launched an ad campaign aimed at selling bigger and more expensive diamonds in the United States. The lure was sex, wrapped in romance. Young American men would be persuaded—no doubt by their fiancé or future in-laws—that diamonds are a gift of love and an engagement ring is a promise. So "A diamond is forever" symbolized that their love would be everlasting, just like a diamond.

Again there was a persuasive double meaning. How could any young man on the threshold of marriage argue with something so tender and promising! Both may be taking a gamble, but at least his fiancé offset the risk with the security of knowing that "diamonds are a girl's best friend."

Hair styles and shades of color also have their place in fashion trends. But, whereas many women went artificially blonde in the twenty-first century and left their dark roots to show their bravado, hair colorants were socially unacceptable in the 1950s. Whether or not a woman colored her hair wasn't a question to embarrass women with at that time. Evidently they were ready and willing to make a change, but it was not something they would admit to openly, in case it might be thought unnatural, superficial, or vulgar to pretend to be what you are not. But, apparently the manufacturer knew the demand was there, since the following advertisement for Clairol hair colorant increased sales by over 400 percent:

Does she . . . or doesn't she?

Foote, Cone & Belding were Procter & Gamble's ad agency. They cleverly turned their headline into innuendo by using a witty and titillating double entendre to launch a new hair-coloring kit to do-it-yourself at home, so that no one would know if a girl dyed her hair. "Only her hairdresser can tell," said the advertisement reassuringly.

A later advertisement for the same product depicted a glamorous blonde "Miss Clairol" with a small child, to show she was really a responsible mom and still demure, as young ladies were supposed to be. *Demure* in French means later rather than sooner, hence the innuendo in the headline that she might no longer be a virgin.

Another famous advertisement also tempted women to be naughty but nice. It said:

You've come a long way, baby . . .

It managed to convince women to smoke a cigarette brand called Virginia Slims in 1968. They were narrower to suggest feminine elegance. By that time, women wanted to be more like men, only smarter. Although an inviting "permissive society" was developing in the mid-1960s, it was still considered vulgar for well-brought-up women to smoke in public. So Philip Morris decided to link their brand to an aspirational image. The advertising agency exploited the opportunity with a message aimed at women's desire for emancipation and empowerment, by suggesting they were no longer "babies" to be protected in a paternalistic society, but grown women who were now free to choose for themselves. Once again the advertising used innuendo and wit to make readers pause to consider the double meaning.[6]

Inverted commas suggest an admiring but unseen male making a remark that we would consider patronizing and unacceptable today.

Significantly, the feminist image that served the advertisers so well at the end of the 1960s turned out to be a disadvantage later on in the 1990s, when women consumers in the age group of eighteen to twenty-four were turned off by the priestesses of feminism, whom they didn't consider were really feminine at all. So Philip Morris innovated the brand by using new slogans and bringing out a king-size product in the Virginia Slims line.

Ambiguity

It brings up six fundamental questions that advertising agencies have to ask their clients, and entrepreneurs and marketers must ask themselves: (1) *Who* do I want to target as potential customers? (2) *What* do I need to tell them? (3) *How* should I speak to get their attention and engage with them? (4) *Where* is the best forum for my message? (5) *When* is the best time to advertise? (6) *Why* would they want to buy from me?

The answer to the first question is hidden in the answer to the last one. Hidden, because we won't know the reason *why* until we uncover the *real* motivation—sex, hunger for things, prestige, money or power, or fear of aging, loneliness, or death.

We see why and can understand its subtlety and complexity when we ask what appears on the surface to be a simple question, like "Why does a woman buy a new dress?"

"Why?" is an ambiguous word—meaning that, although we might reasonably expect suitable answers to the first five questions, people *don't know why* they make a decision most of the time. So they'll say whatever pleases the questioner. Embarrassment often inhibits people from telling the truth. But most people simply misunderstand the question. One reason a woman may buy a new dress could be because she can afford the price or because it happens to be in stock. But those are only "prevailing market conditions." So we have to rephrase the question to why did she *want* a new dress?

People buy for hidden reasons which they are generally unaware of at a conscious level. And "People think they are led by what they see, when they are really driven by what they *feel*." Those remarks form the basis of psychoanalysis—to find out what people *really* think, feel, and want. And it is axiomatic, from Freud's findings, that what people make manifest is unlikely to be the truth. Or it may only be partly true, whereas the real truth is buried deep in the mind. Psychoanalysts are like archeologists in that they have to probe and dig into the unconscious mind.

Today's neuroscience confirms psychological in-depth studies by revealing that up to 90 percent of the time, decisions to purchase are formed deep within the subconscious.[7]

So, short of putting people with similar characteristics as your target market through an fMRI machine to pose questions to them and study their brain reactions, we should reconsider why that fictional woman *did* buy a new dress. In other words, what conditions prevailed without which the purchase would not have taken place, other than current market factors? An entire brand-building strategy, or an advertising campaign to launch a new product, could be wasted through failure to understand the reason why people buy particular products or services. That is why free-association interviews, projective tests, and nondirective questions can uncover hidden or unconscious motives and bring them to light.

Surface explanations that appear to be rational may be only convenient fibs to conceal the embarrassing truth. For example, the real reason might be that the woman in question has two children, just met an attractive man, and plans to cheat on her husband. So perhaps the key words an ad agency would use in a communications strategy document should be "yielding to sexual temptation."

How to Influence People

Since people are driven by what they feel, advertising must appeal to emotions. Even so, their actions need justifying, if only to themselves. But how can a marketer or advertiser justify irrational purchases arising from emotional needs? Only by persuading buyers that there are also logical reasons for making a purchase.

It means finding a way to convey an appeal to emotional temptations and also to reason at the same time. So advertisers need to prepare a communications strategy.

"How many ads have you seen lately that seem in desperate search of a strategy?" asked the chief creative officer for McCann-Erickson Worldwide advertising agency: "It's like meeting someone who knows how to talk, but doesn't know what to say!" That is why advertisers use an agency with creative copywriters who know how to seduce and satisfy customers. It is a rare and much-envied skill. David Ogilvy used the expression "creative potency" to describe it.

He also warned us that "agencies are infested with men and women who cannot write." It is even truer today when literacy standards have dropped. And if *they* are helpless at writing, we are left only with examples from advertising geniuses like Ogilvy and Caples, and also Rosser Reeves, who invented the expression a "unique selling proposition" (or USP), which every headline should convey.

They remind us that, whatever we do, we must keep in mind that the power of an average working advertisement to sell goods and services can be divided along the following approximate lines, despite Ogilvy's hyperbole: (1) Picture and Headline: 75 percent; (2) Body copy and baseline: 15 percent; (3) Layout, typography, and graphics: 10 percent. And despite the relatively low values credited to the more subsidiary ingredients, each of them depends on the other, like links in a chain. Leave only one of them weak and the advertisement could be less effective or even totally useless.

Online Advertisements

When we attempt to adapt our ideal communications to the media of the Internet, we find that "Only the highest ranking ads are eligible to show at the top of the page" (say Google). Ranking is caused by an advertisement's Quality Score and an advertiser's bid. Since Google ads are geared to a search engine driven by algorithms, not only the operation, but also the "Quality" of the ad (in Google's terminology) is linked to the number of people who respond by clicking on it. This is altogether different from what was used before the digital revolution to induce consumers to buy goods or services.

Google evaluate ads by three criteria: High relevance, Good performance over time, and Competitive Bids. That too is an entirely different approach than using traditional print advertising. Nevertheless, the previous rules still apply, even if Google's means differ since Google targets intended consumers through keywords and text.

What does that really mean? Algorithms assume (if they could be said to assume anything) that if an ad consistently generates clicks from readers, it must be tailored correctly to meet consumer needs and wants. But what if readers just click out of curiosity or just for fun, and not with any intention to buy? That is a problem which questions the integrity of the digital methodology. And it is by no means the only one. A lot of assumptions are being made by suppliers since the Internet. And consumers are left to muddle through and docilely accept the fact that nothing in life is perfect. We are already accustomed to trade-offs in our lives. Why should we expect advertising to be different?

For example, when Starch tests were used to measure readership of press advertising nearly half a century ago, an analysis of 20,347 ads in forty-seven major magazines in 1970 showed that only 44 percent of respondents even *noticed* a particular advertisement. Even fewer respondents (35 percent) could identify the brand afterward. And only 9 percent actually *read* most of the advertisement.

As for television, when Gallup used his telephone survey to research viewers on the day following a TV program, on average only 12 percent who saw the program could remember the commercials. That amount is likely to be considerably less today with more television channels and other communications devices vying for attention, like the Internet and mobiles. So we have to get used to the fact that nothing in life is entirely the way we want it to be.

Nevertheless, advertisers and advertising agencies want to know how to obtain more visibility to ensure they reach their intended target markets. And that's not all. Glib old hands in the agency business used to boast, "There are only three things to remember—*domination, domination, and domination!*" But it wasn't true, for several very good reasons. Even if you manage to dominate the space or the time, your message may not work. It may even create the wrong impression or image for your brand and turn people away from buying your products or services. What's more, any positive momentum and brand loyalty you *had* succeeded in building up over previous years could be reversed in an instant by a badly conceived commercial film that is confusing or ambiguous, or an awful press campaign that insults the customers' intelligence.

Even if you find a way, your communications must be built around a properly structured selling message that will produce results. So you might want to undertake a reality check by researching to be absolutely certain *who* you want to target, *where* they are, *what* they want, and *why* anyone would want to buy your products. The best strategic communications are designed by first preparing a communications strategy with tactics. The following framework was used by Unilever's group of global companies in the 1960s.

Communications Strategy

Client: *J.B. Harvey Ltd*   Date: *30 April, 2016*

Product Type: *Tips Teabags*   Brand Name: *Floral Tips*

1. TARGET MARKET(S).

   Primary: *Middle-income groups age 25–65. Urban Males & females.*

   Secondary: *Rural.*

   Tertiary:

2. UNIQUE BUYING PROPOSITION (or USP).

   Floral Tips provides an uplifting, tasty and invigorating cup of tea.

3. REASON WHY?

   Only the strongest-tasting tips of leaves are used in this unique blend.

4. SUPPORTING CONSUMER BENEFITS.   EVIDENCE

   A. *Economical:*   *Less tea needed with strong tips.*

   B. *Blended for connoisseurs:*   75% Ceylon to 25% Assam.

   C. *Not only for social occasions:*   *Now in a new $5 economy pack.*

5. APPEAL TO THE SENSES.

Sight: *A beautiful and inviting tan color.*

Touch:

Hearing:

Smell: *A seductive aroma of sunny Indian tea plantations.*

Taste: *Sharp and invigorating.*

6. EMPHASIS: *Good taste and hospitality.*

7. BRAND IMAGE.
Your discriminating guests will love this delicious and stimulating, refined tea, and respect your good taste.

That succinct document was designed by top multinational advertising agencies under the direction of their major global client, as the first step in a plan to improve the value of advertising, which is described in the following pages. But first we should see how two geniuses of advertising approached and solved its problems.

After expanding Ogilvy & Mather globally in 1963, David Ogilvy wrote a book about his experiences in advertising. He called it *Confessions of an Advertising Man*. Everyone who becomes the client of an advertising agency, or briefs a boutique commercial art studio or an independent designer, or is obliged to produce their own advertising should read it, if they want to know how to persuade consumers to buy their products or services. It should be a compulsory read for students or graduates of advertising, marketing, business management, or mass communications. It is probably already studied by those who staff leading advertising agencies, since it is continually reprinted.[8]

If advertisers and agencies want to make their advertising budgets stretch further by reducing the large amounts that often gets wasted, they should also read *Reality in Advertising* by Rosser Reeves. He worked for Ted Bates ad agency and believed the effects of advertising on consumers could be measured. Proof of its effectiveness is that it too is continually reprinted.[9]

It is significant that both books appeared in the 1960s, since it was a period of economic expansion. And it was the time when Unilever's chairman famously complained that half his advertising budget was being wasted and it was time for advertising agencies to be more accountable for how they used or misused their clients' advertising dollars. As a result, Unilever instructed four or five of their agencies to propose how to produce more cost-effective advertising that sold more goods. This is how they went about meeting the challenges.

A Plan to Restructure Advertising

Major agencies servicing Unilever were Ogilvy & Mather, J. Walter Thompson, and Ted Bates (all now part of the WPP group) and Lintas (now Lowe Lintas). All were skilled in creating advertising that moved billions of packaged goods to consumers from dealers' shelves over the years. But it seems that discontinuities had harmed the organizational knowledge and creative skills of some agencies that were slow to recover—like firing entire creative teams when major accounts were lost, downsizing during economic recessions, and coping when creative people and executives left to join other agencies or start up their own. And some of them took valuable clients with them, resulting in more staff cuts. Working for an ad agency was precarious as a consequence.

Choices of media had already become more complex, so that media departments split off to form specialized media agencies with the newly invented computers. They could calculate such complexities as the cost to reach targeted audiences through a whole mix of different media, each of which reached consumers with a different spread of demographic and psychographic characteristics, some with different size overlaps and other wasteful features.

More often than not, it was clients with cost-cutting or subjective CEOs or CFOs who were to blame for inferior advertising, inefficiently targeted budgets, and inferior or unintegrated marketing. So one of the goals was to provide more regulation and controls in the ways and means of producing advertising campaigns that could exclude uncreative, uninformed, and unskilled individuals who frequently interfered and reduced the effectiveness of the advertising.

What Is a USP?

Good advertising that aims to sell goods or services always offers a USP, in the headline or immediately beneath it. It is a guarantee that promises what consumers can expect from buying them. And it concentrates only on the most important persuasive selling idea available. That promise is likely to have been researched beforehand to ensure it is what consumers really want, and not just what a supplier *thinks* they want. An effective USP is not only unique, but must also be competitive.

Unilever insisted that good advertising must be clear, uncomplicated, and easy to understand immediately and completely. They emphasized that "Good advertising persuades readers that a brand will deliver the basic consumer benefit by offering convincing reasons why, and supporting evidence wherever possible."

They added, "Good advertising is competitive. It convinces a consumer that the benefit promised can best be obtained from one brand only." Most importantly, "Good advertising involves the consumer. It presents the brand's benefit to the consumer and its proof, in a human and dramatic way which arrests attention, evokes sympathetic emotional response, arouses desire for the product, and leads to the type of action required to purchase it."

If we take the aircraft industry as an example, Lockheed Martin's F-35 Lightning II claims "Air Superiority" as their USP and explains it on their website, "Designed to dominate the skies." It is as minimalistic as it can be.

Lockheed did not go into the realms of fantasy by claiming it *will* dominate the skies. It is simply *designed* to do so. They listed four supporting benefits: (1) Fifth generation characteristics of radar evading stealth; (2) Supersonic speed; (3) Extreme agility; (4) Most powerful and comprehensive, integrated sensor package of any fighter aircraft in history.

That certainly makes it a unique claim. And it sounds convincing. But controversy over the price of Canada's alleged procurement of the F-35 for the Royal Canadian Air Force in 2010 brought Lockheed's claims into the spotlight. Opposition parties in Parliament questioned the overall value for the immense amount of taxpayers' money. One question asked by a critic was, "Can Lockheed *prove* its claims of superiority over all its competitors?"

In short, a USP is a valid claim only if it can be shown to be genuine.

Working with an Agency

Working with an advertising agency has clear advantages if it is a well-respected one, but there can be a number of damaging disadvantages if it is not. Many of the disadvantages can be avoided by following a similar protocol that Unilever's advertising managers used, even in the days when Lintas was a department of that company and not an independent agency as it is now.

Once the communications strategy was agreed upon by the client and agency, the agency's responsibility was to transform the basic template of the strategy into a unique and creative advertisement designed to sell the goods and services to that section of the public who were agreed to be the most suitable target for their selling communications. It would embody all the desired elements they had discussed and agreed on. The agency would recommend the most appropriate media mix, supported by readership or audience ratings for each medium and the cost per thousand consumers to be reached.

Meanwhile, the advertiser would establish a checklist to use at preliminary agency presentations of concepts, rough layouts, and provisional copy, to determine five facts:(1) Does it promise a basic selected consumer benefit or USP? (2) Does it offer a convincing *reason why?* (3) Is it unique and competitive? (4) Does it clearly identify the brand? (5) Is it clear and uncomplicated?

If advertisements did not answer all five questions in the affirmative, the meeting would immediately cease and the agency would be told to return to the drawing board. That routine simplified the process and saved time. It also helped to redirect the creative people toward their client's objectives. And it excluded uninformed and uncreative people from the debate, to prevent them from steering it off-course.

An example of how a creative team followed each of those five firm instructions was an advertisement created for one of Lipton Tea's overseas subsidiaries, named Pitco Tea. It was designed to launch tea bags in South Africa, which was behind with the technology for several reasons at that time. One was that most South Africans loved tea in loose leaves. Serving tea was a ritual that showed hospitality and made guests feel welcome. Even when visiting an office on business, a silver teapot would invariably be produced on a silver tray. Tea was not only a pick-me-up, but a very sociable custom. People of English origins and Zulus alike had discerning tastes. Poorer black Africans would buy a special small ten cent pack to be able to afford the very best tea blend. People of Dutch extraction, on the other hand, preferred coffee with a high chicory content. South Africans of Indian ancestry bought tips teas rather than leaf. So the question of how to introduce tea bags and whether they would be successful in South Africa was a complex and subtle one based on demographics.

A creative team at the J. Walter Thompson advertising agency was briefed on the tea blend and the social situation. And since headlines had become shorter by this time, it was a challenge to create a selected message to get attention and provoke buying action in approximately three to five words which would reflect all those different tastes. It takes inspiration and considerable creative skills. But knowing the USP was ease and speed made it much simpler than first thought. The copywriter came up with a solution that inspired the art director to start work on a suitable layout. It used only three words to persuade him. They were, "Have a Quickie!"

It was 1968, and the titillating double meaning suited the cheeky social character of the permissive society of the late 1960s. The innuendo was obvious. The picture the layout artist executed was simple and well designed; it showed a tea bag being lowered by its string into a welcoming teapot. There was no distracting clutter. The Pitco logo was at the bottom line of the advertisement, where it should be.

A subsidiary benefit, at first, was that tea bags were easier to clean up than removing piles of wet tea leaves stuck in the pot and the kitchen sink. But the primary claim was unique and competitive because Pitco was the first tea blender with tea bag machinery in South Africa.

Buyers Beware!

It is not only when we come to the Internet that we find dishonesty, deceit, and fraud in selling, advertising, or marketing—it has always existed. The Internet makes us more aware of it because it enters our home like a dangerous virus. And it is more blatant than we have been accustomed to. Some online ads have the bad manners to follow us around the web with *behavioral targeting*. It is a nuisance at the very least and a blatant invasion of privacy at worst, because online frauds take place like burglarizing our homes. Like many of the tricks cooked up online, it attempts to catch users off guard and makes them commit themselves by clicking on impulse.

The stupidity and avarice of those advertisers deludes them into imagining we will be overjoyed to do business with them, instead of avoiding them as quickly as possible. All the amateurish deceptions and frauds make it even more important than ever that we buy only from companies with an established and untarnished brand, and certainly not from companies more obsessed with their technology than dedicated to providing customer service.

Behavioral targeting is a different matter than being trailed by a live salesperson in a retail store where customers intend to buy. Consumers are bound to appreciate good advice from someone knowledgeable before committing themselves to the purchase of a high-ticket item. But being an online pest targeting victims at home is a dishonest show of desperation and deceit.

9

Pictures That Sell Goods and Services

"Visual understanding is the essential and only true means of teaching how to judge things correctly," wrote the Swiss educational reformer Johann Heinrich Pestalozzi. Visual understanding of concepts at Pestalozzi's school could be said to have launched the scientific career of Albert Einstein with his thought experiments and his talent for abstract and mathematical thinking. Thought experiments and abstract thinking also come into play when producing traditional advertising. But it can hardly be said for digital advertising online that depends largely on decisions made by artificial intelligence.

Nevertheless, the transition from print to Internet advertising is not nearly as complicated as it might at first seem. In 2013, for example, Samsung ran a video advertisement lasting for about thirteen seconds on Facebook. It was a little different from traditional cinema advertising, but without having to go to a theater to see it. What made it different was the convenience of having it arrive on one's own screen. There were other trial approaches of a different nature for different products, like the launch of a new book published by one of the conglomerates, which looked more like a personal website about to be researched for its degree of effectiveness. Both stood out because this type of advertising on social media is still new.

Nevertheless, they, and YouTube videos, generally resemble David Ogilvy's classic print layouts for newspapers and magazines, since about 60 percent of coverage consists of either a squared up picture or the video picture itself. The rest is much the same as previous commercials on cinema screens, so that our eyes and minds are already accustomed to online advertising. Whether the concept is being portrayed as well as the outstanding commercial advertising films once produced by J. Walter Thompson is another matter altogether.

Some other types of online advertisements are similar but static, as if we are watching the pages of a glossy magazine—with the claimed advantage that the subject advertised should suit our individual requirements according to what Google's algorithms discover from a consumer's recent online browsing. But, although we know that algorithms cannot assume anything, their programmers can certainly make any number of incorrect assumptions. Other small Internet advertisements that run down the side of the pages of social media like Facebook are more like colored classified newspaper ads—except they are *not* classified and frequently vanish before we have time to register them and choose to click on them. Catching a viewer's attention still relies on a picture, and getting the reader's interest depends on a short eye-catching caption, like "Have a Quickie!" So the transition from print to Internet is fairly simple for consumers. And, again, there is the advantage of having the advertisements served up at home or in the workplace.

What is original is the concept of ads being almost personalized when targeted at our own specific screen. Whether it is a good or bad thing is a purely subjective opinion. Some Internet or mobile users might find it annoying after the novelty wears off, whereas it might be considered to be great news by teenagers eager to buy more and more of almost anything.

As an example of the similarity of digital advertising to traditional ads, a Samsung Galaxy II smartphone advertisement displayed an eye-catching picture with a three-word headline that said "Vivid. Fast. Slim." Words in a smaller font beneath it said, "> Go to feature." When you click on *feature* for information, you get the body copy and description of features on a different page, which avoids clutter in the main advertisement.

The seductive colored illustrations are not sexual like Google Street View, but more like a delicious box of glossy chocolates designed to tempt us. They depict an enticing, shiny toy, like an elegantly thin, old-time Asprey platinum cigarette case or a silver Dunhill lighter, tastefully designed to make you want to handle it. And what we are promised if we buy this pocket-mobile is a treasure trove from Aladdin's cave with all the most up-to-date applications to draw us into different worlds, like a virtual vacation from reality. On this page, the headline "Vivid. Fast. Slim" is elaborated on with the words "Enhanced readability. Slimmer design (8.49mm). Better battery consumption. Quick multi-tasking. Efficient gaming. Luxurious design and easy grip." Perhaps the most significant word is "gaming," since the whole novelty of the mobile device is based on a human propensity for playing games, particularly among thirteen to twenty-three-year-olds.

Fulfilling a Hope and a Dream

Looking at these magical mobiles and smartphones designed to tempt and seduce buyers, not just with their exotic colors and textures, but also with their range of uses, we can see how a team of innovative designers, electronics engineers, and entrepreneurs created a hope and a dream to fulfill the wishes of twenty-first-century buyers who grew up in a consumer society that enables them to buy whatever they want on credit.

Steve Jobs recognized that it is the hope and the dream promised by the technological devices, rather than the products themselves, that overcomes any resistance to buy—in much the same way that teenagers order Coca-Cola to buy into the dating fantasy that Coke promises, and apparently also appears to fulfill.

Steve Jobs is featured in these pages as a prime example of innovation and entrepreneurship, rather than as a role model, because even though we can't help admiring what he achieved, he is also an example of what *not* to do. It is arguable whether he made more or less mistakes than successes. But the fact remains that his penultimate success just before he died must be envied by most entrepreneurs and marketing managers. He envisaged Apple out of nothing but his unconscious mind and turned it into a business organization now valued at $246,992 million. Its glittering electronic devices evolved from his dual nature and his awareness that his unconscious mind was preparing the way for his innovations. It was why he believed so insistently on his instincts and probably why he sometimes appeared to be schizoid. It makes him an interesting object for scrutiny and analysis.

At the same time, readers should be warned that high-growth companies, like Apple, are also high risk for investors—closer to speculation or even gambling than more conservative Blue Chip ones. Prudent investors like Warren Buffett stay with blue chip companies, like Heinz, which was taken private by Buffett's Berkshire Hathaway, after a deal said to be worth $23.3 billion, for which he will own 55 percent of Heinz.[1] It highlights the difference between the volatility of a technology company making devices that can rapidly go out of fashion, or become obsolete when competitors copy and improve on them, and the stability of a daily mealtime commodity like baked beans and tomato ketchup.

121

Strategic Advertising

The following seven colored advertisements all possess specific and significant ingredients in common. The first ingredient is the double meaning that makes readers pause to reflect, solve the semantic riddle, and smile at its ingenuity, wit, and suggestiveness. Perhaps even the emotions of admiration or respect come next. It means the advertisement makes four or five impacts on the reader's mind and emotions, instead of only one, which makes it far more likely to be remembered in a flash. It happens because the advertisement is not just glimpsed and ignored, but it activates the brain cells and lights them up. Another ingredient is the sex appeal inherent in four of them. Add to that the sheer effrontery or *chutzpah* of all the designs. And there is the irony in the two Conservative political posters, of the opposition Labour Party being shrugged off as a hopeless case of misplaced dedication to an outdated socialist fantasy.

Flashbulb memories are ones of significant events that make such an impact on the senses that consumers are more likely to recall them vividly later on.

If we use the previous advertisers' checklist with its five direct questions about the inclusion of a USP, the reason why, unique and competitive features, brand identification, and a clear and uncomplicated message, we find that every one of the following outstanding contemporary advertisements answers them in the affirmative in its own distinctive, original, indirect, and subtle way. Each is designed to overwhelm readers with its atmosphere so that each message illuminates the brain cells without needing to be baldly spelt out in writing. That is why the headline for five of them is not splashed across the top of each advertisement or immediately beneath it, as in the past, but is more subtly placed in small type at the bottom of the page, as if the picture alone made its message clear—whereas it doesn't entirely. Even an illustrated poster needs a written message to persuade readers to act.

What we see is a trend over time from using thirteen to fourteen words, down to about three to five, and finally to just a few words at the bottom of more sophisticated advertisements that almost tell their story without them, but find they need them after all. As for the two posters that follow, they convey words and picture almost simultaneously. And all of them have a talent to amuse.

"Sex Is No Accident. Always Use a Condom."

Grey Advertising of Germany chose a format of a colorful five-frame comic cartoon to get their story across to their targeted consumer segment. In the first frame, they showed a casual young man in T-shirt and shorts, roller-blading in a city street while listening to music from an iPod. Suddenly, in frame two, he sees an oncoming streetcar and trips on the rail with surprise. Across the street in frame three, a young, leggy, blond teenager bends down in a miniskirt to put her shopping in to her automobile. We see panic on the face of the oncoming roller skater as he realizes he can't stop and is aimed directly at the rear end of the girl bending over into her car. The final frame shows the direct result of the impact of boy-meets-girl in an unconventional way, not exactly head-on since the girl is sent sprawling as he enters from behind.

Of course, it's intended as a joke, a fantasy of wish fulfillment. And it is the explosion of the weird collision, and the joke, that creates the impact of the message: *always wear a condom for sex.*

Since it was probably printed in a comic or magazine, the message appears in small type at the base of the cartoon, for readers who already saw the joke to get extra amusement from the message. And it is likely to be remembered because it is a *risqué* joke that was endorsed by laughter.

Viagra

M&C Saatchi also found an amusing and original way to symbolize sex in a metaphor of a protuberant phallic symbol. It is a dark shiny red bonnet of a sleek sports car that appears to be battered with a number of hits. On a second look, the dents appear to be in regular rows, and we realize they represent the impression of the studs that fasten a mattress.

The message along the bottom of this magazine advertisement says, "See the world differently." It features a blue diamond-shaped pill and adds, "Ask your doctor about the new Viagra value pack today."

It too is a joke whose originality will be recalled with amusement and admiration for the concept. And it informs consumers that it cannot be bought over the counter.

100% Electric

The bright yellow background color of this magazine-type ad has a black shape silhouetted at its center. And like one of those shapes in a puzzle that can be seen as either one of two different objects, it is either the silhouette of an automobile seen from the front or back, or an electric plug hanging on a cable with two prongs.

Placed quietly at the bottom is the traditional Citroen logo and a message, "100% Electric. The New Citroen C-Zero." The cleverness of the subtle rendition of an electric car is both admirable and amusing.

123

Its *double entendres* is a visual one, instead of being verbal. The ad agency is Euro RSCG.

Morphy Richards Depilatory

Dominating the magazine page is a stunningly beautiful young woman holding a pair of tailor's shears nonchalantly in one hand. It takes a moment to realize that she only just decided to cut her skirt short to reveal her long slender legs. The shredded remains of her dress lie scattered around her on the floor. The reason for not concealing her legs behind the original long skirt is evidently the benefit of having used a hair remover by Morphy Richards.

The advertisement, by Contract Advertising of India, shows audacity and originality that will shock some readers and amuse others. It is certain they will remember it, particularly young women who will use her as a role model. And they know what product to use in order to obtain the same gorgeous effect.

For Beautiful City

A young woman is also featured by McCann-Erickson advertising agency for their client, the City of Belgrade. But since she is shown from the rear, it is her bottom that dominates this advertisement. She bends down in blue jeans. Beside her is a lovable dog with its tongue lolling happily out. "Clean after your dog," says the message at the base of the ad. And that is exactly why she is bending over on the pavement while her pet looks on.

Once again it is an original approach, and likely to be remembered with a smile.

A picture tells the story in each one of those five advertisements. The modest written message at the end is more like a punch line to a joke that everyone knows is coming, or a nudge in the ribs. But the following two horizontal advertisements are different because they are posters for billboards. Both were commissioned by Britain's Conservative Party and designed by the irreverent Saatchi & Saatchi. One shows a disgruntled business executive holding a briefcase open by the handle to show it is completely empty. The headline says, "Labour's Spent."

Again there is a dual meaning. In the first place, the Labour Party has spent all the taxpayers' money and left the nation broke. And, second, Labour (or Socialism) is a spent force. Running along the bottom of the poster is a subsidiary message: "Thanks to Labour's Debt Crisis, there's no money left. Britain needs change." The final word is a *double entendre* too, meaning Britain needs a different government and is desperate for hard cash.

"I Took Billions from Pensions. . ."

According to Saatchi & Saatchi, all this poster needed was the self-satisfied smirk on the face of the Labour Party leader who came after Blair. So there is Gordon Brown looking witless beside his message: "I Took Billions from Pensions—Vote for me." It conveyed a clear impression that Brown was too empty-headed to know what he was saying or doing. It led to his downfall, because both of those posters echoed what many long-suffering voters had already concluded—it was time to vote Conservative. And they did.

It is a prime example of taking the lead by reassuring the public that what they think is true, in order to get them to act on it.

How Did They Put the Sell into the Advertising?

Every well-constructed advertisement is aimed at stimulating five sensitive psychological consumer instincts in the following order and manner, according to an acronym called AIDCA. "A" represents catching a buyer's Attention. "I" is for creating Interest; "D" for arousing Desire; and "C" for establishing Comprehension and Conviction. The second "A" is a call for Action. The AIDCA formula was borrowed from the art of selling and is described more thoroughly in chapter 15 about the psychological process of selling.

Despite the brilliance of John Caples, the master of advertising wordsmiths was, arguably, a copywriter named Clyde Bedell, who came later. His famous book, *How to Write Advertising That Sells*, is repeatedly reprinted.[2] He used the AIDCA formula as a framework to go into deeper details for writing selling copy into promotional material. For example, "GET ATTENTION! *Make your headline work—be brief if you can.* (1) Mention the prospect and his (or her) interests. (2) Promise benefits. (3) Use news to the point. (4) Provoke curiosity. (5) Mention the product favorably—using selling points. AROUSE INTEREST AND CREATE DESIRE."

Without elaborating or fine-tuning his copy, as he does—in this case with thirteen different classifications—he follows on with CREATE CONVICTION (with seven classifications of that theme) and TRY FOR ACTION, with another six classifications of that approach. His book is the Baedeker guide to copywriting, whether for advertisements, public relations editorials, or a supplier's own website, which is otherwise merely an online catalog or brochure. Readers who are seriously interested in improving their copywriting or commercial editorials can buy Bedell's book and see for themselves.

One illusion suffered by many advertisers, and also small commercial art studios, is that an advertisement is just a pretty picture. To disabuse them of that notion, Starch tests of different print advertisements for the same product, with the identical headline, often demonstrated how the uglier one obtained more responses than one with a more professional layout. The reason was thought to be that it provided more conviction for down-to-earth products like furnaces, or automobile tires, for example, that hardly possess sex appeal.

Another illusion is using a *gimmick* or slogan rather than a well-thought-out USP. Because, by definition, a gimmick is mere show without the substance to sell anything.

Although most of the advertisements on the previous pages were witty and amusing, wit is very different from clowning like a slapstick comedian. David Ogilvy warned against advertisements that are cute, funny, or smart-alecky. One of his sayings was "People don't buy from clowns." He also warned against stupidity by reminding us that "the consumer is not an idiot, she is your wife."

Sex appeal often tempts readers to stop and study an advertisement and seduces them into buying all sorts of products and services, from high fashion clothes to artificial nails, slim diets, and suntans. Some people will do and pay almost anything for the sake of sex—even for an illusion of it. It is an essential ingredient in the world of advertising and public relations because it mirrors life. On the other hand, scintillating glamor figures easily distract readers from the main message if they are not relevant or not presented prudently and tactically. Men and women admire pretty young women, but they can distract from an advertiser's intentions. For example, an advertiser of a low-calorie sweetener used a slender model caressing an elegant borzoi to impress the idea of slim elegance and diet consciousness on readers' minds in a commercial film. But consumer tests revealed that not a single viewer had read the message or remembered the brand, or even the type of product, because they were gazing at the pretty woman and the elegant dog.[3]

The effectiveness of appealing colored magazine advertisements comes partly from displaying only the minimum number of components to avoid clutter that distracts from the main message. The same factor applies to advertising videos and short commercial films.

The question of whether new technologies, so loved by Hollywood blockbuster movies today, are also beneficial for commercials is a serious consideration because of the distinction that separates selling and entertaining. The boundaries have become more blurred because of the enormous youth market that keeps consumer economies going. They are thirteen to twenty-three-year-olds, who love to dramatize themselves in order to be the center of attention. Some of the newer and younger advertising agencies reflect this with technological glitter and noisy sound effects and cloudbursts of fireworks to capture their attention and engage with them. But, as with every other type of component in an advertisement, there can be too much and too many effects that distract from the key message.

Nevertheless, as soon as a blockbuster movie uses technology and fantasy, futurism, comic strip-cartoons, or space wars to channel young cinemagoers to cinema box offices, some advertising agencies will repeat those effects in an advertising commercial aimed at the youth market. What their outrageous effects generally reveal is that the creative people have run out of original ideas.

What a Good Advertising Agency Can Do

These types of costly distractions from selling can be avoided by using a good professional advertising agency. The problem is how to find one. For one thing, most creative people are introverts who live in a fantasy world of their own of pretty pictures, well-executed layouts, smart ideas, and often irrelevant gimmicks that have nothing to do with selling goods or services. And many don't bother to keep up to date by reading or studying research results. Most have no idea how a real business works. It's not their sphere and would be more likely to obstruct their wild creativity.

Although an account executive or an art director is supposed to direct creative people toward realistic marketing goals, art directors have to be (and generally are) overwhelmingly creative too. And account executives are caught in the middle with a double agenda: they must please the agency that pays their salary, and also their client. They are supposed to impose a reality check on the creative team. But it is not easy to do without crushing their creativity and discouraging ideas. That is why it is important to find a responsible and well-managed agency from the start. They must have a creative department with a record of original ideas and a portfolio of successful ads that sold their clients' goods and services.

127

So, despite David Ogilvy's skepticism about copywriters, he advises us as follows: (1) Select the right agency; (2) Don't make them feel insecure; (3) Brief them thoroughly; (4) Don't try to compete with them creatively.[4]

He added an important rider which is proved in the advertising arena time and again. "If I were a manufacturer, I would look for an agency which had no new-business department." The reason is that agencies driven by their own bottom line and double agenda tend to focus their A-team on making presentations to open new accounts, which are then placed on the back burner with the B-team. The result is often an anticlimax that leaves the advertiser wondering why he isn't getting the ideas and service that were promised. Ogilvy also warned that, if you choose a second-rate agency, they'll blame your advertising manager for not briefing them properly. And it is not unusual for the agency to get him fired.

Benchmarks Measure Results

Just as consumers' buying motives have to be explored and measured before designing new products or services that advertisers hope to sell to them, so benchmarks are needed to measure any improvements or losses in sales after an advertising campaign. This precaution may prevent any dropping off in sales or possible damage to the brand resulting from the wrong advertising approach. Rosser Reeves of Ted Bates Advertising showed how it can happen, by providing a number of case histories in his landmark book in the progress of advertising. The following are three examples, edited for brevity:

1. An advertiser spent $2 million a year, but put his message into the heads of only 5 percent of his targeted market. Yet his biggest competitor registered *his* story with over 60 percent of those consumers in less time and with fewer dollars. Why?
2. Two advertisers spent $10 million each to change their stories at the same time. A year later, one had registered his new message with 44 percent of US consumers, whereas the other had penetrated the minds of only 1.8 percent. Why?
3. A food advertiser had a strong story, but used a dramatic device that overwhelmed it. The result was only 9 percent remembered the copy, whereas 38 percent recalled the useless device he'd used that conveyed no message at all.[5]

None of that would have been discovered without first setting up benchmarks from research and then taking regular measurements for comparison afterward. That is where cool objectivity and meticulous attention to detail enter the marketing equation. Service industries and manufacturers are unlikely to be objective about their own advertising, because they are in love with their own products, and love is notoriously blind.

For example, Steve Jobs' divided attention or split personality was described earlier on. Its result was that when he designed, manufactured, and launched NeXT Computer, he did just about everything wrong in order to satisfy his own personal whims and standards, and not the market's. He was in love with his factory, with his product, with the materials he used and the design he created, and blind to his own mistakes. Instead of designing NeXT computer for potential users in the market, he made it for himself. Or, one suspects, it was to show off to his craftsman father. But a market of one won't pay the overhead costs.

It is often said that people, creative people in particular, must be passionate about what they are doing. It is what underscores the duality of the marketing process because creative teams who design and develop a product *must* be passionate. The advertising agency must be passionate too. But business people have to be clinically objective in order to make realistic evaluations. Otherwise they will be shortsighted or blind to design flaws and defects. Hence the split personality of Steve Jobs attempting to be creative with one part of his mind and also run a business enterprise that required hard-headedness.

An advertising agency can be most effective when it has a small team of intellectuals at its core—as J. Walter Thompson and Afamal had at one time (and perhaps still do).[6] Intellectuals of the type previously described at Bletchley Park in World War Two, were known for their instinctual imaginative uprushes that penetrate to the core of a problem and are able to resolve it, whereas the average intellect and outlook may be unable to stretch its boundaries widely or deeply enough. It is one of the advantages of being able to hire a global advertising and marketing agency that dedicates an entire team to a client's account.

An agency is most effective when the client is disciplined and prepared to leave the ideation and imaginative interpretation to the tender love and care of a dependable creative agency. That is why successful clients appoint an experienced advertising manager to brief an agency dispassionately, scrutinize their presentations analytically, and keep the agency to its promises in an objective and businesslike fashion.

Timing and Testing

As well as measuring everything first and last, market leaders also test everything they produce, whether products, services, or communications.

Unilever's marketing system and procedures for producing advertisements that repeatedly sell millions of their products to users over dealers' heads is based on testing everything first, to make sure it works effectively. There is no point in spending millions on advertising a less-than-perfect product. And yet there are plenty of products on the market with a design flaw left unchecked because of poor or nonexistent quality control. We know there is no such thing as perfection, but we have to aim at it until we are satisfied we are achieving results that are at least as good as, or better than, our biggest rivals. Similarly, it would be wasteful and purposeless to let down all the work of research and development by accepting inferior advertising. That is why market leaders research consumer needs in the marketplace and in their homes, or on the streets.

They look for and study the most suitable consumer motivations, in order to fulfill their needs. They test the taste of foods and beverages until they are satisfied with the blends and certain that buyers have confidence in their brand and will want more of it. They test scents, toiletries, and cosmetics for the same reasons, because dealers they sell to want regular repeat orders from customers. They test skin sensitivity to deodorants, shaving creams, laundry detergents, and household cleaners. They research the effects of their brands on consumers to create Brand Awareness and ensure Brand Preference and Brand Loyalty. Brand champions watch to avoid anything that might tarnish brands under their care. They test their products to ensure they fulfill the claims of their USP. They also test their communications in much the same way, before and after a new product launch. So do Colgate-Palmolive, P&G, and other leading marketers of fast-moving packaged consumer goods. So do leading manufacturers of small and large appliances, like General Electric, Matsushita, Apple, Nokia, and Samsung.

Ensuring that the advertising in every new campaign works as well as the products is part of the marketing culture. Unilever, for example, used four criteria for testing their advertisements, known by the acronym ACCI.

(1) *Awareness:* Did passersby in the street, or shoppers or cinema audiences or whoever else, remember noticing the advertisement in any media when reminded and shown a copy of it? (2) *Comprehension:* Did

they understand the USP or the main product benefits? (3) *Conviction:* Did they believe what the advertisement claimed? (4) *Intention to buy:* Will they definitely buy it or are they likely to buy it, or may do so, or not? All responses would be rated and analyzed, with a reason why. If the marketing people have any doubts that the advertising impact is not powerful enough or if the message is confusing, the new or innovated product launch should be postponed to research and design a new advertising campaign. And perhaps more work may need to be done to improve the product, as a result of consumer feedback regarding the possibility of design flaws.

There are other more sophisticated tests of all media which have become more complex to measure as a result of the Internet and the introduction of social media and all advertising in it, because Internet advertising is still in its infancy. No doubt bigger advertising media, like *Google* and *Facebook,* are already analyzing reactions to their advertising and their media. It is still too early for any informed book to be published on the results of online advertising that now includes mobiles and smartphones that duplicate or overlap television and the Internet.

Timing is essential. Just as a new product has to be launched at the right time and in the right place, so does advertising—hopefully at peak periods of audience ratings. Timing plays a crucial role in all strategic plans and tactics, since (as in battle) there may be only a hair's breadth of difference between success and failure, with only one moment to achieve success. Time is the most valuable and the most perishable of all resources. Now it's here, now it's gone!

Clicks, Likes, and Teasing

The assertion by David Ogilvy that "People don't buy from clowns"—or advertisers who fool around—has stood the test of time, because he researched the results of his advertising campaigns and was on intimate enough terms with his clients to know their sales figures. So he was in a position to know which headlines and what other components were responsible for influencing people to buy.

Of course, he wasn't in business during our own fun-loving era of blatant consumption based on extended credit, with banks falling over themselves to offer us loans at 20 percent interest. His was a different world in which he knew the hard end of business with its profit-and-loss accounts and its cost–benefit analysis. His clients were among the biggest companies in the world, with huge advertising budgets that had to produce massive sales volumes in return. Today we see a very different consumer society with excited kids and impulsive teens of both sexes happily treating shopping in the plaza or the mall as if abandoning themselves to all the joys of a public holiday, and eagerly waving their plastic cards at checkout counters as if they were growing an endless supply of banknotes in their backyards. But Ogilvy had to work ingeniously to find ways to get people to buy his clients' products and services in a highly competitive environment where consumers were cautious with their dollars.

American capitalism is a ruthless sink-or-swim system with no safety nets, in which you have to keep selling to a lot of people just to break even, pay your overhead costs, and cover a regular monthly payroll. So he was careful to research his ads and the responses from consumers. Regardless of all the glitter and pizzazz of product designs and promotions up-front, he knew that selling is a serious business in which buyers need to trust the products, the services, and the company, before they buy. And he was well aware that they won't buy from people who fool around.

A company has only to make a fool of itself once for any trust and confidence in it to evaporate. Buyers must know unreservedly that they can rely on suppliers. But it is tempting to play games on social media like Facebook, or in a YouTube video, where everyone is showing off, teasing, or playing games to get attention, as if they imagine they are being followed by a TV camera.

So there has been plenty of clowning on the Internet since the digital revolution and the introduction of online social media. We have been regaled with all sorts of gimmicks designed to get our attention. Of course, cheeky teaser ads have always existed. But going into hoots of laughter isn't a recipe for buying anything.

In fact, teasing videos posted on YouTube get millions of views—like the baby falling on its face and crying, or an infant being bitten by a pet frog and looking surprised. Then there are those weird and sometimes hilarious short phrases linked to social media, which are more like shopping lists, but apparently get millions of clicks and "likes." They are so successful at obtaining those knee-jerk reactions that there are commercial studios filled with bloggers who are well paid to come up with sentences that tease or shock, like, "TEN GHASTLY-LOOKING CELEBRITIES" or "TEN OF THE MOST HIDEOUS BOOBS" or "THE TEN UGLIEST BACKSIDES." They don't claim to be ads, just teasers to nudge you into clicking for the following page where advertisers can display their ads.

But clicking isn't buying. Nor are "likes." So they leave us puzzled as to why they think anyone would want to link their advertisements to those types of remarks and risk tarnishing their image for life—since they will always be there to be scorned or ridiculed by millions of viewers.

Trick or Treat?

On the other hand, there can be no doubt that Google's staff are very smart people and their approach to advertising is an ingenious money-maker for their media, although we don't yet know whether it actually works for advertisers or not. Perhaps it is still too early for an objective in-depth research study to show us how many sales each algorithmically motivated ad produced and whether it was cost-effective.

Certainly, leaving consumer targeting and visibility on the Internet to algorithms programmed to recognize specific key word sounds scientific to those who believe that artificial intelligence has all the answers. But, of course it doesn't. And only advertisers themselves can determine which headline, or photograph, or ad, persuaded enough people to use their advertised service or buy their products.

No doubt those quick-witted Google nerds are continuously improving their product, since the technology is still new and advertisers are still trying to get a handle on it. Google are the runaway leader in digital advertising with 31.45 percent, with Facebook 7.93 percent, Twitter 0.87 percent, Microsoft 2.54 percent, and Yahoo 2.52 percent.[7]

Meanwhile, readers and advertisers and ad agencies have plenty of opportunity to study, in these pages, what the most skillful and creative advertising agencies did to increase the sales of products from Procter & Gamble, Lever Brothers, Colgate, GE, Apple, and other global market leaders who grew rich and famous from the results of professional state-of-the-arts advertising and marketing before the introduction of digital media. The overwhelming question likely to dominate this discussion is whether algorithms or artificial intelligence can equal what human intelligence managed to devise from the 1920s to the 1980s, which was scientifically proven to work.

Share of Advertising Media

In fact, traditional media continues to dominate. Latest research studies show that, of a total advertising budget of nearly $187 billion, digital media's share is likely to be less than 30 percent. But it is growing faster. Nearly $79 billion is spent on TV advertising. Then comes digital advertising. Print is in third place.

Modest growth in current ad spending is symptomatic of caution when contemplating digital advertising and apprehension about the shrinkage of the numbers of readers of print media. Social media is likely to see most growth (31 percent), followed by video (29 percent) and mobile (20 percent), with search engines 45 percent.

Changes in ad spending by media in 2015: digital: +13 percent, outdoor: +4.8 percent, cinema: +3.4 percent, radio: +1.8 percent, TV: +1.7 percent, print: −7.9 percent.[8]

10

The Value of Branding and Marketing

The Top 100 Global Brands increased in value by 14 percent year on year in 2015 to a value of $3.3 trillion, according to Millward Brown. "A successful brand," they claim, "is made up of three key components": (1) How relevant or meaningful a brand is in our lives. (2) How different it is to our competitors. (3) How well we know and trust the brand and whether it is salient. Brand strength drives value.

Five of the Top Ten Brands dropped out during 2006–15 and were replaced by others. And no brand occupies the same rank today as it did ten years ago. Perhaps unsurprisingly after the digital revolution, the top four global brands are in the technology category. And the number of Chinese brands in the Top Global 100 increased to fourteen in 2015.

Top Ten Most Valuable Global Brands (2015)

	Category	Brand Value ($millions)	Rise or Fall (percent)
1. Apple	Technology	246,992	+67
2. Google	Technology	173,652	+9
3. Microsoft	Technology	115,500	+28
4. IBM	Technology	93,987	−13
5. Visa	Payments	91,962	+16
6. AT&T	Telecom	89,492	+15
7. Verizon	Telecom	86,009	+36
8. Coca-Cola	Soft drinks	83,841	+4
9. MacDonald's	Fast foods	81,162	−5
10. Marlboro	Tobacco	80,352	+19

The next ten Top Brands are Tencent (technology), Facebook (technology), Alibaba (online retail), Amazon.com (online retail), China Mobile (telecom), Wells Fargo (bank), GE (conglomerate), UPS (logistics), Disney (entertainment), and MasterCard (payments).[1]

Brand Power

Brand power was crucial in the past ten years, which were divided into two halves: those before the global financial crisis and the others afterward. Consumers spent more cautiously in the second period and no product or service category was spared from disruption. Millward Brown went on to stress that "Brand Purpose" increases the growth of brand value (the reason why consumers purchase a specific brand or are prepared to pay more for it). Brand Purpose means having a purpose beyond making money, like improving lifestyles or making the world a better place. It is a factor that "predisposes a consumer to purchase a particular brand" because it has a strong brand proposition, which comes first, before the advertising. Superior brand value and growth occur from a combination of a unique and compelling core proposition, a distinctive brand identity, and great advertising. As for innovation, it is no longer an option: "Innovation drives brand value."

Research shows that there is a strong and productive correlation between a brand being innovative and being loved by consumers. On the other hand, consumers may try a brand once or twice, but they won't stay with it unless they trust it.

Another prediction from BrandZ is that half of media budgets will go to digital media, although no one can forecast when.

The momentum of brand image is not often discussed. And yet, a broad and in-depth study was once made to discover whether there is one single ingredient that might be responsible for a company's success. Although it found that success depends on a whole bundle of different factors, the reputable and thorough publication, responsible for accumulating all the facts and analyzing them, decided they had unearthed enough evidence to pinpoint "momentum of image" as the overriding factor for success.[2]

The New Normal

Millward Brown is one of the leading consultants on branding. He had already described 2013 as a "Year of recovery, refinement and relevance." There was a new tone, according to BrandZ. They called it "the new normal," resulting from the disruption of the digital revolution and the global recession. It emphasizes, once again, that a rising economic tide generally favors strong brands, which recover faster than weaker ones. The fact is clear, according to Millward Brown, that "the Top 100 most valuable global brands in 2013 rose 7 percent in value, with the rise spread across most categories." By 2015, the value of brands had doubled. It indicates that what *has* changed is that far more ambitious companies must now brand their goods and services or improve their existing brands to a more sophisticated level if they want to remain competitive.

On the other hand, the alleged rise in market values of branded goods brings up a troublesome but intriguing subject, reminiscent of Oscar Wilde's witty remark that "Nowadays people know the price of everything and the value of nothing."[3] The subject was raised by *The New York Times* book critic when writing about Alan Greenspan's new book, two years ago. Greenspan is one of the most famous living economists in the world. He stated in his book that, while the value of the US economic output has increased since the 1970s, the weight has not. "If everything 'Made in the U.S.A.' in 2013 was placed on a giant scale," Greenspan wrote, "it would weight about as much as everything 'Made in the U.S.A.' in 1977."[4] So what do those two rises in value really mean?

It gives us pause to wonder if Greenspan was, once again, questioning the prices of company shares as a consequence of irrational exuberance on the stock exchanges, compared with their *real* value. Perhaps the rise is due only to buyers and sellers being carried away by the adrenaline rush of competition and excitement in the stock markets.

The "new normal" may be something quite different. It may really be consumers rejecting once-eminent brands which are now tarnished by outsourcing manufacturing to Asian factories, in favor of buying cheaper products, on the grounds that, if goods are tarnished or flawed, they may have to be replaced. Offshoring, particularly to China, resulted in huge lineups at Walmart's returns counters, for example, with electrical appliances that failed to work, quick-boiling kettles that could not be switched on or off, branded glass ovenware that cracked or exploded in the oven heat, and any number of other complaints regarding shoddy materials, design flaws, zip fasteners that failed to function, and other poor workmanship and failures in quality control. Have once-famous names that offshored their manufacturing lost control of their brands? And has the goal of branding, which was consumer preference, been lost by greed for cheap labor?

Such doubts beg another, even more overwhelming question. Have companies that switched to offshoring their manufacturing, instead of protecting their brands, made the same mistake as those big publishers who tarnished their brands by switching to celebrity platforms instead? And will this be the year when all the clocks stop, all over the world, and run backward to the far-off days before sophisticated marketing? Or are consumers and investors already aware that those brands may have actually lost their value through neglect? It seems that a company can't be both factory oriented and brand or marketing oriented at the same time. Marketing objectives should have taken precedence over saving on factory costs.

Most Trusted Brands

The objective of branding is not only to establish an image of quality and dependability, but also to market a positive identity as both a tangible and an intangible consumer benefit, by creating awareness and raising it to such a height that it gains the largest share of that category in consumers' minds. It should be so socially relevant to the needs of consumers that it becomes a household word like, for example, Hoover and Frigidaire once did.

It means the brand will have a dominant emotional impact, as well as a rational one, over all other similar brands, as a symbol of what it stands for and what it stands behind, since a brand is intended to be a guarantee. It should not only dominate a shopper's mind when preparing a shopping list or browsing in a store, but also dismiss previous attachments to other brands in a brand-switching process. At the summit of those ascending intentions is maintaining loyalty to the new brand against all-comers.

One problem is that brands lose meaning every time a company is bought out and merged into a bigger one, unless they continue to receive tender loving care thereafter. And the danger of them being tarnished is even greater if they are no longer manufactured by the same company but offshored instead.

Brands continue to need personal attention and care by a brand champion, to ensure they do not become tarnished in any way, either by wrong decisions inside the company or by campaigns outside. They might include overpricing, on one hand, or inferior shelf positioning in stores, on the other. On the inside, that care requires that marketing and brand managers are part of the R&D team from the beginning of a new product design. Brand management must take continuous care to retain a brand's pristine public image, because it will be a visible, attractive, and vulnerable target for every competitor in the same or similar category to attack.

A brand will only reach that measurable pinnacle of brand awareness if it continues to fulfill consumer needs. If it does, it will have achieved trust. The Top Ten Most Trusted Brands for five or more consecutive years, in 2015, were Toyota Cars, Iams Pet Food, Quaker Snack Bars, Kellogg's Cereal, Sun Life Financial Insurance, Jamieson Vitamin, Sensodyne Toothpaste, Coppertone Sunscreen, Toyota Hybrid Cars, and Yoplait Yogurt.[5]

Brand champions watch for changes in consumer needs, which may make a product irrelevant. Lux Soap Flakes was trusted as "kind to hands" when women washed fragile undies themselves. It lost its relevance when laundry appliances became affordable and laundry detergents were formulated to remove stains better than pure soap. But Lux Beauty Soap, launched by Lever Brothers in 1925, strengthened its market position by association with four hundred of the most glamorous Hollywood actresses, and now with Bollywood stars. Lux is still the best-selling toilet soap in the world, according to ACNielsen (with Dove in second place and Lifebuoy fifth, both of them Unilever brands). Every day twelve million Lux products are bought, demonstrating Unilever's masterly professionalism in branding their product ranges.

Global CEO Jez Frampton of Interbrand echoed former CEO of General Electric, Jack Welch, by remarking at the end of 2013, "Those who lead today's brands can no longer rely on once immutable truths or principles of leadership honored in times past."

But there is irony as well as strange *déjà vu* in the way that things change, yet remain remarkably the same. That is because, while technologies change in cycles of discovery—with steam, mechanics, electricity, electronics, and algorithms—human nature changes only gradually, if at all. As he points out, "purchasing increasingly shifts from a physical experience to a virtual one." With that shift, consumers also shift to relationship-based interactions where "new skills and sensibilities are needed." Consumers carry more weight, and "less tangible strengths like emotional intelligence and psychological insight are just as key to leading a brand today as the ability to generate high ROI and increased shareholder value."

Earning Loyalty

Loyalty is always suspect, since consumers continually switch brands. Plastic customer loyalty cards of all types are intended to build up purchasing points, like air miles, that habituate customers to continue using the same supplier, even the same bank, in good times and bad, like wearing an old-fashioned wedding band. To what extent they work is hard to tell. It is an ongoing rebate for being loyal, instead of a discount. Do distributors raise their prices to accommodate the costs?

Of course they do, if they want to stay in business. Customer loyalty cards have been described as "a tiresome burden" for customers. They are primarily intended to benefit suppliers, or they would not distribute them in the first place.

Some loyalty programs are better than others. One study undertaken in Canada compared the top twenty-two loyalty programs on the strength of each one's overall value. Perhaps the most significant of its four main findings was that "In some cases, the cost to own a loyalty card (i.e., the annual fee) is so high that a reward will never be truly earned."[6] That example also tends to indicate that loyalty programs without a fee are paid for by charging consumers premium prices, since the cost of the program must come from somewhere. If so, there is no benefit for customers.

Like loyalty to brands, it demonstrates how make-believe has always been more important than reality—since consumers switch all the time.

Earning or Losing Trust

That questions the one-sided approach to loyalty programs that offer benefits while actually creating problems for consumers who suspect they are being cheated. If companies and institutions want loyalty, they have to earn consumer trust first.

For example, the human face of organizations has vanished in a welter of electronic voicemails and departmental menus. It initially came about from the loss of well-trained, charming, and caring women who really seemed as if they wanted to help us on the phone. They were seen by consumers as being on their side and not on the side of faceless and manipulative corporations. The first real attempt to solve consumers' problems came about when boys were replaced by girls on phones, because they were more reliable and their gentle voices were imbued with a helpful smile. More recent electronic operations eliminate costs by reversing that helpful practice. The smile is replaced by an electronic scowl. Consumers would be justified in imagining it was intentional, to avoid the responsibilities of providing customer services and keep the complaining public at bay.

At the beginning of 2014, neither the role of voice-boxes nor departmental menus nor many company websites were aimed at helping consumers. Instead, new technologies are generally adopted to save companies time and money. The question of marketing efficiency, or effectiveness, is something that most companies are either blind to, or have not yet mastered, or have forgotten as a consequence of cost-cutting concerns during the global financial crisis. It is the old conundrum of whether to produce revenues by caring about what customers want and providing it, or simply by cutting costs. The result of cost-cutting is that personal service has been dying by inches. It has been replaced by special and deceitful limited-time promotions aimed at retrieving former customers who switched to other companies because of poor service.

How much business gets lost when consumers struggle their way through a maze of phone numbers that a recorded voice tells them to click on, only to be returned to the beginning without hearing a helpful human voice, is impossible to determine. And the bigger the company or institution, the less likely it is that customer complaints will even be heard because, as usual, the problem is at the top where top managers have isolated themselves from customers and markets behind electronic barricades. Near-monopolies, institutions and NGOs in particular, deceive the public by filling their websites with elaborate and confusing information that repeatedly claims to offer service, while contact addresses are carefully eliminated to avoid it. If a phone number appears for emergencies, waiting time is long, dismal, and confusing, and calculated to discourage contact.

Just as the engineering stage of product marketing was fraught with product orientation instead of consumer orientation, the same problem applies to computer programmers or engineers who create communications without any thought of user-friendliness. Their priority is technological efficiencies instead of consumer appeal. The net result is irritated consumers frustrated by disinterested recorded voices telling them that "your call is important to us." It demonstrates the opposite. Time lost by consumers struggling to be put through or waiting in a virtual limbo can never be recovered. Nor can the insult be reversed. It results in brand switching.

Outsourcing messaging and customer services and complaints means that top management doesn't receive feedback from consumers. So there is evidently a lack of understanding of the marketing process in which every one of a company's staff should be oriented to customers and sales, including outsourced services. Companies have to establish their priorities in this sphere, as in any others, if they want new business or wish to keep existing consumers loyal. Is their objective to encourage sales or turn business away? Paying lip service to consumer needs while actually damaging relationships leads inevitably to brand switching instead of brand bonding. And bonding is particularly important for service industries that need continual repeat monthly business.

Brand bonding and brand switching are measured regularly for major marketers by companies like Interbrand and BrandZ, each in their own distinctive ways. Two questions often asked by clients are, where should my brand be positioned in the market (bearing in mind all the similarities and differences of competing brands) and what share of the market can I realistically expect to obtain? The answers depend on many factors, including the amount of budget available to promote the brand. That is where those brilliant, creative, and intellectual mathematicians in the global advertising and marketing agencies score with their leaps of imagination and their "sense of location" (as military strategist Carl von Clausewitz called it, as if imagining all the possible moves on a chessboard before commencing play).

Inevitably, the 80/20 principle crops up in measuring brands too. In their case, a small number of consumers account for a large number of sales, just as a small number of the population accounts for the most wealth. Sometimes called "the Pareto principle," it is based on economist Vilfredo Pareto's discovery that only 20 percent of the pea pods in his vegetable garden contained 80 percent of all the peas.[7]

One example of this fine focus is a US luxury home builder. Toll Brothers concentrate on prospective purchasers who go to the opera, with Toll Brothers Metropolitan Opera international radio network. They exemplify good use of psychographics in targeting people who evidently enjoy finer things and richer experiences in their more leisurely and appreciative lives.

Past, Present, and Future

Looking over our shoulder to compare where we came from with where we are now, we may remember the chairman of British Airways, Sir Colin Marshall, remarking that "Marketing is both the business of the future and the future of the business."[8] It was a watershed period after Britain had failed as a manufacturing economy, and the United States had already been overtaken by Japan not many years before that. From a Fellow of the Chartered Institute of Marketing in the United Kingdom, it sounded like a wake-up call and a rallying cry after numerous successes as chief executive of BA when he made the airline more competitive. Now the disruptive forces of digital technology run counter to marketing, since they are factory-oriented and take management a step backward in time, unless used prudently, when the right tool for a specific task.

He died in 2012, having "turned British Airways from a sleeping giant into a world leader."[9] Before that, the formerly nationalized airline was "a loss making discredit to the nation" with its bloated bureaucracy, and "operated largely for the benefit of the staff and civil servants." Marshall arrived from New York to wake up the airline during Prime Minister Margaret Thatcher's reign—which he was able to do as an outsider and someone dedicated to the marketing philosophy. BA is now the largest airline and the "British flag carrier." It was privatized by the Conservative government in 1987 and took him eight years to transform it from failure to success.

British Airways became a success story and a credit to the integrated marketing philosophy, whereas, in contrast, former market leader Eastman Kodak was failing in the United States through lack of attention to marketing. They sought bankruptcy protection in 2012 after 131 years in business. We can learn a number of useful lessons from the airway's success and the camera company's failure.

How did those trials and tribulations come about? Taking British Airways out of the dead hands of socialism was an important beginning to bring the airline back to life, but a great deal of deconstructing and planning and restructuring had to take place in the following years, finally resulting in success.

But how could Kodak's once fine brand become so damaged? And could failure have been prevented? We have to look back at the mid-1980s, because it is easy to forget that Japan was the most innovative and competitive economy in the world for nine consecutive years until 1995, when the US economy faltered and reduced its imports from Japan.[10] Even now Japan is the third biggest global economy. Both Peter Drucker on management and W. Edwards Deming on quality controls had attempted, since the 1980s, to persuade American companies of Japan's superiority in management, manufacturing, and marketing. And paperback books on Japanese formulas for success abounded at every major airport. But US arrogance and complacency made American suppliers remarkably rigid. They mirrored Britain's complacency after the English Industrial Revolution, when America and Germany easily stole markets from them. Now it was the Asian Tigers who scooped up trade that would otherwise have gone to Britain and the United States, who didn't even appear to notice the loss of business.

Nations and institutions and business organizations believe in their own superiority because of historic success. And Britain and the United States had been supremely successful in the past. But part of a nation's and a company's culture is to project historic growth as their due, and continue to repeat what they did in the past (even repeating the same

143

mistakes) until they are suddenly confronted by discontinuous change for which they are unprepared.

Complacency is addictive and corrosive. Complacent leaders believe there is only one way to run a business, and it's *their* way. They scorn competitors and lose sight of what others are doing. And that is not their only failing: They focus on short-term plans and often reduce budgets aimed at future growth, like research and development of new products; they make the common mistake of hiring managers who think like *they* do; and they prevent *new* thinking by promoting only from within. Since disengaging from the marketplace outside allows more time for internal politics, they become distracted from their goals. Complacency leads to loss of engagement, drive, and vigor in the marketplace. Unproductive accountants and cost-cutting have the upper hand. Companies become defensive instead of offensive. And battles are not won by being on the defensive.

Complacency Breeds Arrogance

One example of how complacency breeds arrogance occurred in 1973, in the accounts department of the biggest South African conglomerate, S. A. Breweries. It is the dominant brewery and the biggest producer of Coca-Cola brands in southern Africa. Their headquarters at Number Two Jan Smutslaan was known as "The Kremlin." Its brainpower was respected, not only because of its position as market leader, but for its diversification by means of a number of subsidiary companies, each of which was the market leader in its own different sphere. The group was one of the most sophisticated holding companies in southern Africa. It included Sol Kerzner's Southern Sun Hotels, which modernized the hotel and tourist industry; the Food Corporation in food and beverages like Coke and Carling Black Label beer; the Associated Furniture Company; a diversified shoe conglomerate named Shoecorp Ltd; a highly successful chain of stores named OK Bazaars; and Scott and Edgars Group that specialized in fashions.

Shoecorp was far and away the footwear market leader in southern Africa, with Bata Shoes lagging a long way behind. It consisted of five well-managed factories, each producing its own different brand of shoes, from women's fashion shoes to "Jack & Jill's" children's shoes, the greatly admired quality Barker brand for men, more casual "Hush Puppies," and nonbranded cheaper dress shoes. It had six provincial warehouses which were well managed; a very large wholesale distribution operation called Lipworth, which was also well run; and forty-five national shoe salesmen. All was well until the so-called financial whiz-kids in their accounts department proposed a cost-cutting program by centralizing the entire organization, ostensibly to trim off any fat.

Potential savings looked so good on paper that no one bothered to ask the opinions of their major wholesale distributor or the regional managers or their factory managers or the national salesmen—all of whom would have told them why it wouldn't work. And they were the ones in touch with consumers and the trade, and not the head office. If asked, they would probably have looked puzzled, or remarked, "If it ain't broke, why fix it?"

Nevertheless, by 1974, Shoecorp had built a new and automated central warehouse beside Jan Smuts airport, which didn't work and was holding up deliveries and preventing new sales. They had also centralized the marketing of five entirely different brands aimed at different market segments and formerly with different marketing policies. Then suddenly (or so it seemed to the newly imported CEO at the head office) Shoecorp plunged from a highly profitable company into a loss position for the first time.

Consultants from the United Kingdom pointed out that it was because the company had failed to design the program on marketing data and objectives, as they should have done. Instead, the financial whiz kids at head office, who clearly did not understand the marketing concept, had been seduced by their tunnel vision into believing their own projected numbers. What, after all, did they know about running a business! And yet, someone at the top had listened to them uncritically and also been mesmerized by their projections as if they were real. In fact, their entire proposal had been a delusion by theorists without hands-on experience.

Shoecorp's resources quickly evaporated. And most on the board were fired when the company downsized in a restructuring program aimed at surviving.[11] S. A. Breweries no longer possesses any manufacturing or retail outlets.

Discontinuity

A second example of failure to orient to marketing also took place in South Africa, a few years earlier. It involved an American brand, General Electric, which was then the global market leader. Here again, there was complacency and arrogance at the top. Complacency stemmed from being a Top Ten brand. Arrogance came from Americans at the head office who considered the South African market to be a far-flung colonial outpost and not at all like the bustle of New York. They were wrong.

GE's southern African division consisted of small and major domestic appliances, sometimes erroneously called white goods. It was then run from the New York office or from their factory in Louisville, Kentucky, not long before Jack Welch was appointed CEO in the United States. Their problem was they were not in touch with the extraordinarily rich and varied South African market, whose biggest growth (unbeknown to most companies even in South Africa then) was in the burgeoning urban black market. With the exception of Unilever and Colgate-Palmolive, who possessed a sophisticated knowledge of growing black populations, most companies had not done the research required to reveal that cities like Soweto were being transformed by an emerging black African yuppie middle class who wanted all the new consumer goods with their bells and whistles and glittering LED lights. That exciting market segment was abandoning old tribal customs, like drinking highly nutritious sorghum beer, in favor of Carling Black Label from S. A. Breweries, which was advertised for white yuppies.

Instead of doing their homework, whenever losses mounted in GE's Johannesburg division, and the New York office was too out-of-touch to know why, cost-cutting was their substitute for creative ideas or a more aggressive marketing policy. And so the American CEO would be replaced by a new one with a financial background and a sharp pencil. He would fire the marketing director, the market research manager, and the sales and advertising directors. A productive department once created to research and market the most suitable goods would suddenly be abandoned. Cost-cutting would show a temporary paper profit to satisfy New York for a while, until sales took a dive once again.

With profits vanishing before their eyes, they would hurriedly replace the CEO again—this time with someone who had enough marketing experience to hire a new marketing director, a new market research director, and new sales and advertising directors who would have to start again from scratch, with lost knowledge, lost personal contacts, and lost momentum. Time-consuming trial and error would be invested in studying a complex and segmented market and trying to understand and master it, in other words, discontinuity, which meant a period of lagging behind in confusion and uncertainty. That was how the last marketing team described it.[12]

The failure, as always, was somewhere at the top of the management pyramid in far-off New York or Louisville, who still apparently did not understand the South African market, or even the marketing concept. And that was strange, since the concept had been clearly described in General Electric's own 1952 annual report. But all the staff changes during the ups and downs of the economy over two decades had evidently created discontinuities that resulted in loss of corporate knowledge and skills. It seemed that the top management in the United States had forgotten about their mission statement and objectives and been flying by the seats of their pants instead.[13] It took Jack Welch's appointment to change all that and steer GE in the right direction.

A Failed Culture

The following example of Eastman Kodak's monumental failure brings us up to date. Kodak had been in business for 131 years and frequently been a leading global brand. And yet, they were obliged to file for bankruptcy protection in January 2012.

The reasons for Kodak's failure are many and varied, but all point to an inability to change its culture in the face of new technologies that caused social changes. It required new thinking, imagination, innovation, new attitudes, and new approaches. The core problem was that, after more than a century in the photography business, they failed to understand why consumers took photos. Evidently they had isolated themselves from their customers and the marketplace and prevented feedback. Digital photography meant customers shared online instead of having to make prints.

Complacency apparently left Kodak completely unprepared for this new turn of events. It was not structured for marketplace discontinuity. That suggests a failure to focus on marketing with its dedication to continual consumer and market research, particularly consumer motivational research which can place a company ahead of the pack. As a consequence, they failed to anticipate the shift from analogue to digital cameras. It also meant a failure to transform in time from past technology to new technology, as Fuji Film did. Their list of failures does not end there. There was failure to innovate, failure to compete with Apple for market share, and failure to recognize that the dominant product would be the mobile phone camera.

Since Fuji, Canon, Nikon, and Olympus took market share from Kodak, there appears to have been poor judgments and bad decisions at the top. There was the failure to understand changes in communications media and sharing on social media like Facebook. Added to that was poor timing: too slow, too little, too late. Perhaps the fundamental

147

problem was that Kodak had excluded marketing inputs from R&D decision making. Although collaboration with marketing operations did take place in the end, the new customer focus came too late. Revenues of $15.97 billion in 1996 slipped to $4.11 billion by 2012.

It is always difficult to understand top management mind-sets without being personally engaged in a situation, but it is said that academic theory ruled over reality. Therein lies the problem that academics (unless they are scientists) feel more comfortable with what happened in the past, rather than being gifted with prescience about the future. And, as Peter Drucker's famous study of General Motors' top management revealed, GM knew without a shadow of a doubt that academic theories get in the way of the momentum and practicalities of running a business. Consequently they hired practical, down-to-earth managers more accustomed to dealing with real situations than unproven classroom theories.

With the offshoring trend, we might also question whether one of the reasons why Kodak was so isolated from consumers and the marketplace was because of outsourcing manufacturing to China. Then there is the branding situation. If Kodak had a brand champion, they failed. If not, they should have hired one who reflected the age and social customs of the primary market, and listened to her. It emphasizes again a lack of bottom-up feedback. Unilever's former chairman, unknowingly, spoke Kodak's epitaph (if indeed they should fail to survive after restructuring) when he said that "Brands die when they cease to be meaningful to the consumer."

New Ways of Thinking

Why is it so difficult for some companies to understand marketing? Perhaps some idea can be read from Jack Welch's remark when he became CEO of GE, which is worth repeating: *"For you to succeed in the future you will have to abandon every single thing you've learnt in the past."* Confronted by such discontinuity and complexity, old-type leaders and managers who predict the future from the past, and are unprepared for the unexpected, express an inability to let go of the old way in order to create new ones. Meanwhile most companies continue to hire people like themselves, when new ideas and experience are needed from a diversity of fresh attitudes, new skills, and different thinking.

Many CEOs are scared to make the leap because they can't handle other opinions, attitudes, or ideas that differ from their own, nor the type of nonconforming individuals who come up with new ideas.

The following is a fairly recent example of how new ideas occur and benefit consumers and suppliers.

"Librarian of the year" Joanne Budler noticed crowds of waiting passengers at a Manhattan airport who weren't reading books, as in the past, but talking or texting on their smartphones instead. She recognized an opportunity to convert them into readers by introducing a new program called "Books on the Fly." It enables waiting passengers to access Kansas City Library's eLending service.[14]

Evidently airport bookstore kiosks were not addressing their potential customers' needs by selling engrossing novels and the latest business books for busy executives, as many had in the past. Whether it was a result of discontinuity or simple management sloppiness, they seemed to think it was enough just to create a presence by hiring someone to take the cash. And yet, the recent merger of Penguin Random House emphasizes the significance of a time when W. H. Smith's famous UK bookstores recognized such an opportunity.

As early as 1848, Smith saw passengers waiting on railway platforms, and envisioned a new market with a new need. He opened kiosks to provide them with newspapers, magazines, and affordable books. We owe our High Streets to Smith, because he invented chain stores. Then, in 1935, Penguin Books invented paperback books to sell at sixpence each (5 cents) and proved that a mass market would buy serious books if they were offered at the right price. W. H. Smith kiosks sold them to waiting passengers. Penguin is now the biggest global publisher after merging with Random House in 2013. Now, with far longer waiting times for flights today than ever, W. H. Smith recently opened new stores in major airports across India and has planned thirty new kiosks in China.

That is a case of the exact opposite of discontinuity harming business, but rather one of a continuous stream of challenges resulting in innovations for 167 years, while sticking to what a business knows best.

But some brands invite failure by shortsighted neglect of opportunities and addressing customers' needs in preference to gambling on fluctuating stock prices. It may satisfy major shareholders temporarily, but result in the fall of once-admired brands, like Sears, and other chain stores and department stores, forced to close hundreds of unprofitable branches through feeble management and marketing, and unload millions of employees onto the job market because they failed to compete with more professionally managed companies. Tarnished brands also include industries that isolate themselves from consumers by outsourcing customer services and complaints to call centers, and keep customers at bay with unfriendly electronic menus and voice-boxes, in a short-term belief that they are saving money by cutting costs.

The invention of the World Wide Web, on the other hand, is an entirely new communications medium with dramatic possibilities for influencing online sales and social trends that provides opportunities for new and original ways to exploit its immediacy and reach and interactivity. But, so far, its biggest users search the Internet primarily and repeatedly for pornography. Most others do so for largely superficial or frivolous reasons that suggest it cannot be taken seriously, and that, like most other digital consumer devices, it is little more than a toy for playing juvenile games. Nielsen's research shows that only about 4 percent of Internet users appear to be searching for serious information.

We can't repeat enough that it is still in its infancy, so there is a great deal of uncertainty about digital media. Nevertheless, recent research by Nielsen revealed that (1) 71 percent of marketers will increase their use of mobile advertising, (2) 81 percent planned to increase their use of social media for advertising, and (3) marketers reported running 33 percent more digital brand advertising campaigns than direct response campaigns.[15]

11

Removing Uncertainty and Ambiguity

Of all the dualities in human nature, and therefore in running a business enterprise, perhaps none is more perplexing than the dual nature of uncertainty and also the manifold nature of ambiguity. Most companies find them difficult to handle. On one hand, there is the uncertainty of choosing between the creative side of business (particularly marketing, which requires budgets) and cost-cutting by a chief financial officer. It involves a balancing act by a CEO between *making* money by marketing or *saving* money by cost-cutting—the very problems that confused Shoecorp and GE, who made unwise choices, since our objective should be growth, not defense. It means a choice of life over death.

There is also the ambiguity between short-term planning to make a quick buck and long-range planning for the future survival of a company. It often goes hand in hand with the argument between development and cost-cutting. Audacity (compared to cringing and waiting to die in a defensive position) is a very different state of mind that arises from a company's culture.

Since the Japanese are skilled at ambiguities and uncertainties, we can benefit from their management and marketing practices, before moving from the general to the particulars of marketing. Here are twelve different attitudes more typical of Japan:

1.   They accept ambiguity, uncertainty, and imperfection in their organizations as a normal part of life.
2.   Although they like predictable order, they are also flexible—like the legend of the bamboo and the oak.
3.   They view situations objectively instead of personally, as conditions one has to find ways to live with, rather than pumping up adrenaline to fight un-winnable battles.
4.   In the West, ambiguity implies that a situation is incomplete, unstable, and unresolved. But ambiguity is accepted in Japan as an either/or

situation and a matter of fact in life—it may be either desirable or undesirable, depending on a particular circumstance.

5. They are driven partly by work ethic, partly competitiveness, and partly as an obligation to society. Money is not the primary motive, as it is in the United States.

6. A tradition of lifetime employment to ensure social and economic harmony differs from the United States, where capitalism is hostile to social safety nets.

7. Slow and profound evaluation and promotion in Japan, versus rapid evaluation and promotion in the United States.

8. Nonspecialized holistic career paths in Japan, versus narrow specialized ones in the United States.

9. Collective responsibility in Japan, versus individual responsibility in the United States.

10. Problem-solving orientation in Japan, versus success orientation in the United States.

11. More holistic concern in Japanese companies, rather than solving individual problems on their own merits. *How will it affect other departments, other markets, other consumers, or the economy?*

12. A longer term view on possible outcomes when making short-term decisions: *How will it play out over time? What are likely to be the unintended consequences?*

The net result of all those differences was that Japan and other Asian countries happily enjoyed much of the global economic growth from 1975 to 1995 and laid the foundation for their present success, until the collapse of Western economies which were their customers. Their expansion took two decades without the West being even aware of Japan's greater competitiveness, or why. Meanwhile, most Western economies, including Germany, ended up with much the same global market shares as when those two decades began. It involved twenty years with virtually no growth in the West during a period of global economic expansion.

What did we do wrong that Asia did right? And is it possible that some, or all, of those characteristics could have made a difference to the North American and EU economies?

The Most Polished Retailers

If we could choose an entrepreneur or a CEO who embodies most or all of those characteristics, it would surely be Heather Reisman, Canadian founder and CEO of Chapters and Indigo retail book chain. It is rare to find a president who grew up with the marketing philosophy as part of her own attributes. She was educated as a social worker at McGill University in Montreal. She then had the unusual advantage of founding a business consulting firm in Toronto, advising clients on strategic change.

She started her own company with retail stores named "Indigo Books and Music," then bought out her major competitor, "Chapters," in 2001. She is the biggest book retailer in Canada with 249 stores by 2011 and claims she is the biggest in the world. Reisman is very likely the most polished retailer in Canada. Visit any of her stores; there seems to be nothing to improve and everything to admire. She is a self-confident perfectionist, from store layouts and displays, friendly staff who enjoy their work, the most up-to-date technology for choosing or ordering books, and promotions with flair to create store traffic. Her website is impeccable.

"We are the healthiest book company in the world today," she claimed at the closure of a major store in Toronto in February 2014. "But we have invested every single thing we've made back into the company." Reisman loves books. And she is determined not to overextend her business like Borders did. The closure of a city store was a practical response to rent increases. Meanwhile, her admirers are watching how she handles the disruptions in the book industry.

Formerly President of Cott Corporation and Governor of McGill University and the Toronto Stock Exchange, Reisman is a prime example, to her fingertips, of what a twenty-first-century marketer should be: she learned and executes all the most modern management and marketing techniques with seamless perfection and panache, despite the onslaught from new technologies and media, mergers and acquisitions, and social change.

An attractive feature of successful modern retailers is that customers should have no worries, since they will always be looked after as a priority. It enables, for example, customers of Walmart to relax with confidence and do more shopping than they would otherwise do by knowing that the customer service department will always take back merchandise, whether it is faulty or the customer made a mistake. They don't want to waste time asking why it is being returned, but prefer to do everything to encourage more sales. And they were not the first retailer to treat customers like royalty. Nor was Selfridges in London's Oxford Street, Fortnum & Mason in Piccadilly, or Harrods in Kensington.

Marks & Spencer was founded in 1894, and still made a media splash in 2013 with a pretty teenager modeling bras and panties from her "Rosie for Autograph" collection.

153

"Marks and Sparks," as it became known with affection, was started by a Polish immigrant who barely spoke English and a Yorkshire book-keeper. Marks borrowed five pounds to open his Penny Bazaar. His policy was to sell only British clothing under the St Michael's label (and then St Margaret's). Their branding was a guarantee of quality at affordable prices. Quality food was introduced in 1974.

M&S focused on consumer needs from the beginning with a policy that "The customer is always and completely right." They made it easier to shop with confidence by accepting returns with a full cash refund. There are now 360 M&S stores in forty countries. They began selling online in 1999. The five pounds that Michael Marks borrowed now yields a return on investment of close to ten billion pounds a year.[1]

Marks' approach was an innovation at the time, almost as much as Gordon Selfridge's was, by inviting consumers to come into his stores instead of passively waiting for the carriage trade to deign to patronize him. They knew that other consumers had money to spend too, if their prices were more affordable and their goods and services were dependable. And they wanted customers to tell their friends how well they were looked after and bring them in too. It was a new way of thinking that aimed to satisfy consumer needs and wants. That is why M&S is such a successful brand.

Retail store chains and department stores that don't follow their example are in trouble today, when just surviving in a poor economy and with disruptions from digital media is a serious challenge. But M&S have continued to do what they do best and remain customer oriented. Consequently, its present CEO, Dutch-born retailer Marc Bolland, is being given credit for its first annual profit rise in four years, dividend increases to shareholders, and "an outstanding year in a difficult market."[2]

Fulfilling Needs and Wants

Before our self-indulgent consumer society burgeoned, and almost right up to World War Two, most suppliers catered to basic *needs*, like food, clothing, and shelter. Society's wants were catered for by upmarket specialists like Tiffany in New York, Asprey in London's Bond Street, Fortnum & Mason, or the Army & Navy Stores. The pendulum swung more to *wants*, because of today's more comfortable and widespread lifestyles, with its easy credit facilities.

The scope of marketing now encompasses everything consumers want or need from the market. The breadth and depth of activities required to fulfill their needs is so great that most people are still confused about what marketing is and what it does. It does far more than merely direct the flow of goods and services from producer to distributor or customers.

The range of goods and services, and the complexity of managing a chain of grocery stores, like Sainsbury or Waitrose in the United Kingdom and Walmart in North America, is so great that it would be surprising if customers didn't wonder how they manage to keep their food so varied and fresh, with all the time it must take to decide what customers want, finding it, and displaying it for them to buy, and all the different managers of processes it must go through first.[3] The only way to control and execute such activity efficiently and on time is to set goals and budgets that lead to a company's objectives and mission, and meet them according to milestones in prearranged time schedules.

PERT software is available to create a chart to manage each project by Program Evaluation & Review Technique. Reviewing marketing programs means first diagnosing present conditions from a situational analysis, to develop a marketing strategy that plans for the future. Since a business can be successful only if it offers the public something of value, the SWOT analysis would involve appraising what products or services competitors are marketing successfully and what is available or in the pipeline. It also involves researching to find out what consumers want that they are not yet being offered.

There are at least twenty different types of research available, from product to consumer research and market research, to enable marketers to depict their market, chart their own position in it, and establish where they want to be in future. It means appraising a company's resources as well as consumer needs and ensuring that all those resources are sufficient to achieve the agreed objectives.

A Warning about Plans

Planning involves selecting not only the most appropriate strategy to meet objectives that should penetrate a marketer's selected consumer segment (and possibly attempt to dominate it) but also the most suitable tactics and the ways and means to do it. Marketing managers are key initiators and innovators in updating an annual overall business plan, with the cooperation of other department managers.

Planning is the foundation of all other business activities: it considers the future today. And yet, managers from the president down are notoriously disinclined or unable to *read* marketing plans, however succinct! It is part of our illusion of literacy. Consequently, as Professor J. G. Kotzé wrote, "Evidence also abounds that a significant number of top executives do not always understand the nature of the business environments in which they operate."[4] It is not mere shortsightedness but a form of mindlessness.

Of the two companies in South Africa described previously as suffering from myopia at that time, the market research manager of GE's southern African division developed an excellent comprehensive annual plan. But nobody read it.[5] Nor did Shoecorp's board of directors read the business consultants' diagnosis of what their failing company was suffering from, or how it could be restructured to survive. Instead, they continued to occupy themselves with irrelevant and self-defeating activities, because they failed to understand their priorities and had no conception of the marketing philosophy. They were old-time bureaucratic administrators who never bothered to stay abreast of new trends, and certainly had no conception of lifetime learning.

Irresponsible top management behavior imposes considerable stress on marketing managers who are expected to produce profitable results, since they have to obtain inputs from other managers and the president's approval for necessary budgets. It means hiring a marketing vice president with a strong character, determination, and persistence, as a right-hand man (or woman) who can fill in the CEO's gaps of knowledge and rectify the typical failings of a business leader; one of which is often impatience with reading documents. Often he hasn't the time. Or it may be because he, or she, feels more committed to engaging with the chairman or shareholders than with marketing.

One way to overcome the planning problem is to integrate marketing in every department, from the CEO to the receptionist, particularly among all individuals who come in contact with consumers, since all of them are responsible for public relations, and therefore, indirectly, for sales.

The success of an entire business enterprise depends on whether the marketing planning was undertaken in a thorough and imaginative way. Terms are clearly defined and objectives and goals agreed beforehand. Milestones describe how and when they will be achieved, what budgets are required, and sales targets agreed for each product. An operations manager will, therefore, know how to schedule production on assembly lines to meet shipping dates. Management by Objectives enables all that to happen, because managers and staff will know exactly *what* is to be done and *why*, and *who* will undertake each particular function.

An annual business plan will clearly state methods of achieving goals, the required resources, timing, and interactions with other departments and individuals. In that way, each manager can be responsible and held accountable and individual performances can be measured.

Managers can plan for and react to competitors' activities, using ongoing market research that might reveal any erosion of brand awareness or of market share and such situations as labor strikes, raw material delays, or shortages that may interfere with sales.

Although macroeconomic changes are often discontinuous and beyond control, a prescient marketing manager will plan for possible alternatives. Plans also act as a useful checklist for a marketing department.

Most managers in the West have a tendency to imagine that once a job is done, it is done for good. But, since everything is continually changing, nothing is ever final. Nor should it be. And forgetting things fast is a human characteristic. So plans are invariably forgotten in the day-to-day running of a company, once hard copies are put away in drawers and soft copies closed up in laptops.

One way a marketing vice-president can ensure the annual plan is *not* forgotten is to prepare a bar chart on a wall where weekly or monthly product meetings can take place. Different colored strips representing each product can identify its stage of preparation and the movement of every product toward its next position on the date schedule—almost like movements in a chess game. It is an ideal place for a small conference table where product and brand managers and Q-Circles can meet.[6] Marketing orientation means being open to new ideas and providing them for continual improvements, which should be part of a company culture. Nothing should ever be static in a company that is alive and alert to change and challenges. The concept is what Japanese businesses famously call *Kaizen*. Despite respect for traditions, they know there are always possibilities for improvement.

Product Differentiation

Ambiguity and uncertainty are avoided in the marketplace by displaying an enormous variety of goods in big box stores, in particular, that are not all aimed at the same type of consumers. A typical supermarket displays at least 80 percent of its goods for customers who want something they don't need, and most probably less than 20 percent for essentials we have become accustomed to, or which are better for our health. A glance reveals they are divided into frozen dinners for bachelors or working families who can't be bothered to cook a meal from scratch, organic foods for people who are concerned about not being contaminated by chemical fertilizers or insecticides, slim or fat-free foods for weight-conscious consumers and, on the other hand, outrageously self-indulgent foods like Ben & Jerry's ice cream, or extra chocolate brownies. And those are only foods designed and made to meet the particular demands of different mind-sets and lifestyles.

Nearly a century ago, Henry Ford began his mass production business by having all his automobiles sprayed black, because he was oriented to his factory conditions and cost-saving practices. But when consumers didn't like it and competitors provided different colored vehicles in different designs, he had to do what the market wanted. By now, manufacturers like Ford and breakfast cereal suppliers are only too happy to provide every segment of the market with goods and services according to its taste. One result is an abundance of shelf space devoted to snacking (a habit that barely existed only a few generations ago, hence the growth in obesity and diabetes).

It raises questions as to whether suppliers should care about the quality of their food and the results of eating it, if only because of the rising cost of health care. This was the final argument that led to pressures on suppliers of cigarettes and tobacco. But human rights activists claim that consumers should be free to follow their own whims, whatever the cost. So food processors cater to them.

Few products appeal to everyone. And those that do are usually undifferentiated commodities that are vulnerable to price competition. But even simple commodities like breakfast cereals have become differentiated to suit different tastes, follow novelty trends, and suit the changing whims of children.

Who Consumes?

A glut of magazines displayed in supermarkets and book stores is testimony to targeting market segments by gender, age, ethnicity, marital status, profession, income group, hobbies, or life cycles. Consumers are categorized by social and psychological profiles according to what they want, to fit their lifestyles or different tastes. Product differentiation mirrors the different needs of market segmentation.

Ford and General Motors are not the only suppliers who aim to provide a different product for every significant income level, gender, and taste for styling, or choice for safety or speed. But Ford became the most successful automobile manufacturer in the world, once it was forced to meet competition by switching from factory orientation to consumer or market orientation to stay in business. A strategy of differentiation is intended to exploit every possible market segment. And consumers like novelty, with new designs celebrated each year.

It places great responsibilities and pressures on marketing people to innovate new annual models which will be different enough from previous ones to induce consumers to trade in their old vehicle for a new one. Some marketers focus on opinion leaders as first responders to a new product or service, often featuring a celebrity in their advertisements as an endorsement. They are the most popular and eye-catching ones, since viewers and readers identify with their role models and even copy their clothes or accessories and the cars they drive. But celebrities are costly, so some marketers will use a "blind testimonial" by an unknown expert or "regular people." It is all part of the illusion that businesses create. And fashion changes apparently inspired by fashion leaders make impressionable people view their old model and themselves with disappointment as being unattractive, out of date, or shabby.

When marketing was becoming a fine art as well as a meticulous science, the question arose as to who influences a buying decision? A new male fashion may be aimed at husbands, but suppose it is really the wife who influences the purchase? And who is the initiator who purchases a new coffee brand or breakfast cereal in the home? Is it the teenage daughter? What about cosmetics? Is the daughter influenced by her peers at school? Research finds the most suitable decision maker to target advertising to.

For example, adoption of medical drugs by physicians is influenced first by *innovators* who take the lead, then by *influentials*. *Followers* are the largest group. Finally comes the small group of *diehards* who are slower to change their habits. So if a marketer has to focus her attention and budgets on the most productive segment, diehards will obviously be ignored in favor of one of the other categories. But which one?

Some manufacturers produce standard products or no-name products, as well as ones differentiated by style and brand which are made to order (MTO). It reduces costs by keeping investment in machinery and machine-minders continually producing returns. Other firms differentiate product types by using different factories designed to make particular products more cost-effectively. New products are often developed in a separate facility by a specialized new products team—preferably away from a bureaucratic head office that is likely to stifle nonconformity, originality, ingenuity, and invention.

Psychologist Carl Jung pointed out that every judgment a person makes is conditioned by his personality type. So populations are broken down by mind-sets or attitudes, as well as typical demographics. Psychological profiling resulted in psychographics that influence different consumers' different points of view.

For example, researchers identified a partial genetic explanation for novelty-seeking behavior. Novelty-seekers tend to be extroverted, impulsive, extravagant, excitable, quick-tempered, and exploratory, because they possess a slightly longer version of the D4 dopamine receptor. Dopamine is the chemical most strongly linked to pleasure and sensation-seeking. Such psychographics have been selected for other psychological types too, like Achievers, Contenteds, Aspirers, Hedonists, Introverts, Socialites, Pessimists, and Strugglers. Each type would have special needs and wants that a marketer can fulfill with different products or services. Even more certainty about consumer wants may emerge from studying the brain with new technologies like fMRI machines.

Nevertheless, it is the feel-good factor of dopamine that led to the ever-open door of the refrigerator at home and snacking throughout the day—a custom that didn't exist only a few generations ago, before our age of anxiety. Now, the number of jobless people has grown, and hundreds of thousands have given up looking for work. So it should come as no surprise that it is in the area of snacking throughout the day, and junk food, more than any other, that we find mutual agreement between the cold and calculating exploitation of consumers by food processors who provide what consumers want, and the consumers themselves. Those consumers are more than willing to be exploited, as long as they can buy snack foods containing an abundance of sugar and salt and fat to arouse the taste buds and relieve their boredom.

On the other hand, there is a highly critical consumer segment that rejects processed foods in preference for organic foods and studies the contents carefully on every package.

Products versus Brands

Compared with a product manager who is responsible for marketing a commodity that sells mostly on price, a brand manager has an advantage that the product she markets was designed specifically to fulfill the needs of a particular consumer segment, in accordance with results of studies made by consumer and motivational research. It will therefore have a unique selling proposition built into its design. The brand manager's goals are to create brand awareness by packaging, advertising, and promoting it differently and uniquely. Benchmark measurements will reveal the degree of consumer awareness achieved. The aim is to increase that awareness in terms of share of mind.

With food and beverages, share of gut is as important as share of mind. (The thought may come before the deed, or the instinct before the thought.) Valuable brands often have a brand champion who does nothing but administer to the needs of the brand, like a caregiver with a patient, to ensure that the amount of brand awareness is increasing, and not being eroded by market forces. Her next step is defining relationships with competing brands in the same product category or brand preference. She will aim at greater preference for her brand after establishing a benchmark against which any fluctuations can be measured.

Since a considerable amount of brand switching goes on (for all sorts of different reasons) she will research for brand loyalty—a comparison between how many consumers switch to her brand, as opposed to those who switch to a competing one. Reasons why will be researched in each case, and results will be used to create advertising and promotions aimed at increasing the volume of brand bonding—since some consumers love their chosen brands.

Maintaining the brand's sanctity will ensure the brand is never tarnished by wrong claims, unsuitable media, inappropriate events, bad company, or (as with Kodak) outdated technology. The brand must always be meaningful to consumers, however much social customs, fashions, or the environment may change. Marketing moves in lockstep with the social evolutionary process.

The dynamics of the global market are changing again because of social media. Success will go to companies that staff for change and organize to embrace the market dynamics. We are more connected and networked than ever before, with a rise in constant consumer use of mobiles, regular use of tablets, and an addiction to texting. Google, Facebook, LinkedIn, and Twitter have changed social customs by providing an outlet for narcissism. Never before has it been so evident that masses of people believe the world revolves around them and their needs and wants. They believe that everything is about them, and they want to tell everyone, including total strangers, all about their daily activities, their likes and dislikes, and their sexual preferences(like Gay Pride processions in city streets) and are eager to display different photos of themselves online, continually upgrading to what they think are improvements in their personal appearance.

161

The Tyranny of Software

Meanwhile, the marketplace has become more complicated as a result of new communications software and hardware. We already suffered from information overload before the turn of this century. Now there are more distractions and a great deal of irritating information online, as everyone competes for our attention and cyber parasites interfere with our computer screens. And our security is breached.

We have to prioritize and simplify to reach our goals, and not become distracted by technology. One aspect is the tyranny of badly written software, designed more to tell us how clever software engineers are than to help users by making processes easier and quicker. Like the fervor to invent apps that most people don't need, they regale us with so many alternatives, including trying to think ahead of us (almost always wrongly) that we could be forgiven for longing for a simple electronic typewriter that does not conceal all the tools we need to use it properly, or compel us into a maze of unnecessary labyrinths as a consequence of the software designer's own confused mind. It may be possible to make a fortune by designing and marketing no-frills software for a word processor that helps to speed up the writing process, instead of hindering it by distracting users with the technology. Everything else is changing faster than before. Top brands designed to fulfill consumer needs do so much better when they listen to consumers and users and act on their preferences—that is what being marketing oriented means.

"In the past," said former Unilever Chairman Sir Michael Perry, "innovation started with a marketing brief, which went to R&D, which changed the product, which was rushed to the agency . . . Essentially it was linear . . . Thinking in terms of 'marketing functions' and 'marketing departments' is *old* thinking." What are required now are simultaneous activities aimed at putting the consumer at the heart of the business. It is general management's responsibility too.

New Product Development

It means that every business has to ensure it has new products in the pipeline, to avoid a hit-or-miss situation. It has to plot the life cycle of each of its products and services to predict its momentum in the marketplace, such as when it requires support against competitors, when its popularity may decline, when it needs promoting, and when it should die and be replaced by a new brand that is more meaningful to a new generation.

To avoid ambiguity and uncertainty, sophisticated marketers use screening techniques before they launch each new product. 3M followed three criteria to aim at a successful new product: (1) Is it the first of its kind in the market? (2) Is it useful, and of a quality which will command a profitable price? (3) Is it novel enough to be patentable?

They averaged thirty-three technical successes out of each hundred laboratory starts. Only three were considered commercial successes. They are well aware that thirty thousand new consumer products are launched annually and 95 percent fail. 3M estimated that half their profits came from products that didn't exist ten years previously. It shows the impact of change on the market and their ability to change with it by knowing what consumers want.

The enormous S. C. Johnson—which still describes itself as a family business—used two major criteria to reduce the number of failures in launching new products. One of them is screening, when they ask themselves, Does it have a demonstrable "product plus"? They estimate the total market for the product. They estimate growth possibilities of the total market. Their marketing people estimate what they consider to be their attainable share of market. And they calculate potential gross profit margins.

They also use a sponsor group for broad participation, which includes the conceiver of the new product, a laboratory technician, a marketing person, a financial officer, a production person, and a new products manager. Companies of that stature and experience obviously benefit from their know-how.

As another example of what sophisticated and established market leaders do, Borden Co. introduced 179 new products in 1963. Over 22 percent of its total sales were from products added in the previous ten years. They used six criteria for choosing new products, all of which are remarkable in being company oriented instead of consumer oriented. Will it upgrade profit margins? Will it benefit from our know-how, experience, and reputation? Does it have prospects of being an established item in our product line? Will it retain the status of a "specialty?" Does it fill out a product line or have prospects of development as one? Does its potential volume warrant the management attention necessary?[7]

Those suppliers of consumer goods and services follow a marketing culture, whereas some other organizations mentioned for their failings were oriented, instead, to factory production, or the imposition of bureaucratic administration, or shareholders, or speculation, gambling, or family or social priorities, personal foibles, or to the whims of accountants or the theories of academics, instead of to consumer needs and wants.

It is sobering to consider that *cultural attitudes and activities change brain structure.*[8] That finding from the latest brain scans indicates that once a CEO or company veers away from a goal of fulfilling consumer needs, for whatever reason, their fixed mental attitude is almost impossible to change until disaster strikes.

Those companies mentioned were remarkably forthcoming with information at that time—no doubt because they were proud of their successes. In today's age of anxiety with a more competitive global market, it is harder, if not almost impossible, to persuade companies to reveal such sensitive information about what makes them successful. They are far more likely to sue each other for infringements of copyrights and patents, or trade secrets allegedly passed on from former employees. So, although those explicit figures may be out of date by now, they do give us an idea of what can be achieved by integrated marketing and organized teamwork.

12

Creative Thinking and Reasoning

The cognitive revolution began as an intellectual movement that dates from the 1950s, now known as cognitive science. It is the study of the human mind and its processes. It combines perception, language, memory, reasoning, and emotions, while researching intelligence and behavior through a number of disciplines including psychology, philosophy, neuroscience, artificial intelligence (AI), anthropology, and linguistics. It was influenced strongly by the burgeoning fields of computer science, artificial and robotic intelligence, and neuroscience. It led to making testable inferences about human mental processes. "It can best be understood in terms of representational structures in the mind and computational procedures that operate on those structures."[1]

It is ironic that the Behaviorist school of psychology had previously considered mental processes irrelevant to the study of how we behave. They believed that we are what we do, not what we think. Behaviorists studied only observable behavior that responded to environmental influences that could be seen and measured. They dismissed all mental activities like conscious and unconscious thought. Their founder John B. Watson and his devoted follower B. F. Skinner led the Behaviorist school which dominated psychology in the first half of the twentieth century.[2] Although psychology was originally defined as the science of the mind, Watsonian Behaviorism replaced it with a chain of conditioned responses to outside stimuli, using laboratory rats for his studies. Watson thought he was being scientifically objective, but was biased.

In its dogmatism to study only observable and measurable responses to rewards and punishments, Skinner encouraged his rats by rewarding them with pellets of food when they solved problems he arranged for them, and punishing them with electric shocks when they did not. The analogy of rats to business executives attempting to solve daily intellectual and creative problems of a different kind should not be lost on us.

It replicated a management theory of the times when executives were, metaphorically, rewarded with a carrot and punished with a stick.

The principles of Behaviorism were applied to changing patients' behavior for the better by classical conditioning, which had originally been demonstrated in the early 1900s by the well-known pioneer work of Pavlov with his dogs, which he taught to salivate without seeing or even smelling any food. Instead, the dog reacted to various sights and sounds it already associated with food. He found that the dog behaved according to both unlearned and learned components. In other words, its responses were inborn or innate, but also resulted from learning.

Two brilliant skeptics of Behaviorism were scientific journalist Arthur Koestler, who criticized Skinner's assumption that human beings behave in the same way as rats, and philosopher Bertrand Russell. Russell remarked sardonically on the curious fact that "the type of problem which a man naturally sets to an animal depends on his own philosophy, and that this probably accounts for . . . the results."

Since Behaviorism was all about manipulating behavior, we need to be reminded that it developed at a time when fascist ideas were gaining ground in Europe.[3] Behaviorists continued to be a dominant force in psychology until the late 1950s and 1960s.[4] But, by that time, many psychologists realized they could not understand or explain human behavior without referring to mental processes.[5] Cognitive Psychology, on the other hand, seeks to explain observable behavior "by investigating mental processes and structures that *cannot* be directly observed."[6] Cognitive psychologists study how people process memories in adapting to their world.

Cognition means "how information is processed and manipulated in remembering, thinking, and knowing."[7] (Hence motivational research to replace erroneous assumptions.)

There is some irony in the outcome of our cognitive revolution which released all kinds of creative and practical ideas that now line the shelves and display cases in distribution outlets all over the world, and advanced medical equipment in hospitals and surgeries, as well as business and industrial technologies, since Watsonian Behaviorism blindly and persistently refused to believe in the power of cognition to influence our motives. And yet cognitive psychology has transformed our economy into the familiar electronic consumer society of the twenty-first century.

Computers stimulated the growth of cognitive psychology because its psychologists saw an analogy between computers and human brains.

They used the analogy to try to explain the relation between cognition and the brain.[8] That analogy was first recognized by mathematical genius John von Neumann in the late 1940s, when he developed the first modern computer, which showed that computers could perform logical operations. It led researchers to believe, by the 1950s, that some mental operations could be modeled by computers to describe something about the workings of the human mind.[9]

Comparisons tempted psychologists to embark on further studies. Pioneer Herbert Simon compared the mind to a computer processing system and described the human brain as the hardware and cognition as the software, with the sensory and perceptual systems providing an *input channel*, "similar to the way data are entered into a computer." When information is inputted into the mind, mental processes act on it as computer software acts on the data. The transformed input generates information that remains in the memory, in much the same way as a computer stores what it has worked on. "Finally, the information is retrieved from memory and 'printed out' or 'displayed,' so to speak, as an overt observable response."[10]

In fact, neuroscientists have since shown that digital computers and human brains do *not* function in the same way, which led to the 1969 analogy being criticized as an oversimplification.[11]

The Neuroplastic Brain

Meanwhile, the discovery of the plasticity of the human brain is now recognized by scientists who acknowledge that it possesses a special capacity for modification and change, in accordance with learning new skills to survive new challenges in the evolutionary process.[12] This revelation underscores the necessity for societies, institutions, business organizations, and nations, to adapt, since everything around us is constantly changing, and we must always find ways to adapt to change or die. Fortunately, our nerve cells are not fixed and immutable structures. And although they possess an inherited biological basis, they constantly adapt to changes in our bodies and in the environment in order for us to survive.[13]

The term "neuroplasticity" is now generally used to depict how our experiences contribute to the wiring or rewiring of the brain with new cells.[14] For example, when a baby reaches out to touch something or gazes intently at a face, electrical impulses and chemical messages shoot through its brain and form, or re-form, brain cells into networks. Similar changes take place throughout our lives, even after we have stopped growing. So the previous belief in immutability has been discarded as wrong.

The study of the brain and our nervous system that directs our behavior is called neuroscience, and people who study it are neuroscientists.[15] Although most of us generally take the complexity of our brains for granted, neuroscientists have been attempting to pinpoint specific functions in particular areas of the brain as a major research strategy.[16] And yet the brain operates in a highly integrated way, through countless interconnections of brain cells and extensive pathways that link different parts of the brain. Each nerve cell communicates with thousands of others in many kilometers of connections.[17] It is how we too connect and adapt to the changing world.

Relatively permanent changes in human understanding and behavior probably always result in changes in the structure of the brain.[18] So that when we think of new ways of thinking or acting, our brain probably always changes as a result.[19] However, since computers and brains work differently, they have different patterns and strengths and weaknesses.

Information Processors

The main difference between computers and human brains is that computers depend on one or two central processing units to process billions of calculations precisely every second. Computers *serially* undertake one calculation at a time. They can undertake repetitive and complex numerical calculations much faster and more accurately than the human brain.[20] They apply and follow rules more consistently and with fewer mistakes than we can. They can also represent complex mathematical patterns better than us.

By comparison, each of our brain cells, or neurons, is a living information processor. It receives inputs from neurons that synapse with other neurons and integrate the information by sending its own signal onward. Thus billions of neurons may simultaneously activate at any moment in time. The brain is a massively *parallel* information processor. And even *"the computing power of an infant human brain far outstrips that of most computers."* Moreover, neurons (and therefore the brain) can respond even to *ambiguous* information from our five senses. In contrast, most computers must receive information from a human who has already coded the information to remove much of the ambiguity.

The capability of our brains to deal with ambiguity indicates the unlikelihood of computers replacing our more complex and important judgments, decisions, and activities in the near future. Experiments with computers to process visual information or spoken language have achieved only limited successes and only in specific and limited situations. Computers are also limited when it comes to learning and generalizing, whereas our brains have an incredible ability to learn new rules, relationships, concepts, and patterns that can generate to novel situations.

Although computers are being designed to improve on their ability to recognize patterns and use rules to make decisions, they do not have the means to develop new learning goals—unlike the fictional artificially intelligent computer named HAL 9000 that took over control of a spaceship in the Arthur C. Clarke 1968 science-fiction book, and in Stanley Kubrick film, "2001: A Space Odyssey." But many communications and media technologists have become distracted from reality by science fiction.

Perhaps the most important difference is that the human mind is aware of itself, whereas "no computer is likely to approach the richness of human consciousness."[21] Nevertheless, the role of computers in cognitive psychology is increasing and has initiated the study of artificial intelligence as a science of creating machines that can perform activities requiring intelligence, although operated by people. One approach "relies on the serial architecture of traditional computers to create software that produces intelligent outputs and sometimes mimics human functioning. The other seeks to combine large numbers of simpler processing units to create a parallel computer that can also produce intelligent outputs, but do so by mimicking the architecture of the human brain."[22]

AI is used for tasks that require speed, persistence, and a vast memory.[23] It is also designed to assist medical doctors in diagnosing illnesses and prescribing treatments, examining equipment failures, and evaluating loan applications.[24] Although AI attempts to mimic the way we think, its capabilities are not the same as ours when we form concepts and solve problems or when we think critically, reason, or make decisions.

Anyone can see, for example, when using a word processor that almost a hundred percent of its predictions as to where our words are intended to fit into an unfinished sentence are likely to be wrong. It probably results from a software designer's human errors that impose an irrational and annoying tyranny over us. In short, AI is still only a work in progress, flawed and incomplete. What is far more interesting is that so are human brains.

Brains Are a Work in Progress

The question now being asked is, "Is technology creating better brains or interfering with our use of existing ones?"[25] To paraphrase the answers of several brain and mind experts on a serious television panel, it was pointed out that brain mass changes with brain experience, because growing brains create new connections—hence *neuroplasticity*. And those connections bring the mind and brain together.[26]

"But is our electronic culture preventing us from thinking effectively, since we constantly interact with a new digital environment of smartphones and tablets and laptops: does all that prevent deep thought by distractions that take control of our attention from outside?"[27] For example, the average North American kid spends ten to eleven hours a day staring at a screen.[28]

It is true that people have an almost infinite appetite for distractions and no longer connect with each other as they used to; and that was what made us human. They are connected instead to all kinds of electronic devices that overload the conscious mind. But, as Dr. Heather Berlin remarked, "It is too soon to know what the effects will be." There is also no doubt that we need contemplation and quiet imagination for the creation of ideas, which is best done in solitude, without outside distractions. Open offices therefore mitigate against quiet and uninterrupted thought and could therefore be considered the enemies of creativity and innovation. The problem is that people become attentive to what is new, even if it is trivial, and become easily distracted from deeper thinking.

There is still plenty of dispute about whether electronic games improve or retard fluid intelligence. Clinical psychologist Dr. Jordan Peterson claimed that playing games simply teaches you how to play them better, without improving fluid intelligence, and that physical exercise has been shown to improve cognitive functions in older people by pumping more blood through the brain.

When the four experts on the panel were asked to name the primary factor in improving cognition, all agreed it was physical exercise.[29] It was also generally agreed that cognitive improvements include brain speed, memory, retention control, ability to record accurately, and coordination of complex actions.

Statistics show that smarter and more conscientious individuals are most productive, earn more, and live longer. And the more flexible the mind (so that they can think on their own) the more satisfaction they feel. It was generally agreed that the brain needs a variety of social experiences and also solitude—in other words, *different* experiences. That includes physical and mental exercise. As the old adage rightly said, "If you don't use it, you lose it."

Forming Concepts

The thinking that managers do on a daily basis in a business organization is generated by concepts that become grouped together with other components to form an original idea. The most common example that many of us know is a hungry chimpanzee in a zoo that gazes longingly at some food on the ground beyond the confines of its cage. As long as it links only two concepts together (the boundary of its confinement and a meal) it will be frustrated from taking positive action. The moment of illumination arrives only when it notices a broken branch lying on the other side of its bars and conceptualizes it as a tool to manipulate the food into its cage.

Human beings possess a special capacity, perhaps even a compulsion, for grouping objects together into meaningful patterns. It is a survival skill. Conceptualizing uses not only objects but characteristics and events to make sense of the information in our world.[30] What we know and what we learn depend on our ability to group things according to similar or common features, in order to identify what our senses tell us.

Concepts enable us to generalize. They allow us to associate experiences and objects, like identifying the school of art a painter belongs to. And every time we come across new information, conceptualizing it triggers a memory of similar information from a concept that enables us to recognize what it relates to. The concept we recall from memory provides us with clues about how to react to the new information and what its further implications are. Memory is crucial, because of the unique encyclopedia of knowledge stored in our unconscious mind.

There are two traditional models of how we structure concepts—the "classical model" and the "prototype model."[31] In the first model, "all instances of a concept share defining properties."[32] For example, we know that a triangular shape must have three sides with angles that amount to 180 degrees. But most concepts are far more complex. The example given by psychologists Santrock and Mitterer is "flying," which might refer to a bird or a pilot. But penguins and ostriches are birds that cannot fly, and a pilot can relate to steering a ship or acting as a guide, as well as flying an airplane—hence the complications of ambiguity, which artificial intelligence cannot handle.[33]

The prototype model recognizes that people decide whether an item reflects a concept by comparing it with *the most typical one* in that category, so that birds generally fly or sing and build nests. But there are exceptions. The problem of the confusion of ambiguities was simplified by Eleanor Rosch, who argued that membership in a concept can be "graded," instead of being all or none.[34] In other words, the better member of that concept (like a robin) possesses more characteristics than the poorer member of that category (like a penguin). So the prototype model maintains that "characteristic properties are used to create a representation of the average or ideal member . . . for each concept. Potential members are then compared to this prototype." So the prototype model is able to explain typical effects.[35]

Results of studies are supported by neuropsychological investigations showing the distinction between explicit learning of more abstract concepts and perceptual learning of more perceptual ones. For example, *explicit* rule-based concept formation involves activating the prefrontal cortex of the brain.[36] In contrast, *implicit* perceptual concept formation does *not* involve prefrontal cortex activation.[37] It involves activation of the occipital cortex.[38]

Problem Solving

Solving problems in order to initiate new ideas is the essence of what marketers and managers do every day. And it is impossible to solve problems without concepts.[39] One example given is driving a vehicle. Most road signs that keep traffic moving in a disciplined fashion are symbols that represent concepts, like Stop, Yield, One-Way Street, Pedestrian Crossing, School Crossing, and Parking. William Eno found a way to solve problems of traffic chaos in New York City, where horse-drawn vehicles made traffic dangerous and pedestrians unsafe.

Everyone is confronted by problems in everyday life that they have to solve. It involves achieving a goal that is not already available. Two steps are required to overcome mental obstacles and develop expertise: find and frame the problem, and develop good problem-solving strategies (like subgoaling and algorithms) and evaluate solutions.

Students are taught traditional ways to solve well-defined problems in the classrooms with well-defined steps. But many of life's problems in the real world outside are ill-defined, vague, or complex and don't appear to possess clearly defined ways of being solved. That is why this book focuses on real-life situations in the gritty workplace and the ever-changing marketplace for entrepreneurs and executives who have to solve business problems on a regular basis.

One psychologist recommends what he calls *uncertainty orientation* when tackling those vague problems in vague situations.[40] His strategy in those circumstances is to weigh several specific alternatives before selecting one. It means finding and framing specific problems before attempting to solve only vague ones. Problem solving is "an attempt to find an appropriate way of attaining a goal when the goal is not readily available."[41]

But many institutions and business organizations are averse to any idea that there are problems that need to be brought out into the open, and discourage staff from identifying them, because it may result in exposure and blame. Since the reason for problems is often at the top of the management pyramid, the very culture of some organizations activates against anyone who attempts to raise problems that need to be solved. Executives are hired to provide solutions, not to create more problems.

They may occur in companies that distribute cancer-causing tobacco or foods that threaten health, meat marketed with life-threatening bacteria, or toiletries or detergents that could harm the skin. Exposing problems is viewed as being disloyal, or even treasonous. While some managers remain silent, others with stronger characters may feel so scandalized or morally tarnished that they become "whistleblowers."

Whistleblowers are individuals who exposed abuses of large corporations or government because they had a problem with them. Many were fired from the job or prosecuted for placing their issues in the media spotlight. Most people are unaware that there is a whistleblower law in the United States that dates back to 1777, so that the government views it as a criminal act. Where such an act is considered treason against a nation's security, the law is pitiless.

When the World Wide Web was invented, it was unlikely that anyone considered the possibility of it exposing to the entire world what the US government considers is secret information. But new technologies always bring unintended consequences with them. So the criminal cases against Julian Assange and Edward Snowden, and a related case against Private Bradley Manning, for allegedly providing government secrets, sparked a global uproar in 2013.

They questioned whether the public should be denied information they may need to know in a free and democratic society—also the questions of government censorship, national security, civil liberties, freedom of speech, and the First Amendment. But US government agencies allege they broke the law by releasing thousands of confidential documents. The two major cases (that of Assange's WikiLeaks, and Snowden) were still being hotly argued in 2015 by the US government and a civil liberties lawyer who believes in clemency, since he claims they acted to protect the public from secret and allegedly criminal activities by government that invades people's privacy and human rights. And yet they were prosecuted under a law intended for espionage.

Whereas George Orwell "feared the truth would be concealed from us, [Aldous] Huxley feared the truth would be drowned in a sea of irrelevance."[42] Both turn out to be right. Julian Assange is still being given political asylum by the Ecuadorin Embassy in London after three years.

Although neither whistleblower seemed to be too concerned about character assassinations by media or government, the US government was outraged at being publicly humiliated by the disclosures. Consequently both major players were holed up in Russia, which gave them asylum, to prevent criminal proceedings if they return to the United States. Meanwhile, Manning was sentenced to thirty-five years in prison for violating the Espionage Act when he released the largest set of classified documents ever leaked to the public, and other offenses.

Their problems were evidently complex ones. Nevertheless, each of them saw what they thought were clear ways to solve them. Between two passionately opposed views on the whistleblowers, we are left to consider which represents true reality and which is an erroneous distortion influenced more by social biases or political expediency. Fortunately, the fact that they are very different types of people helps us to analyze the problem coolly.

The Marketplace of Ideas

The question is bound to arise as to whether all problems can be solved if there is willingness on both sides to solve them. In this case, there is a distinct bias of the political right against the political left that is frequently part of the human condition. And it becomes almost impossible to reach a compromise when the split between two diametrically different mind-sets is 50/50. And yet no right seems more typical of the United States, from its very origins, than the right of free speech. But free speech has powerful opponents, who see it as dangerous to national security. So freedom of speech is never absolute.

For example, Justice Oliver Wendell Holmes surprised his colleagues when he opposed a court decision against agitators and anarchists who spoke against World War One soon after it ended, when fear of international communism swept across the United States at the ongoing Russian Revolution. Holmes argued that, regardless, their speech was protected by the First Amendment that protects freedom of expression.[43]

Holmes wrote, "But when men have realized that time has upset many fighting faiths, they may come to believe even more than they believe the very foundations of their own conduct that the ultimate good desired is better reached by free trade in ideas—that the best test of truth is the power of the thought to get itself accepted in the competition of the market, and that truth is the only ground upon which their wishes safely can be carried out. That at any rate is the theory of our Constitution. It is an experiment, as all life is an experiment. Every year if not every day we have to wager our salvation on some prophesy based upon imperfect knowledge. While that experiment is part of our system I think that we should be eternally vigilant against attempts to check the expression of opinions that we loathe and believe to be fraught with death, unless they so imminently threaten immediate interference with the lawful and pressing purposes of the law that an immediate check is required to save the country."

Holmes had very likely read John Stuart Mill's essay *On Liberty* (1859), in which Mill wrote of "the collision of truth with error." Opening up discourse, Mill claimed, could only champion truth. Our beliefs, he wrote, "have no safeguard to rest on, but a standing invitation to the whole world to prove them unfounded . . . if the lines are kept open, we may hope that if there is a better truth, it will be found when the human mind is capable of receiving it."

Holmes' recognition of competition for ideas in the marketplace, and his concept that ideas either flourish or die according to the extent of their truth, was surely derived from Darwin's theory of Natural Selection. It acknowledges that whereas some ideas may shock some people's sensibilities when they are in advance of the times of the generality of people, it is only because human nature has not yet caught up with them. It is a clear-sighted argument also against ignorance, bigotry, and prejudice.

Neither John Stuart Mill nor Oliver Wendell Holmes could have conceived of the information flow on the Internet and social media that everyone has access to since the digital revolution, nor our private telephone and email messages that government intelligence agencies are intercepting. But no doubt they would both have doggedly pursued their dreams of liberty and freedom of speech today. That is the basis of the argument taken by the whistleblowers. But no president is likely to relinquish a defensive weapon designed to protect the security of the United States, however Machiavellian it may seem. And their justification is clearly spelt out at the tail end of Holmes' declaration, which is quoted above.

For most people, the problem with that argument is a belief they were taught at school that only one answer can be right and that there can be only one solution. But, given the mindfulness of the metaphorical language of game theory, there is a choice between *commitment* or *cooperation*. It is known as "the Prisoner's Dilemma."[44] And it brings to mind mathematician John von Neumann, who had something to say about knowing and understanding the differences between human intelligence and AI, which is explained only a few pages further along.

Algorithms versus Heuristics

As a problem-solving strategy, *subgoaling* means defining and setting intermediate goals that place individuals in a firmer position from which to appraise the final objective with its inherent solution to the problem. That is what business guru Peter Drucker had in mind when he advised us to break down management functions into smaller components and analyze each one before taking the next step on the stepping-stones to a destination that may come to seem inevitable. It means paying attention to the most appropriate research for each stage. Psychologists also recommend working backward as well as forward, by establishing the closest subgoal to the final solution when reached, which may influence individuals to change earlier goals.

Algorithms are defined as strategies that *guarantee* a solution to a problem. They come in all kinds of shapes and forms, and no two are alike. They may be "equations, computer programs, formulas, instructions, or trying out all possible solutions."[45] We use algorithms when following a cooking recipe or solving mathematical equations or following directions on a map. Algorithms allow us to link our sites, or log on or scroll down from one subject to another on different websites, or enable personalized advertisements to display themselves on our site. They seem to possess magical properties. But crossword puzzle enthusiasts use them all the time, to make down- and-across answers fit precisely into their intended squares.

An algorithmic strategy tries out all possible solutions to achieve the only right one. Considering the millions of steps to do so, we should choose either a simpler problem to solve with a smaller number of possible solutions, or a suitably programmed computer to make all the calculations for us. That is why it is far better to use heuristics. Heuristics are "strategies or guidelines that suggest, but do *not* guarantee, a solution to a problem."[46] Particular combinations are more likely to work than others. And the types of problems we face are more likely to be solved by heuristics than by algorithms.[47] They help us to narrow down solutions to ones that work.[48] But we won't know how effective our solution is until we discover *if* it works. So it helps to keep in mind a criterion for judging its effectiveness, whatever you expect to achieve.

An important attitude toward problem solving is continually to think and rethink and redefine the problem.[49] Those who are good at problem solving don't mind going over it again and again, even when they think they've got it right. Consider those brilliant mathematicians decoding German military secrets at Bletchley Park in order to win the war, most of whom cut their teeth on crossword puzzles and enjoyed the challenges to produce the only one right answer. It is what executives must always feel when setting goals they look forward to fulfilling. Innovative market leaders like Samsung and Apple invite feedback at every stage of design, manufacturing, and marketing processes, in order to improve assembly lines and new products being researched and developed. It pays *not* to be satisfied, so as to be continually challenged to improve ideas and products, and the ways and means to produce them.

Once again, the human brain proves to be far ahead of new technologies, since (as Dr. Norman Doidge found out) *"The brain changes its very structure with each different activity it performs, perfecting its circuits so it is better suited to the task in hand."*

People in businesses that interest them are often accused of being obsessive, but you have to be passionate when pursuing excellence, or you won't even come close to it, which raises the emotional versus the rational approach once again.

Stagnation and Denial

When people run out of practical solutions they often turn to myths instead. And computer technologists and bloggers who are fascinated by AI seem determined to turn the brilliant mathematician John von Neumann into the stuff of legend, since he developed the computer as a forerunner of what we have today—the mobile. In fact, he already *is* a legend. The problem is they may be idolizing him for the wrong reasons because they misunderstood his ideas.

John von Neumann was a mathematical prodigy in his teens. He was a Los Alamos veteran, having worked with Oppenheimer, Fermi, Bohr, and the other members of "The Manhattan Project." He was considered to have one of the most powerful brains of the century, and contributed to quantum physics. His proposal to the US government to make an advanced computer was accepted, and he worked on the Mathematical and Numerical Integrator and Computer, known as "MANIAC."

In his book for the Silliman Lectures in 1958, he coined a new expression to describe accelerating progress in computer technology that would change society in an unpredictable future. It is part mathematical computation and part science fiction of the Jules Verne and H. G. Wells kind, brought to the subject of AI. So unpredictable is it that it has become unfathomable for most, and easily misunderstood. Von Neumann used the expression "singularity" in the forward to his original thinking on *The Computer and the Brain*, in which he predicted an explosion of AI.[50]

Technological singularity has become the Holy Grail of software and hardware nerds. It would put technocrats at the center of power, apparently by dispensing with all other forms of management and labor. The moment predicted by apocalyptic futurists for machines to take over all jobs at present undertaken by humans is 2045 (according to Ray Kurzweil) or 2030 (according to Vernor Vinge). Nevertheless, it is still only fiction.

While it is true that in 1951 Alan Turing considered machines might overtake human beings intellectually (as one did with the limitation of logical chess games) it ignores all the advantages of emotional intelligence, the complex and subtle matter of ambiguous thinking, imagination, and creative intelligence, the workings of the unconscious mind, access to lifetime memories, and all that neuroscientists have since discovered about the brain that improves itself with every thought and action its owner takes—none of which can be handled by so-called AI. In fact, as computers developed to their present stage, we were constantly cautioned that they are stupid, since they can only do what their human programmers tell them to do. And, as a consequence of the flawed human condition, many software programs are likely to be poorly designed.

"You must see that in a sense all science, all human thought, is a form of play," explained Professor J. Bronowski, in order to introduce the brilliant mathematician von Neumann, who was a master of game-playing. "Abstract thought is the neoteny of the intellect, by which man is able to continue to carry on activities which have no immediate goal . . . in order to prepare himself for long-term strategies and plans."[51] (*Neoteny* is an unusual word meaning the production of offspring by an organism.)

"Chess is not a game," John von Neumann said. "Chess is a well-defined form of computation. You may not be able to work out the answers, but in theory there must be a solution, a right procedure in any position. Now real games," he said, "are not like that at all. Real life is not like that. Real life consists of bluffing, of little tactics of deception, of asking yourself what is the other man going to think I mean to do. And that is what games are about in my theory."[52]

"In the latter part of his life," Bronowski explained, "John von Neumann carried this subject into what I call his second great creative idea. He realized that computers would be technically important, but he also began to realize that one must understand clearly how real-life situations are different from computer situations, exactly because they do not have the precise solutions that chess or engineering calculations do . . . . He distinguished between shorty-term tactics and grand, long-term strategies. Tactics can be calculated exactly, but strategies cannot. Johnny's mathematical and conceptual success was in showing that nevertheless there are ways to form best strategies."

In *The Computer and the Brain*, he looks at the brain as "having a language in which the activities of the different parts of the brain have somehow to be interlocked and made to match so that we devise a plan, a procedure, a grand overall way of life—what in the humanities we would call a system of values . . . He was a genius, in the sense that a genius is a man who has *two* great ideas."

The Plastic Brain

That "interlocking of different parts of the brain" has since been confirmed by neuroscientists using fMRI brain scan machines, as "neurons that fire together, wire together." It was part of the discovery of brain plasticity. Neuroplasticity refers to changes in neural pathways and synapses which take place through life as a result of changes in thought and behavior resulting from environmental or circumstantial changes.

When we contemplate the IT industry, we need to be reminded once again how people often turn to myths when they cannot handle the truth. And bearing in mind the discontinuities of history with its unintended consequences, it is just as likely that human idiocy or irrationality will result in a world littered with dysfunctional and rusting machines like H. G. Wells famously predicted in his science-fiction story.[53] But despite all the stupidity that our history reveals again and again, recent studies of the human brain by fMRI scanners show it to be very much superior to AI designed and programmed by computer nerds for industry, trade, and commerce. Those are aimed very largely at greater speed and accuracy. Neuroscientists are likely to have quite different opinions about the future of AI than Silicon Valley, which feeds the public's curiosity and credulity with myths calculated to exploit consumers. It is all part of scheming in a business that made them rich.

Meanwhile, Western economies are in a state of inertia after the effects of the subprime mortgage scandal, deindustrialization, and offshoring. One online blogger predicts a "great stagnation" in which 10 to 15 percent of the population will work the smart machinery and the rest will become poor. Then, who will buy products and services if potential consumers are jobless and too poor even to buy food? He refers to powerful capital, and worthless labor that lives off the crumbs that fall from their master's tables (or trickle-down economics). The problem is there won't be enough jobs to feed us all, since the top level are the 1 percent of billionaires who made their fortunes from capital gains and investment income.

Our saving equation, so far, is the Pareto principle that 80 percent of the wealth is owned by 20 percent of the population, which still applies today. And, according to economist Vilfredo Pareto, will always return, regardless of attempts to redistribute wealth.[54] But what was true of an agricultural society or an industrial economy may not be the case in a digital one.

With communications now largely in the hands of bloggers on the Internet and social websites, discussions on the subject at present sway readers by appealing to their optimism or their pessimism, rather than presenting hard facts. They are mere fantasies of science-fiction writers using their imagination in attempts to predict the future. And the future is unpredictable.

Even if the concept turned out to be possible, practical, and realistic, it is more likely there would be a terrible retribution. The Luddites who broke machinery when they lost their jobs in the Industrial Revolution were a minority who were prosecuted, deported, or hanged. But a digital age of automation that benefits only 1 percent of the population and condemns 99 percent to starvation is unlikely to last long.

In any case, the BBC announced online on December 2014, that Professor Stephen Hawkins—one of the world's leading scientists—warned that artificial intelligence could end mankind. "The development of full artificial intelligence could spell the end of the human race," and, "efforts to create thinking machines pose a threat to our very existence."

13

Motivation and Its Antithesis

As well as studying problem solving, psychologists also study the obstacles that, more often than not, prevent people from solving problems effectively. There are three major hurdles: (1) becoming too fixated, (2) Not being sufficiently motivated, (3) Not controlling emotions.

Fixation often causes people to use the wrong strategy when they need to look at the problem from a different perspective. Functional fixedness results from being fixated on a thing's *usual* function, instead of using imagination, flexibility, and innovation.[1] In other words, there are often other ways to solve a problem that suit its particular characteristics better.

Personality characteristics and personality flaws were previously remarked on as possible stumbling blocks. There is also a "mental set," which can occur when a way of solving a problem that worked before fails to provide a solution now.[2] It is essential to break out of a mental rut. One way is to abandon the project temporarily, because of the fixed intensity with its dogged and narrow-minded certainty of finding a solution. It is often better to turn to another, more pleasing activity and return to the problem later on in a happier state of mind. A more joyful attitude is likelier to open up wider possibilities for other solutions to appear. Smiling, even to yourself, is a key to reach out and open doors to the unconscious, where a solution may be waiting to emerge.

On the other hand, despite your problem-solving skills, you may be wasting time and effort in attempting to find a solution when your thoughts are choked by negative emotions or if you are simply unmotivated. Studies (by researchers Sternberg and Spear-Swerling, and Martens and Witt) demonstrated how "children become more effective problem solvers when their motivation levels have been increased by rewarding their success."[3] But internal motivation is the key to being able to persist without becoming rigidly fixated on only one way to solve a problem.

"Individuals who are competent at solving problems are also usually not afraid of making mistakes."[4] It enables them to persist until they find a solution, instead of giving up too easily, as many people do.

Experts and novices think and solve problems differently.[5] Researchers have studied both types in different areas, like physics, mathematics, electronics, chess, history, and even squash.[6] They found that the extensive knowledge acquired over time by experts influences what they pay attention to and how they organize, represent, and interpret information. And the way they encode and store information influences their ability to remember, reason, and solve problems. Experts solve problems differently because they are better than novices in four different ways: (1) their knowledge base, (2) domain memory, (3) strategies, (4) deliberate practice.

Experts organize information simply and more quickly "without going through tedious problem-solving efforts," because their existing broad knowledge base is organized hierarchically, with specific details grouped in chunks and in "concept trees." So it is easier for them to use shortcuts to solve problems.[7]

Experts remember information in their own domain of experience, because they use a storehouse of knowledge to organize and chunk information.[8] Experts often possess more effective strategies beforehand and are more flexible in modifying them while progressing in solving a problem than novices.[9] Years of experience and conscious effort in practicing to become an expert motivate them to improve their skills, which are far superior to a novice. It may be in commodities trading or medicine, chemical engineering or marketing goods and services, practicing law or managing companies.

The word *experts* is synonymous with "superior managers." Nevertheless, it is well to keep in mind that expertise in one sphere of problem solving may not make you an expert in another field.

Curiosity Is a Survival Instinct

In *The Innovator's Dilemma*, Clayton Christensen posed a question, as an academic theorist uninvolved with the shirtsleeve management of a particular company, as to why a CEO who was always successful in the past goes on to fail repeatedly.[10] Was he too inflexible to adapt to changing circumstances? Or was he always a third-rate leader and manager who was just lucky when circumstances were in the company's favor—like the economy or lack of competition—and his flaws are now clearly revealed? In fact, there may be a third alternative: he may no longer be motivated. And the real reason is rarely, if ever, mentioned in books on management. It is simply a lack of curiosity.

What is remarkable about its absence is that curiosity is probably the main reason why human beings have survived. And yet, paradoxically, many people today are not in the least bit curious about what is happening around them. It brings us back once again to what is probably the worst failing of the human condition—complacency. One of its destructive results is that it kills motivation by eroding our curiosity. And yet "the only reliability in the universe [is] curiosity and the only answer is another question."[11]

Curiosity is essential to maintaining a lively interest that drives an executive to keep herself constantly informed. The best managers continually question everything they see and do, including research material piled almost continually on their desk, in order to be properly selective and know which material to ignore and which to set aside for more thorough analysis and contemplation.

Since there are other types of curiosity, it is as well to define three typical ones here, to avoid confusion. There is a narrowly focused curiosity aimed at a specific task to be managed. And there is the wide-angled curiosity of creative and innovative people.

The third kind is entirely different. It is what author Cervantes named "reckless curiosity." No doubt he coined that expression because the famous hero of his classic tale, *Don Quixote*, is vague and purposeless, misdirected, confused, and his time is misspent.[12] Reckless curiosity is also a survival instinct of a kind, since it is a means to escape from reality into a make-believe world. Today it might be described as more like the curiosity devoted to sinkholes like the Internet and social media, through mobile electronic devices, which leave the user wondering afterward whatever happened to their shrinking time. Quixotic means being unrealistically optimistic.[13] It is another form of reality distortion. *Don Quixote* is about escaping into illusions because of an inability to handle the truth. Its author was aware of this human failing long before Mark Zuckerberg designed Facebook as an escape to fantasy.

Complacency not only erodes curiosity, it also perpetuates the mindlessness that caused it in the first place. The unfortunate result is probably best depicted by a famous essayist and literary critic, who wrote of his protagonist in his novel, "I fancy I should be happy if I had something to pursue. But, possessing all that I can want, I find one day and one hour exactly like another, except that the latter is more tedious than the former."[14] His remark shows precisely how

185

complacency causes *ennui* or boredom, which withers the spirit and results in mindlessness.

If we could drive or take a walk to the Tate Gallery in London, we could actually see the result in the famous painting by Walter Richard Sickert, which was considered to be one of the finest paintings in England at the time and was purchased for the nation by a trust. He named it *Ennui*. It features a middle-aged couple who would once have been described as *petit bourgeois*.

The couple avoid looking at each other in the confines of four walls of a sitting room in which they appear to be imprisoned. The woman has turned away from her husband, her shoulders slumped over a sideboard as she stares fixedly at a framed photograph on the wall. Her husband desperately holds onto a cigarette in his mouth as if his life depends on the nicotine. There is a pint glass half-empty on the table in front of him. Most important is the date it was painted—1914. It is a riveting depiction of part complacency with their few possessions and part-listlessness at not knowing what to do next. They are spiritless and entirely devoid of motivation. The painter captured a mood of helplessness and hopelessness in Europe that led to World War One. It catches the mindlessness and helplessness of politicians and military leaders not knowing what to do next, while the uninformed public was driven into what they assumed would be a traditional set-battle overseas, with everyone returning home for the Christmas holidays.

The Loudest Voice at the Table

We may have entered another period of complacency, or *ennui*, or helplessness, a hundred years later. This time by the wizards of Silicon Valley, who are so successful and rich from distorting reality for the consumer society that they may have arrived at an ideological dead end. That is when complacency takes hold. A contemporary artist would probably paint them into a montage with happy consumers playing electronic games, messaging on their mobile devices, or gazing for hours at the Internet. But from the point of view of a serious need for national leadership, and creative managers in business, it is unlikely we shall find them among those escaping from reality by staring into the fictional world of cyber space for much of each day.

Manufacturers, business, and government have driven us into the jobless society we were warned several decades ago to expect. There were 201.8 million unemployed worldwide in 2013, with job opportunities failing to grow at the same pace as the global workforce.[15]

It included seventy-five million young people, or 40 percent of the total.[16] Unemployment grew by another ten million by 2015.[17]

According to *Forbes* magazine, the real unemployment rate is even higher at 14.3 percent.[18] That is because the official rate does not include people finally discouraged from looking for work—known as the "U-6 rate," which is growing because it's hard to get back into the workforce once you're out. Dropouts are viewed as "damaged goods." Even some of those listed as working are only in part-time jobs. After eight months of unemployment, the chances of working again drop by about 45 percent. It is hard to be motivated in those circumstances. Whichever way we view the situation, it is a waste of human resources.

And yet, our political leaders and economists talk about it like the weather—as if there is no point in attempting to do anything about it. So do TV anchor men and women and a multitude of talking heads on every other television channel. So does the BBC Online, and all the other news sites on the Internet. When we stop to consider all the talking that has been going on incessantly for years by now, we realize that no one is actually attempting to do anything about anything. The digital age has already fallen into its own complacency level, because all its communications media are expected to do is tell us what is happening. Extroverts who are spontaneous talkers are hired to talk manically at us and each other, nonstop, in order to keep us watching the screen for when the commercials appear—in the same way that the Internet and social media spew out an endless stream of excessive blogs to keep us on their website so that they can flash advertisements at us. We are inundated with more talking, gossiping, and blogging than at any other time in history. Its sole point is to create media for producing advertising revenues.

One of the idiosyncrasies of talk in the digital era is that it has got faster and faster, as if the addicted talkers know their talk is empty gossip or small talk of no consequence, but they can't stop. Some say they suffer from verbal diarrhea. Hosts of late-night talk shows are paid millions to come up with continuous gobbledygook for juvenile audiences who are so tired from staying up late that they are ready to giggle hysterically at anything. As for politicians, disappointment is almost worldwide. Few make good role models, as we watch them bickering with each other and behaving like kids in a playground, when they are in Parliament. They are full of what the Scots call "blather." It is the type of behavior that would get them fired if they were employees in the private sector where a sense of responsibility is required and executives are obliged to think before they open their mouths.

Here, however, we fall into a distinction between extrovert personalities and introverts who think differently. Whereas it is the extroverts who jump up spontaneously with all the answers, they may not be the right ones. In fact, they are more likely to be merely superficial personal opinions offered without thought. But, in our digital society, it is likely to be those extroverts who win all the arguments, while the introverts are quietly weighing up all the evidence before they open their mouths. They are unheard because they refuse to express a well-judged statement until they have marshaled all the facts.

Are introverts more responsible? Certainly, because they don't wish to mislead anyone by omitting any information that might resolve a debate or solve a problem. And when they finally choose to open their mouths to volunteer a more balanced opinion, they are likely to elaborate on it to ensure they have not left out any evidence that might contribute to the discussion—whereas online and TV media are only interested in two-second bites. Susan Cain, an informative introvert herself, described (far more fully than pioneer psychiatrist Carl Jung did) why we should be patient and not talk so much, but listen carefully to what introverts have to say.[19] Typical of the digital society is that we allow ourselves to be persuaded by the loudest voice at the table, or the one that overwhelms everyone else with its nonstop blather.[20]

There is something about the spontaneity of digital communications—the self-indulgent satisfaction of discovering streams of information just by pressing a key—that instigates a similar effect on human beings the moment a TV camera is pointed at them and they are exposed to public view. They become digital robots, obligated to open their mouths as if someone pressed *their* key, and let instant talk escape of its own volition, without even thinking or applying judgments before it all emerges. It happens at board meetings too. "Think before you talk" may prevent unintended consequences in the same way that "Know before you go" was planned to.

Critical Thinking

Real thinking includes three types of mental processes of a high order, in addition to forming concepts and solving problems: (1) Critical thinking, (2) Reasoning, (3) Decision making. All involve the prefrontal cortex of the brain and an ability to apply judgment. The objective or end result is *evaluation, conclusion,* or *decision.*

Critical thinking can be defined as "thinking reflectively and productively and evaluating the evidence."[21] Those who think critically understand the deeper meanings of ideas. They are open minded to different approaches and perspectives. And they decide for themselves what to believe and what needs to be done.[22]

It is not a new idea: educator John Dewey advocated teaching students to think reflectively in 1933. And it is presently causing considerable interest among psychologists and educators to develop students' ability to think critically.[23] Psychologists Santrock and Mitterer explain that, whereas high-school students may read *Hamlet*, they "are not asked to think about how its notions of power, greed, and conflicting relationships apply to their lives or the wider world. They are rarely stimulated to rethink their prior ideas about these matters."[24] Instead, they are taught to give a single right answer to a multiple-choice question which will be posed at an end of term examination aimed at dealing out grades. Thus, education is minimal and superficial and spoon-fed, instead of stretching the mind as originally intended.

Mindfulness is a characteristic of critical thinking, as opposed to more commonplace mindless behavior, or living on automatic pilot.[25] Ellen Langer describes a mindful person as one who continues to create new ideas, is open to new information, and is aware of more than one perspective. "In contrast, a mindless person is trapped in old ideas, engages in automatic behavior, and operates from a single perspective." It is the type of mindless perspective offered up by digital communications media.

It raises the question whether mindfulness is the opposite of intuition. Acting intuitively suggests a spontaneous and unreflective process, compared with reflective thinking that appears to take time, and is more typical of introverts. Author Malcolm Gladwell claims in his book that intuitive reactions to situations can be as good as, or even better than, deliberate thoughtfulness.[26] That complex and subtle matter of intuition, or gut-feel, is addressed in a different chapter of this book.

Most people tend to take one side of an issue without properly examining or evaluating it from several different perspectives, whereas critical thinking means being open minded to the possibility that there might be other ways of looking at things—hence the passionate anger of self-righteous politicians or religious zealots, or news media editorials, even some academics who believe there is only one right way and it is theirs. Often people are unaware that there may be another side to an issue or of evidence which is contrary to what they have been taught

189

and blindly believe.[27] Being open to every other point of view prevents us from jumping to wrong conclusions that could have unintended consequences. Rationality is the first step to wisdom. And it is impossible to be rational without hearing all the evidence. It is what the introvert tries patiently and calmly to gather and express.

"Reasoning is the mental activity of transforming information to reach conclusions."[28] It can be either inductive or deductive reasoning. Inductive reasoning reasons from the specific to the general.[29] It draws conclusions about all members of a category based on only some of them,[30] whereas an inductive conclusion is never entirely certain and may be inconclusive. Even though it may be right, there is always a chance it is wrong: "perhaps because the study sample may not perfectly represent its population."[31] Or some of the information might be missing.

The fictional English private detective Sherlock Holmes is famous for his deductive reasoning, by examining numerous clues to choose the one correct solution to a crime. Deductive reasoning is always certain in that—as Holmes famously declared—"When you have eliminated the impossible, whatever remains, however improbable, must be the truth."

The Misinformation Effect

"Decision making involves evaluating alternatives and making choices among them."[32] With inductive reasoning, we use established rules to draw conclusions. But when we make decisions, such rules are not established and we don't know the consequences.[33] Nor might we trust all the information in our possession, since some of it may be misleading.[34] ("If you wish to converse with me," advised Voltaire, "first define your terms.")

One research study found people chose the outcome with the highest expected value, whereas, in fact, they may have weighted some of the factors more heavily than others. It was mere speculation.[35]

Confirmation Bias is a tendency to search for and use information that supports our ideas rather than refutes them.[36] For example, politicians often accept news that supports their views and dismiss evidence that is contrary to it. So do the generality of people, which suggests it is probably the biggest cause of irrational behavior. For example, a medical doctor may ignore symptoms because they do not fit his diagnosis of a patient. Or a terrorist may feel justified in killing someone who does not agree with his own beliefs.

Belief Perseverance is the tendency to hold on to a belief in the face of contradictory evidence—like Marxism, self-righteous religions, and other ideologies.

Overconfidence Bias is the tendency to have more confidence in judgments and decisions than we should, based on probability and past experience, being "overconfident about how long people with a fatal disease will live, about which business will go bankrupt, which psychiatric inpatients have serious mental disorders, or whether a defendant is guilty in a court trial . . . ."[37] They have more confidence in their own, often faulty, judgments than objective statistics.

Hindsight Bias is "the tendency to falsely report, after the fact, that we accurately predicted an event."[38]

Availability Heuristic is "a prediction about the probability of an event based on the frequency of the event's past occurrences."[39] When an event has occurred recently, we tend to overestimate its future occurrence, because fear of crime rises whenever the news media highlight a murder story.

Representativeness Heuristic suggests we sometimes "make faulty decisions based on how well something matches a prototype (the common or representative example) rather than on the relevance to a particular situation."[40] In short, we often make judgments of probabilities based on representativeness and fail to consider the size or segment of the population from which the sample is drawn.

One of the most widely studied topics in forensic psychology is judgments formed from eyewitness evidence, because police and the law courts rely on eyewitness accounts which often turns out to be flawed as a consequence of one or more of those biases. Eyewitnesses often make mistakes that send innocent people to prison. It is known as "The Misinformation Effect."

Multiple Intelligences

Old ratings are still used for intelligence testing, such as the IQ or intelligence quotient, initiated in 1904 by Alfred Binet to determine which students did not benefit from instruction in the classroom. There are other tests for achievement and aptitude, in which a psychologist observes and analyzes the individual being tested by sampling his/her behavior, such as how easily a rapport is established, "the level of energy and enthusiasm the individual expresses, and the degree of frustration tolerance and persistence the individual shows in performing difficult tasks."[41] Aptitude tests predict an individual's ability to learn, whereas achievement tests measure what an individual has learned or the skills that person mastered. Such tests are commonplace, but psychologists and psychometrists continue to seek more precise ways to measure intelligence. The reliability of those tests is the extent to which they yield a consistent, reproducible measure of performance.[42]

Neuroscience is now able to offer a new approach to examine differences in individuals' intelligence by using the new technology of fMRI machines to examine people's brains for variations in brain activity.[43]

The question was raised as to whether we may have several different types of intelligence, as opposed to a general ability. Perhaps the most interesting theory for us, with all the multitasking that business executives carry out daily, is Gardner's theory that there are eight different forms of intelligence.

We all know from our own experience that we may be good at playing a musical instrument but not at mathematics; good at painting but not at science; good at natural history but poor at English. Gardner proposed the following eight, but there may be even more: *Verbal skills*: an ability to think in words; *Mathematical skills*: for engineers, scientists, accountants; *Spatial skills*: for architects, artists, and sailors; *Bodily kinesthetic skills*: for surgeons or artisans and craftspeople to manipulate objects or themselves, like athletes and dancers; *Musical skills*: for composers and musicians, orchestra conductors, or music critics; *Interpersonal skills*: for teachers or TV interviewers; *intrapersonal skills*: for psychiatrists, theologians, philosophers; and *Naturalist skills*: for botanists, ecologists, farmers, and landscape gardeners, or teachers of natural history.[44] Gardner limited them to eight "that can be selectively destroyed by brain damage."

The significance to us of recognizing more than one type of intelligence is that entrepreneurship and marketing are not linear activities but require almost simultaneous thinking and multitasking.

Studies to test the degree and type of intelligence of particularly intelligent animals, like chimpanzees, orangutan, crows, and parrots, reveal they possess "flexible thinking" (by transferring knowledge from a known process to an unknown one) and "innovative thinking," which implies creativity. Since they are all social animals in their own natural environment, they are likely to have learnt those skills through sharing information within their cultures. "Culture is a series of activities that shape the mind."[45] "Neuroplastic research has shown us that every sustained activity ever mapped (including physical activities, sensory activities, learning, thinking, and imagining) changes the brain as well as the mind."[46] And, "Practicing a new skill, under the right conditions, can change hundreds of millions and possibly billions of the connections between the nerve cells in our brain maps."[47]

Harvesting Ideas

"Many of the traditional ideas we have about ourselves and how society works are wrong. It is not simply the brightest who have the best ideas; it is those who are best at harvesting ideas from others . . . those who most fully engage with like-minded people."[48] And it is useful to be reminded that creative thinkers are divergent thinkers who can produce many answers to the same question, whereas academic exams today insist on only the one answer previously studied in a classroom. Perhaps it is because academics are specialists in only one subject. It must be frustrating and discouraging for intelligent and creative students, particularly those who (like all those boy-billionaires we admire for creating companies like Google, Microsoft, Dell, Facebook, and Apple) possess simultaneous awareness and an ability to think about things in new and unusual ways and arrive at unconventional solutions to problems.

They also possess four special characteristics that might be essential ones for successful entrepreneurs: (1) Flexibility and playful thinking, (2) Inner motivation, (3) Willingness to take risks, (4) Objective evaluation.

Creative thinkers "play with problems"—whether scientists, mathematicians, code-breakers, artists, or designers, or inventors of electronic devices. A particular clue to their activities is that "humor greases the wheels of creativity."[49] People who joke around are more likely to consider any possibility, however bizarre it may at first seem to others. Hence brain-storming sessions, as long as they are well led, undertaken with good humor, and avoid censorship.

Creative people are internally motivated by the sheer exuberance of inventing new ideas and the artistry that makes them willing to take risks—as opposed to staid and conservative organizations with foundations in the past that must not be shaken in case their people veer off in the wrong direction or make mistakes. That is why bureaucratic organizations are suspicious of creative people and do not welcome them with open arms.

For one thing, creative people are often eccentric. It is how they are able to reach out and capture new ideas from the air. Some are also inclined to vie for attention and approval by shows of narcissism or histrionics. And yet they also possess an ability to evaluate their own work objectively. A painter knows when to stop painting. A short story writer knows how short her story should be. And when they come up with an original new idea, they generally know if further creative thinking will improve it, or not.

Motivation

One of the most important questions for any business organization is how to motivate executives and staff to produce the best performance they are capable of every day, and even how to stretch them further to increase their capabilities. We know that creative people are self-motivated because they enjoy the challenges of what they do best. But, despite that, they still need approval and appreciation for their imagination and skills. That is why performing artists love the adulation of audiences who rise to give them a standing ovation. It keeps them young and energized, thrilled and thrilling, and always ready to display their talents and improve on them.

The same applies to marketing people, because of the large amount of creativity involved in their work. What surprises many people is that it also applies to successful salespeople. But motivation is unlikely to persist if unnecessary obstacles are placed in their way that prevent them from performing as well as they would like. Those types of hurdles are generally set up almost unconsciously by the entirely different mind-set of bureaucrats who lack the imagination and sensitivity to understand and foresee the unintended consequences of their actions.

Ample evidence of this can be seen by watching a YouTube video of, for example, mezzo-soprano Elina Garanca enjoying an audience showing spontaneous appreciation of her talent with their excited applause; and her relieved glance at the conductor, which seems to say "There, I managed it that time!" We see her small smile of contentment as she walks offstage with the applause still sounding in her ears, knowing that all the hard work of practice and rehearsals resulted in a performance that delighted millions.

The reason for the need of outside approval is that motivation and emotions are closely linked. "Motivation moves people to behave, think, and feel the way they do."[50] The Evolutionary Psychology approach emphasizes the biological basis with its instinct for survival. Psychologist William McDougall claimed that all behavior involves instincts for acquisitiveness, curiosity, pugnacity, gregariousness, and self-assertion. And Freud claimed sex and aggression in particular were powerful instincts. But neither satisfactorily explained why. Denys de Catanzaro in 1999, and psychologist David Buss in 2004, argued that it is necessary to examine our evolutionary origins to understand motivation, and that it depends on the competitive advantage of each individual.

Arguments ensued between a *drive* (a state aroused by a physical need) and a *need* (meaning the deprivation that triggers the drive; known as "drive reduction"). For example, a need for food is a hunger-drive. The aim of the drive is to achieve and maintain equilibrium, as all our chemistry and biology tends to do. But some psychologists are lukewarm on the theory. Optimum Arousal Theory—seeking stimulation and challenge, as active sports enthusiasts do—suggests that some individuals enjoy a state of alertness and activity, even living on the edge, like mountain climbers or hang-gliders. But it does not apply to everyone.

The "Yerkes–Dodson law" claims that, on the contrary, performance is best under conditions of moderate arousal rather than either low or high arousal—that neither lethargy nor overexcitement is likely to provide an ideal condition for the best performance. Other studies show that, although moderate arousal does serve best on an average or normal day, there are particular times when low or high arousal results in optimal performance.

One example of that situation is when a sales force is divided into competing teams, from time to time, and both the best performing salesperson and best team are rewarded financially with large bonuses if they exceed their targets. It makes the effort and stress during the period of the competition worthwhile. Although bonuses may appear to be an extrinsic motivator, the sales promotion with the challenge of competing and the teamwork, and excitement encouraged by a champion, involves an intrinsic reward too. It exemplifies the continually successful achievements of all those market leaders mentioned previously in digital technology companies, since "nothing succeeds like success."

The current view of motivation emphasizes cognitive factors, as opposed to rewards and punishments.[51] It involves a positive attitude toward the task, which is likely to be helped by a positive attitude toward the company. Some explanations presented particularly vividly by psychologists, like "Maslow's Hierarchy of Needs" or "Gardner's theory of Eight Intelligences," make an impact that remains in our consciousness because of their vivid concepts that encourage repetition in textbooks, even when there is some doubt that they are entirely satisfactory.

For example, although most of what Maslow says is original and persuasive, his goal at the top of the pyramid, *to achieve full potential as a human being,* remains out of reach for most people. And it would be hard to name even one or two individuals who have reached those Nietzschean heights of a superman or superwoman, although they may be motivated to try. Nevertheless, the personal reward is in the trying, because that is what activates the brain cells and stretches the plasticity of the brain.

The Three Great Motivators

It is worth elaborating further on what used to be called the "three great hidden motives." The Big Three in our consumer society were claimed to be Sex appeal, Hunger to buy things, and Money or Power and Prestige. While the financial rewards of an executive job provide security, legitimate bonuses for successfully stretching the parameters of what can be achieved enable people to buy more things to keep the economy spinning in today's society, where shopping is big news, worthy even of the front page of some publications, and forever on nightly television. As for prestige, American companies discovered long ago they could deal out prestigious titles to executives instead of money. Senior executives, managers, and CEOs of companies were happy to be given status instead of a salary increase, since it lent them sex appeal.

Sex appeal is something special and takes many different forms. It is a strong motivator for getting people to buy almost anything. That three-letter word, which was rarely spoken aloud before the permissive society of the 1960s, now appears everywhere on the sound waves and in printed news media, in day-to-day conversation and at parties, on the stages of theaters and on TV talk shows, in pubs and cocktail bars, and on the streets. People never seem to tire of talking about it or listening to that three-letter word, although it probably means different things to different people. The excitement and wishful thinking engendered by it succeeds in keeping our consumer society shopping at an electronic pace wherever there is surplus money in the bank account, or credit where there isn't. We build up our debt-loads to the banks as a consequence of sex, and banks continue to make huge profits from the interest on credit cards, which make them sexy.

Sex sells cosmetics and toiletries, attractive fashion clothes, tourism and alcohol, and services like hairdressing, tanning salons, artificial nails, health centers, dating websites, diet beverages, slimming foods, skin creams, cigarettes, provocative T-shirts, cafés and restaurants, social media; and other types of grooming, like fat removal, nose operations, wrinkle removal, and face-lifts. Dancing lessons and drama lessons depend on the allure of sex. Rock bands and CDs, popular singers, pornographic movies, erotica, romantic novels that provide us with models of heroes and heroines drawn to each other by their hormones, scandal magazines and tabloids, the automobile industry and real estate, all rely on sex. It keeps lawyers in business, maintains bank and insurance companies' profits, and contributes to the success of gambling casinos. Perhaps the entire combination of industries in the whole city of Las Vegas, and the irrational exuberance of the stock exchange, can be attributed to sex.

The pleasure principle of sexual behavior itself is centered in the hypothalamus and radiates out to connect with other parts of the brain. And we can thank or blame the influence of our powerful sex hormones for the circulation of all that money—the estrogens in women and androgens in men. The specific aim of those hormones is to encourage sex as soon as it is biologically possible. And a multitude of industries have been invented to help them achieve their objective. "Sexual motivation is influenced by sexual scripts, stereotyped patterns of expectancies for how people should behave sexually."[52]

Personality Characteristics

Psychologist Richard Sorrentino's remarks about "uncertainty orientation" and an "unexplored personality characteristic" are beguiling, since it is time to raise the question of how particular personality characteristics influence the attitudes and behavior of entrepreneurs, business managers, and political and other leaders. Is it personality that makes one succeed while another fails? Sorrentino's studies are devoted primarily to examining the interface between motivation and cognition: "A theory of individual differences in thought and action."

Personality characteristics, as we now know them, were researched, diagnosed, and classified in the nineteenth century, first by psychiatrist Dr. Emil Kraepelin, who compiled his famous manual, which was used by medical practitioners and studied since the time of Dr. Breuer and his young colleague, Dr. Freud. It listed the symptoms and recommended treatments for a variety of different mental disorders, with the intention of creating universal recognition, so that all practitioners could work with the same information and guidelines. Now known mostly for his long-term research of manic depression and *dementia praecox* or senility, he believed the main cause of psychiatric disease was biological

197

and genetic malfunction. His findings have had considerable influence in today's studies of degenerative mental diseases like Alzheimer's. His manual influenced the more comprehensive *Diagnostic and Statistical Manual of Mental Disorders* (the fifth edition of which was completed in 2013).[53] It is in general use today by psychologists and psychiatrists in North America, and known generally as *DSM-V*.

The *DSM* may help us to understand what motivates some business managers and entrepreneurs and not others, since it is known that people with different personality characteristics are motivated by different needs and rewards. The fact that it was written to classify mental disorders should not concern us here, since we are not medical practitioners. It is described as "a resource for clinicians, researchers, insurers, and patients." For our purposes, "disorders" can be construed as either intensification or malfunction of the typical personality characteristics that we all display. Wherever there are different personality disorders, there are different personalities. Some patients and psychiatrists argue that many of the conditions classified in the DSM are not mental disorders at all, but individual personality characteristics or quirks of temperament. Its methodology is only mentioned here to exemplify such behavior patterns as *histrionics* and *narcissism*. And we don't only come across them with creative people. We encounter both those qualities whenever we read the general run of blogs on social media websites, particularly Facebook, since they apply to the human condition far more than we could ever have imagined before online social media sites became popular.

Studies of personality characteristics arose from Galen's first typology of four different temperaments (melancholic, choleric, phlegmatic, and sanguine) and no doubt astrological signs with their attributions influenced others. They led to Eysenck's *Dimensions of Personality* in 1967, which developed Galen's four dimensions by attributing eight to ten different classifications to each of them. For example (without going into too much detail), Sanguine ranges all the way from Stable to Extroverted by way of Sociable, Outgoing, Talkative, Responsive, Easygoing, Lively, Carefree, and Leadership. The polar opposite of "stable" is "unstable," where we have a state called *stable–unstable*, which is known as "the neuroticism dimension." A stable person is calm, even-tempered, carefree, and capable of leadership, whereas an unstable individual is moody, anxious, restless, and touchy.[54] Nevertheless, an intelligence industry or a creative business enterprise may have a need for both types of individuals.

There is no need here to elaborate on all shades of Eysenck's personality traits. It is simpler to focus, instead, on the Big Five, which we began with in an earlier chapter to demonstrate the changing range of attributes required of personnel in today's intelligence and creative industries. They are those *"Supertraits" that are thought to describe the main dimensions of personality—openness, conscientiousness, extroversion, agreeableness, and neuroticism.*[55] Those five factors appear in personality cultures all over the world.[56] It makes its acronym OCEAN easy to remember them.[57]

Evaluating people according to their personality traits enables us to understand individuals better. We recognize that their traits influence their attitudes, so that we can predict their behavior patterns much of the time. It makes it easier to choose the types of people required for their different skills in creative teams.

The *DSM-IV* or *V* classifications of the so-called psychological disorders come in useful, both in the way the manual structures its personality categories and in the way we can see how mental disorders can be attributed, in most cases, to intensifications or malfunctions—leaving the so-called normal or average personality characteristics to Eysenck, since there is continual debate about what "normal" is.

Definitions (in *DSM-IV*, Axis II) depend on "personality disorder clusters," so that, for example, ten personality disorders "are grouped into three clusters based on descriptive similarities." One example is *Cluster A:* (1) Odd/Eccentric, (2) Dramatic/Emotional, (3) Anxious/Fearful. It is the "odd eccentrics" who contribute so much of the original thinking that we call creativity.

However, *DSM-IV* warned that "the clustering system has serious limitations and has not been consistently validated." Even so, it allows us to recognize the different ranges, or shades, of emotions that are designated, for example, "Odd/Eccentric." Minor eccentricities are encompassed at one end of its scale, all the way to extremes of real mental disorders like paranoia, schizotypal, and schizoid. Similarly, in *Cluster B:* "Erratic/Emotional," we find Antisocial, Borderline, Histrionic, and Narcissistic at the extreme pole. And yet, individuals who are often erratic or narcissistic can be motivated to be creative.

In *Cluster C* we find Anxious/Fearful, which ranges from Avoidant, Dependent, and Obsessive-Compulsive. And yet some of the most important problem solving depends on obsessive-compulsives who persist until they find an original solution that never existed before.

Psychologists, psychiatrists, and trained Human Resource people would be aware of those conditions. And the degree of oddness or eccentricity a candidate may show can be judged by how much is desirable for such attributes as scientific leaps of faith, or creative ones that invent or innovate the hardware or software of our cognitive revolution.[58] Perhaps the most useful skill is harvesting ideas from one's peers and developing them in meaningful ways, like Steve Jobs did in order to develop Apple Inc.

14

Influencing Sales and Perpetrating Frauds

For anyone in business, particularly marketing people, salespeople, and sales managers, *The Wolf of Wall Street* promised to be a likely textbook—not for imitation, but as a revelation of how Jordan Belfort trained his young brokers to sell to clients who had more money than sense.[1]

On page 2, we see the author as a "connector" in training at L. F. Rothschild in New York City, who focused solely on sweeping past all the receptionists, secretaries, and personal assistants on the telephone, to reach the business owner, and then pass the phone to the "cold-caller" to pitch a sale. A successful salesman's time is far too valuable to waste in such donkeywork, when he makes a couple of million dollars a year. He is a specialist. The *connector* (Belfort tells us on page 3) is several rungs below a *cold-caller*. But the connector too is a specialist, because he does nothing else all day but make phone connections for the salesman. The connector is at the bottom rung of the ladder, whereas the salesman is at the top. As the author explains, Wall Street in 1987 was "a place for killers. A place for mercenaries."

The division of labor between a connector and the cold-canvassing salesman is straight out of economist Adam Smith's *Wealth of Nations* in 1776, where he describes the economic efficiencies and increased production obtained from the division of labor in the manufacture of pins during the English Industrial Revolution.

Belfort explains how Wall Street greed and ambition and the gullibility of buyers, only two decades ago, threw the world into a financial crisis from which we are still struggling to recover. It was the era of junk bonds and derivatives, which people were eager to buy, despite the fact that they had no idea what they were. But, as the author tells us on page 5, "People don't buy stock; it gets sold to them."

It was another successful Wall Street trader who added, "We were prepared to kill someone, and we did. The battlefields of the derivatives world are littered with our victims. As you may have read in the newspapers, at Orange County and Barings Bank and Daiwa Bank and Sumitomo Corporation and perhaps others no one knows about yet, a *single* person lost more than a billion dollars. At some companies it took more than one person to lose a billion dollars. Dozens of household names, including Procter & Gamble and numerous mutual funds, lost hundreds of millions each, billions total, on derivatives. The $50 billion Mexican currency debacle included its share of derivatives victims, too."

"As the late Senator Everett Dickson once said, 'A billion here and a billion there, and pretty soon you're talking about real money.' If you owned stock or mutual funds during the past few years, a portion of the real money lost on derivatives very likely was yours . . . Some clients tired of having their faces ripped off or being blown up, and business declined briefly in 1995 and 1996."[2]

That extract was from a book about "the gluttony and dysfunctionality of Wall Street in the 1990s," which led up to the global economic crisis of 2008, and the crass and irresponsible attitude with which stockbrokers treated their wealthy clients who lost their investment capital. It seems that no other selling techniques were needed than to stoke the fires of greed. But greed is a personal motivation that often arises from childhood insecurity, whereas companies buy stocks for other reasons, the main one being *desperation*. Derivatives trader Frank Partnoy quotes his stockbroker bosses: "We love desperate clients. We get excited about them. We've made a lot of money off desperate people." Among them are companies that dread showing massive year-end losses that would reduce their valuations on stock markets. Desperation induces them to take huge risks in the hope of obtaining huge rewards in a hurry. The answer, they were promised, was to buy huge amounts of derivatives.

"Without derivatives, the complex risks that destroyed Bear Stearns, Lehman Brothers, and Merrill Lynch, and decimated dozens of banks and insurance companies, including AIG, could not be hidden from view . . . they enabled Wall Street to maintain its destructive run until it was too late."

Belfort's young stockbrokers didn't use logical selling techniques, partly because they probably wouldn't have known how to. Instead, he taught them to bully clients already motivated by greed, into buying, while both were carried away by the adrenaline rush caused by delusions of wealth—what the former Federal Reserve Board chairman Alan Greenspan famously called "irrational exuberance." It worked because Belfort's strategy was a simple one that made selling skills unnecessary. It was to target the richest 1 percent whom he claimed are closet gamblers who "can't withstand the temptation to keep rolling the dice again and again, even if they know the dice are loaded against them."[3]

"Don't hang up the phone until the client buys or dies," was one of his instructions. It was all about taking control of the conversation. But clients who thought Belfort's brokers were doing them a favor by giving them confidential tips were in for a shock when they found out that what he preached to his brokers was part of the double agenda of an agent to "only appear to be on the side of the customer and to not actually be on the side of the customer . . . The effort was strictly cosmetic."[4]

Perhaps he has finally answered the question about the difference between investing, speculating, and gambling, by recognizing that although different words are used, they all amount to making bets.

Do the odds against winning vary in each way of betting? Even someone with Warren Buffett's experience of evaluating the economic dynamics of a company or industry, and working with actuaries to assess the impact of risk and uncertainty on undesirable events, and with his knowledge of the uncertainties and imperfections in the markets . . . even he would be likely to smile knowingly and avoid answering.[5]

"The cultural embrace of illusion, and the celebrity culture that has risen up around it, have accompanied a growing system of casino capitalism, with its complicated and unregulated deals of turning debts into magical assets, to create fictional wealth for us, and vast wealth for our elite. Corporations, behind the smoke screen, have ruthlessly dismantled and destroyed our manufacturing base and impoverished our working class."[6]

On Monday, February 27, 1995, the British bank named Barings collapsed after 233 years in business. Its reputation was so high because among its clients were the Queen of England, other royalty and wealthy individuals, and famous British companies. Why did it fail? Because a twenty-eight-year-old derivatives trader named Leeson made enormous losses from buying and selling that Barings didn't have enough money to repay. "He began his career in the back office . . . where he processed trading records. By 1995 Leeson had moved up to the Barings futures trading desk in Singapore, where he was following a low-risk 'arbitrage' strategy of trading Japanese stock. Instead of betting that stock would go up or down, Leeson bought and sold futures contracts on Japanese stocks to take advantage of price discrepancies among different stock exchanges."[7]

Betting is the key word. There is no pretense on stock exchanges that it is anything else but a gambling casino, except for insider trading, from which brokers can make billions of dollars, and which is illegal.

"Remember, a future is an exchange-traded obligation to buy or sell something at a set time and price. The futures Leeson bought and sold included Nikkei-225 futures contracts, the obligation to buy the top 225 Japanese stocks at a certain future time and price. Leeson had discovered that these futures contracts were traded on exchanges in both Singapore and Osaka, Japan. If the Singapore contract was cheaper than the Osaka contract, he could buy in Singapore, simultaneously sell in Osaka, and lock in a riskless arbitrage profit. Buy low, sell high."

But he abandoned his conservative approach and began betting on whether the Japanese market would go up or down. He bought on margin (paying only a fraction of his bet as a down-payment). Remember that Leeson was a trained and experienced trader in one of the best known and best regarded banks in the world. Nevertheless . . .

"First, he bet that the Japanese stock market would go up. Almost immediately after Leeson placed this bet, Japanese stocks went down. As he increased the size of his bet, stocks went down even more. Leeson increased this bet repeatedly, until he had bet a total of $7 billion that stocks would go up or, equivalently, that Japanese bond prices would go down. (Remember, interest rates and bond prices move in opposite directions.) Again, Leeson began to lose money almost immediately. He increased this bet, too, and it continued to move against him. Leeson ultimately bet $22 billion that bonds would go down."

Barings executives began to realize that, since Leeson's losses were capped at a limited downside, he lost only about $1 billion. Whatever it was, it exceeded the bank's net worth. They called the Bank of England, but no bank was prepared to lend Barings money to repay their debts, including the Bank of England. Barings was pronounced dead and buried. Meanwhile, Leeson and his wife skipped town. He was finally found in Europe and extradited to Singapore, where he served six years in prison for financial fraud.

Are Buying and Selling Dishonorable?

Even an old hand at finance and stock markets like Alan Greenspan was taken completely by surprise at the lack of control in banks, mortgage assessors and valuers, insurance companies, stockbrokers, and other financial institutions, and has been tormented by financial investment bubbles ever since the global economic crisis.[8]

Are stockbrokers criminals taking money from clients to put into their own pockets? Is capitalism corrupt? Is money dirty? And is selling dishonorable? Those are questions that have been asked for a very long time. They make some honest salespeople uneasy. But there is a huge difference between greed when there is plenty of money and stockbrokers and the wealthy are ambitious for more and more, compared with desperation when the poorer-off and victimized have to survive by using food banks and are fearful of having their home repossessed by a bank, and of sleeping in the streets like all the other homeless people who fall by the wayside.

In the hustle to make money in the 1920s and 1930s there were no social safety nets if you failed, so failure was not an option, and salesmen never took no for an answer. Fear of poverty drove salesmen to exploit every possible opportunity and study every book on self-improvement, go to night classes, and learn how to talk people into buying your goods or services. There was a big demand for salesmen when the industrial age spawned factories that made things. Even uneducated young men could learn how to sell. But you had to be always on the go and motivated to get rich. The primary ingredient for success was persistence, the motivation was fear of failing.

Since sales management was not properly understood, salesmen were left to their own initiatives and drive. They had to be self-motivated. The lure was the opportunity to rise into the wealthy middle classes.

What was called a "born salesman" had to be an *efficient* one who used his time most effectively, since he worked on commission and had to sell to earn. It meant not only making repeat sales, but making them speedily and "scientifically," so that they stuck. Employers were not happy to waste time and money from returned goods or canceled orders due to customer remorse. And salesmen wanted satisfied customers who would provide them with referrals and repeat business.

If you made cold calls to offices or canvassed from door to door, a demanding schedule was required, because of the volume of rejections and not-at-homes. Carbon salesmen had to complete forms for their sales managers, giving details of twenty calls a day, as mutual fund firms do now.

Buying and Selling Online

In today's hustle to succeed, fewer sales people go to night school or read books on self-improvement. Sales people rely more on laptops and mobiles that help to keep them organized, while more and more companies have set up their own beguiling websites to entice consumers to buy online. Total online sales were estimated at $1,151.2 billion in the first quarter of 2015[9]:

- Global B2C eCommerce sales were $1.5 trillion in 2014. Asia Pacific is now the world's largest regional eCommerce market.[10]
- Forty percent of worldwide Internet users bought goods online from their desktop, mobile phone, tablet, or other device, amounting to more than a billion online buyers.[11]

Most recent breakdowns of online sales categories show that more than 44 percent consisted of computers, apparel, and consumer electronics. Accelerating online sales are fast taking away revenues from shopping malls and their anchor stores, like Sears.

By the summer of 2015 more than a hundred billion apps were downloaded from the Apple site. The following breakdown of categories of the most popular Apple apps downloaded in 2015, show that—like the use of the Internet for searches, the subjects chosen were far and away devoted more to leisure or playing games. Games: 21.8 percent; business: 10.33 percent; education: 9.79 percent ; lifestyle: 8.57 percent; entertainment: 6.6 percent; utilities: 5.05 percent; travel: 4.42 percent; books: 3.67 percent; music: 3.05 percent; health and fitness: 2.81 percent; productivity: 2.81 percent; sports: 2.6 percent; food and drink: 2.5 percent; photo and video: 2.43 percent; finance: 2.26 percent; reference: 2.34 percent; news: 3.32 percent; medical: 2.05 percent; social networking: 2.03 percent; navigation: 1.16 percent.[12]

Application stores are digital distribution platforms for app software provided as a component of an operating system on a PC, a smartphone, or a tablet.

Selling products and services online is little different from the way that the creative people who produced the successful advertisements in the preceding pages did, and much the same way that salespeople in this chapter sell. Of course, there is a whole range of special techniques typical of the Internet, like algorithms, interactivity with key words and search engines, deceptive offers, and all the rest of the chicanery of deception, as well as the digital technology, and not to forget branding and a USP. Nevertheless, it always has creativity at its core.

But new technologies always come at a cost (we can't repeat that too often): in this case the cost is largely distraction or complacency and often dishonesty. Despite the remarkably huge increase in online sales, nothing can replace face-to-face selling when it comes to high-priced or original and exceptional goods and services with brands and labels as warranties of quality. The selling arena is where relationships are opened up and built. Its value is engaging with others and being able to observe their body language. It is how genuine friendships are made. That is when you can negotiate more favorably, and it is still the best way to close a sale with confidence and trust. It is also the best way to obtain new referrals. Relationship marketing provides opportunities to obtain repeat orders. And it can establish consumer preference and customer loyalty.

In spite of the increase in online sales, selling even nameless commodities and simple services require product knowledge, technique, and confidence engendered from personal selling, in other words, the *art* of selling, accompanied by strategies and skills. Company websites are merely online displays of brochures, catalogs, and price lists. However much they attempt to encourage interactivity, and however successful they are, they are more like dealers' display shelves where the buyer has to take the initiative.

Today there is as much demand for effective salespeople as ever, and a shortage of really good ones who can be depended on to move high-ticket items, like automobiles, regularly out of manufacturing plants and into, or out of, retail and wholesale showrooms and stores. The same thing applies to real estate, where the main online objective is to inform prospective purchasers and leave the selling to the sales center which is fully equipped with onsite displays as sales aids.

Any reasonably intelligent individual with an open mind and sufficient self-confidence can be taught to sell. There is nothing difficult about it and no mystique, because it is not multifaceted like marketing. And yet, salespeople phone us incessantly at home who have no idea how to engage customers or talk them into buying. And it is clearly obvious from their fumbling attempts to engage with us that their employers have no clue how to train them. All they want to do is exploit us. And, to judge from their pathetic attempts, they don't even know how to do that. It's just a numbers game in which you hire someone desperate enough to make endless phone calls on commission and with little hope of success, except that someone just might happen to be in the market for your product or service at that particular moment.

Learning How to Sell

In 1924, Henry Holt and Company of New York published *"Bond Sales-manship"* by William W. Townsend. It is doubtful if any other book on selling is more candid, knowledgeable, and insightful. But, overloaded as we are today with information, 469 pages may provide too much of it. Today's mass market is the restless youth market who are anxious to do other things that won't wait. So, for the sake of brevity, ease, and speed, the following are selected gems garnered from this remarkable book—one of two on the bond market which so fascinated the young Warren Buffett that he was prompted to become a successful billionaire investor in companies.

Women readers should note there were no saleswomen in 1924—hence the gender-specific title of Townsend's book. Today, women probably dominate the selling arena, for several very good reasons, as we shall see.

Although Townsend wrote his book to explain the intricacies of bond trading, he succeeded in describing how to sell *anything*. That is because he focused on the way an individual salesperson is instrumental in changing a potential buyer's attitude toward a product or service and closing a deal on it, so that it matters little whether the deal is a jet plane, a cooking range, a laptop computer, or mutual funds.

There is often such a big gap between the regular volume of sales of the top salesperson and all the others in a sales team that a question often considered by administrators and other staff in business enterprises that rely on selling, like the retail trade, is: "Are good salespeople born or are they made?" They certainly have to possess particular characteristics to succeed. But it is more important for them to understand the selling process and know how to carry it through to its goal of making a sale. In particular spheres, like selling real estate or stocks and bonds, product knowledge and perseverance may be the keys to success.

Selling consists of both art and science. Some extroverts are born with the art but have to learn the science to succeed. Others learn the science and develop the art with experience.

Most sales courses teach that just because a customer says *"No,"* doesn't mean he doesn't *want* it, only that you haven't persuaded him to buy it! And many customers buy *after* they said "No." That is why sales-people in training are often told never to take "No" for an answer. The art is engaging with people to make them receptive to your proposal, and then overcome any obstacles that may arise. The science requires careful study and concentration on what you are doing and saying at each step of a procedure that leads toward closing a sale. Salespeople must know *why* they are doing it and *how* to do it correctly to achieve results.

And yet, the actual proposal must be made without any appearance of contrivance or effort, and not the smallest indication that the salesperson or the company is desperate for a sale. The ability can be learnt, but inclination stems from motivation linked to reward—either money, ambition, or a sense of purpose. For some salespeople, a sense of purpose may come from a need to confront challenges and solve problems. For others it may be necessity. Positive and manipulative individuals enjoy solving mysteries and view all problems as opportunities. Selling gets their adrenaline flowing. Those instincts often result in *super*-salespeople.

Townsend listed twelve characteristics he considered essential for an effective salesperson. The following captions are exactly the same as he used, but elaborated on with insights from today's experience in a very different environment.

1. *Instinctive honesty and truthfulness.* If you can march into a buyer's office or home, and meet his (or her) eyes, with your hand confidently outstretched for a firm handshake, and with a genuine engaging smile, you will have taken the first step toward making a sale, by engendering a powerful and honest image—not so very different from what an advertisement does in print or online.
2. *The instinct for helpfulness.* It pays to *want to help* other people, because it shows.
3. *The capacity for leadership.* A seller's job is to *lead* buyers into making the right decisions. It is what Belfort described as taking control of the conversation.
4. *The capacity for accomplishment against odds.* Sales goals won't be achieved without perseverance, and a sense of achievement at doing it right.
5. *A forceful or pleasing personality.* This characteristic is obvious, and yet some sales people turn off a potential buyer because of a personality flaw or poor technique, lack of focus or complacency, lazy-mindedness, or desperation.
6. *Physical poise.* No one is likely to buy from someone who seems insecure, or down-at-heel, clumsy, uninformed, or awkward. Even though

a customer may *want* the product or service, a salesperson can destroy confidence to buy from her. The customer will go elsewhere to buy.

7. *An alert and well-disciplined mind.* It is partly derived from confidence after studying and knowing the products and services the company offers, until it becomes second nature to describe them as consumer benefits.

8. *A good memory.* Unless a salesperson can fluently remember the essential benefits of buying products and services from the company, and believes in them, there would be no point in learning selling techniques.

9. *Constructive imagination.* Effective sales people are goal oriented, creative, and do not lack imagination, or they are unlikely to be able to sell. Their imagination must be constructive and disciplined to enable them to consider all possibilities at a moment's notice, like overcoming obstacles, deciding to switch-sell, or sell-up to a better product if required.

10. *Self-respect.* People have to know themselves to improve themselves. And they have to respect themselves in order to be able to lead others.

11. *A saving sense of humor.* This is essential for a sense of proportion and a realistic attitude toward life. It enables a salesperson to like the buyer, despite recognizing his or her human flaws, as well as their own failings.

12. *The determination to sell.* It may even take the form of a *compulsion*, in the same way that an artist has a compulsion to paint or a novelist to write. Their skill is the source of their identity and success. Salespeople must enjoy selling, or their resolution may falter. A careless attitude or expression can break a deal.

Creative Temperament

The temperament that drives good salespeople to succeed can also make them seem strange to employers, because administrative management is involved mostly in regular practical routines, whereas selling is emotionally volatile. Managers must recognize that an entirely different mind-set is needed for different functions. Salespeople who are the center of attention in a selling arena can be as temperamental as prima donnas, because they are always called on to perform. It is their creative temperament that enables them to stretch the boundaries of their imagination in order to make sales.

Despite the fact that a business can't be in business unless it makes a sale, it is remarkable how many large companies in the West are blandly indifferent to selling, particularly when they are no longer owned by the founder, but in the hands of managers. The owner of most entrepreneurial companies, on the other hand, will be likely to have a slip of paper passed to him unobtrusively at the end of each day, wherever he is, with that day's sales figures scribbled on it as soon as possible, so that he can react to the situation tactically.

What is required is a supportive attitude by management to encourage the best performance from salespeople, because they are the heroes of the enterprise—they make the sales that pay everyone's salaries.

Some employers don't understand sales management and prefer to outsource selling to a company that specializes in recruiting, training, and supervising their own salespeople. It is the entrepreneur's choice. But it is better for a business organization to control its own sales and its own company image, and its after-sales service. It keeps companies in continual touch with the market by providing useful feedback. Outsourcing is fraught with problems. On the other hand, a big enough organization may require nationwide or global agents or distributors with their own sales forces. A smaller or medium-size company needs an experienced sales manager to organize sales teams, train, and motivate them. The job involves setting realistic sales targets and ensuring the company has the right salespeople to meet forecasts.

A professional sales manager knows how to handle attitude and temperament, since salespeople often can't recognize their own faults. For example, books and classes on selling in the great age of salesmen who aspired to earn riches in the 1920s and 1930s often commenced by focusing on salespeople's appearance, which can either encourage or discourage sales. It is as true in the retail trade today as it was when authors like H. G. Wells wrote about the drapery trade when he was a young man in 1910 and staff usually lived in dormitories over the shop.[13] Are they properly dressed? Do they suffer from bad breath or body odor? Are their fingers stained with nicotine? Do they have bad habits? Can they talk coherently? Are they literate? Do they have off-putting nervous mannerisms? Is their hair properly cut? Did they remember to polish their shoes? When buying online, on the other hand, there are few such clues to inspire trust, and the entire image of the website is artificially designed to conceal the premises, the workers, and the owners.

Salesmen in Townsend's days often came to the city for work from the countryside, or escaped from deprived families, and lacked social polish. Those problems rarely exist since glamorous Hollywood film stars became role models. And any possible drawbacks to employing them can be corrected by a caring sales manager who looks after his or her sales team like a competitive, temperamental, and often dysfunctional family. Even so, it means hiring salespeople who have the character to *want* to improve their skills by responding with enthusiasm to training and constructive criticism.

Ethics are important. And it appears, from memoirs and auto-biographies, and the daily news media, that when salespeople get close to really big money, buyers need to beware. For example, former stockbroker and nonexecutive chairman of the NASDAQ stock exchange, the financial swindler Madoff, is still behind bars for fraud after being sentenced to 150 years in prison for operating his so-called "wealth management" business as a Ponzi scheme, resulting in a number of bankruptcies and suicides. Because of his prestige, he had only to offer investors 11 percent interest for them to come begging to invest. The result was they lost everything for the sake of a few percentage points, since their money simply went into Madoff's own pocket.

Did his behavior give capitalism a bad name? Being driven by profit and personal gain is hardly a crime in the United States, particularly when greed was declared to be a good motivator. Nevertheless, it *has* earned a bad name once again. That is because, as long as increased wealth goes only to the top 1 percent of society—widening the gulf between rich and poor—the economic progress credited to the financial sector and Silicon Valley (who can afford to make huge fortunes on the stock markets) is only an illusion.

In fact, the distribution of wealth is much as it was when the nine-teenth-century social economist Vilfredo Pareto studied it to confirm his 80/20 principle—that 20 percent of the population possess 80 percent of the wealth. What has changed is the widening gulf at the very top between millionaires and multibillionaires.

The Subprime Mortgage Scam

Salespeople will come under closer scrutiny today as a result of the spate of dishonesty, fraud, and deliberate misleading of the public by the big banks and other financial institutions, mortgage and insurance companies, and real estate organizations, which caused the subprime mortgage scandal, resulting in the global financial crisis at the beginning of the twenty-first century. It was not the first fraud in the financial sector, but it was the biggest. Townsend wrote his famous book soon after the trial of con-artist Carlo Ponzi. Ponzi was sentenced to prison in 1920 for manipulating the scheme now named after him, and arrested again when he was released in 1922, to be sentenced as a common thief. He was still behind bars when Townsend decided to write an honest and businesslike book on buying and selling stocks and bonds. Ponzi died later on in poverty.

A Ponzi scheme becomes a magnet for investors and speculators by making extravagant claims of offering more interest than the norm. The swindler takes the investment money but does not invest it. Instead, he fraudulently pays out fictitious returns from the deposits of new and unwary investors. In Ponzi's case it took only a year for the cash flow to run out. Madoff appears to have carried on his swindle for about three decades before the money ran out and police made enquiries.

Deceit and manipulation are central features of digital communications media like the Internet. Scammers, con-artists, and fraudsters are natural liars who should never be believed or trusted. They are indifferent to hurting or mistreating others. Two words which describe them relate to known personality disorders. They are *Histrionic* and *Narcissistic*. Histrionic is defined as "pervasive and excessive emotionality and attention-seeking behavior . . . Individuals with HPD (Histrionic Personality Disorder) are uncomfortable or feel unappreciated when they are not the center of attention. Often lively and dramatic, they tend to draw attention to themselves and may initially charm new acquaintances by their enthusiasm, apparent openness, or flirtatiousness. Quickly turns into demands to be the center of attention . . . If not the center of attention, may do something dramatic (e.g. make up stories, create a scene)."[14]

It is often difficult to differentiate between those two personality disorders, because of the similarity of some of the symptoms. NPD is defined as a "pervasive pattern of grandiosity, need for admiration, and lack of empathy that begins by early adulthood and is present in a variety of contexts . . . A grandiose sense of self-importance . . . Routinely over-estimate their abilities and inflate their accomplishments, often appearing boastful and pretentious (& devalue the contributions of others) . . . They may casually assume that others attribute the same value to their efforts and may be surprised when the praise they expect and feel they deserve is not forthcoming."[15]

Personality disorders of that kind involve individuals in some type of delusion. In this case, it was a collective delusion of the financial industry. At the core of the subprime mortgage scandal and its social disruption, from which we are still suffering, is the very point that economist Keynes warned us about: it was based on a whim, without any firm foundation. And it was undertaken with sublime ignorance and astonishing incompetence, motivated by greed. Once the fraudulent scheme was underway, its perpetrators happily believed that if 5 percent of borrowers were unable to repay their loans, they'd still make about $2.5 billion out of them. But if 10 percent failed to repay they would lose $2.5 billion. Where did those numbers come from? Out of the air. As it turned out, more than 40 percent of borrowers couldn't afford to repay their loans, resulting in the collapse of the whole house of cards.

"The crisis of 2008 had its roots not just in the subprime loans made in 2005 but in ideas that had hatched in 1985."[16] Those roots grew from a moment when Wall Street stopped pretending that investing was anything else but gambling on bets—in which the stock exchange was a giant casino and banks had no more control over the systems than they had over their subordinates, who were doing what the "Wolf of Wall Street" was doing behind the respectable masks of long-established brand names that investors trusted.

Wrote Michael Lewis (who knew the game from the inside), "Maybe the best definition of 'investing' is gambling with the odds in your favor." But the financial system had gambled with the odds against them.[17]

You Don't Have To Be a Thief to Succeed in Business

The book you are reading is about honest persuasion by marketers who offer consumers something they will enjoy, and not the dishonest and pathological manipulation of credulous people with more wealth than good sense, or gullible victims who cannot afford to buy. It pays to be skeptical if you are on the buying side. But gamblers are impetuous or obsessive in their pursuit of a delusion of wealth that exists only in their own mind.

While it may be interesting to find out why some people seem almost addicted to taking money from other people's pockets when they are already wealthy themselves, their frauds and scandals mean that salespeople will have to work harder to transform suspicion into trust, particularly if they are selling stock or bonds, or mutual funds, or are otherwise in the so-called "wealth management" business, which must surely inspire wariness by now. (Can you really trust other people to manage your money better than you can?)

Even so, it is important to understand you don't have to be a thief to make a living by selling. Honesty is more likely to result in repeat sales. Meanwhile, every sales person juggles with *four invisible elements* that are instrumental in success or failure. And Townsend spells them out:

(1) *The quality inside the self.* Not only strengths or weaknesses, but skills and techniques that require individuals to *be themselves* and

not follow a process that doesn't suit them. In short, don't be a phony! If you have to say, "Trust me," the chances are you can't be trusted. And although that way may lead to riches, it can also result in prison. (2) *The personal attributes of a potential buyer.* We have to know the buyer more deeply than settling for a stereotype—for example, his or her life cycles. (3) *Know his or her business.* Business-to-Business needs a broad knowledge of the marketplace and plenty of research before contact, to know their history, needs and tastes, and financial scope. (4) *Know the buyer's immediate problem.* Or the immediate opportunity a buyer wishes to exploit. A salesperson won't be able to solve the buyer's problem otherwise.

But buyers don't always know what they want; so a salesperson has to ask relevant questions to find out. For a salesperson who knows the products, three direct questions may be enough. For example, in selling furniture, it may be the material of the frame—wood or steel? Or the upholstery color. Or the type of pattern. But perhaps they want plain fabric. The result of asking such direct questions should lead to the customer saying, "That's just what I'm looking for!"

Don't be deceived—the sale is not complete until you offer an alternative. Or she'll go elsewhere to check out competitors. Ask, "Which one do you want—this or that?"

Understanding life cycles made IKEA the biggest furniture supplier in the world. They noticed that young people's homes have smaller rooms, and designed downsized furniture to fit them. Cheaper upholstery was designed to be replaced and upgraded later on when buyers could afford something smarter or better. The same applies to selling automobiles, real estate, insurance, and investments, even business and industrial equipment—it is often primarily about a buyer gearing up for the next business cycle or life cycle.

Risks and Rewards

The simplest and lowest-paid form of selling is in stores where the company provides the traffic, buyers know what they want and make their own choice, and you only have to take their money. That is not *real* selling, just order-taking. A more complex need of a buyer may be to find a financial instrument to provide a lifelong income from interest or dividends. That customer may visit a bank, or you may visit their home. Each type of selling requires a different personality and different skills. The same applies to a new home builder's sales center compared with selling used homes on the open market through a broker, since one type prefers what they think of as security, while the other is more self-confident in their skills and therefore interested in aiming at bigger earnings through open-ended commission.

The greater the complexity, the higher the rewards. So the type of products or services a salesperson chooses to sell will depend on a capacity to handle complexity and take risks. Either way, a salesperson has to understand the subtleties of two different spheres—the clients' business or industry (microeconomics) and the economics of the marketplace (macroeconomics).

Making a sale may enable an individual to pay the immediate monthly bills, but there are another eleven months in the year waiting with outstretched hands. So a salesperson's job isn't done until she has built a reputation with satisfied customers who view her as a friend or neighbor or business associate. Opportunities abound in every neighborhood community if a salesperson asks for referrals.

The individual everyone went to for advice in a rural village or small community was known as a maven (certainly in New York, which is made up of small communities) meaning someone who acquired varied knowledge. Salespeople can establish themselves as the maven in their own community, particularly if they are in real estate, and draw potential customers to them, instead of cold canvassing. Join all local organizations and create personal networks. They may look to you for leadership. On the other hand, individuals will achieve nothing if they only maintain a defensive stance. General Patton's advice is always worth repeating: "Infantrymen who are waiting for orders in defensive positions are waiting to die." You have to take the offensive to win.

Your reputation for honesty and helpfulness can become your brand to promote by letter, online, texting, selectively targeted advertising, leaflets, and social networks. The immediate problem is to find out what a customer wants—then find out what is available, so that you can sell it to him, or more often her. This is a simple two-step principle for most products, but particularly for exclusive ones that may be hard to find, like collectibles. If what they *want* is not available, find out what they really need.

Finding alternatives is an essential part of selling. But salespeople must know the reasons why the alternative will solve a client's problems much better, because of the benefits she will enjoy if she buys. Finding the most valuable reason for buying may be the key to making a sale.

Suppliers of products to Walmart compete on the same shelf in the same department. But those who made a commodity similar to all the others, instead of creating a product differentiation, are merely providing a slow-mover to collect dust on the shelf. That differentiation is its "unique selling proposition" (or USP) that offers a particular benefit to a buyer. Most sophisticated marketers use that approach. For example, most small countertop ovens that grill or bake create unnecessary cleaning work by having to remove spilled food or crumbs that contaminate the bottom. But Black & Decker provide one with a floor that easily slides out to be cleaned. The USP is the ideal argument for a salesperson to make, as well as an advertiser, because it was built-in to the design as the most valuable reason to buy it at the start.

But, when cold canvassing from door to door, or calling on a trade buyer in commerce or industry, marketers have known for centuries that you must get a prospect's undivided attention to open up an opportunity to sell, or the sales pitch is doomed. Selling is a natural psychological process that uses mindful or emotional stepping-stones. That statement should give us pause to consider once again the primary motive that advertisers appeal to as the most powerful one.

Unfortunately, the Internet is a distracting force that harbors a disruptive ingredient which seduces with the most powerful motive of all. As Dr. Norman Doidge wrote in *The Brain that Changes Itself,* "Pornography growth has been extraordinary. It accounts for 25 percent of video rentals and is the fourth most common reason people give for going online. An MSNBC.com survey of viewers in 2001 found that 80 percent felt they were spending so much time on pornographic sites they were putting their relationships or jobs at risk."

If 25 percent openly admitted that pornography was their main motive for searching the Internet or renting videos, we can be sure the number is far greater because of viewers who were too embarrassed to say so. Since most users of the technology are in the main hormonal arousal age group of fourteen to twenty-four, it could be more like 33–50 percent. It raises the question of how much the Internet is only make-believe and unreliable, instead of real. Together with its porn websites, it is a prime example of reality distortion. So advertisers need to know the psychographics of the people they actually reach when they advertise online, and how much weight the Internet carries. Significantly, men are the heaviest online video users and watch them longer.

The huge pornography industry is addressed in the final chapter. But we can learn what else consumers search for online from the Nielsen Social Media Report (Q3 2011). It revealed that 22.5 percent of total time spent on the Internet is devoted to social networks and blogs, and 9.8 percent to playing games. Email involves 7.6 percent of the time, portals 4.5 percent, videos and movies 4.4 percent, search 4.0 percent, instant messaging 3.3 percent, software manufacturers 3.2 percent, classifieds and auctions 2.9 percent, and current events and global news 2.6 percent.

"All of a sudden," Michael Lewis realized, "the Internet was just another technology, less important than the steam engine, the cotton gin, the telegraph, or air-conditioning. It was nothing more than a vast delivery service for information."[18]

Divided Attention

Maybe. But the unintended social consequences are something else. We live in an Internet connected world, says Nielsen Research. Users enjoy the freedom of being connected anywhere at any time. It is a challenge for brands, and also a social challenge, because it results in fragmentation of the mind. For example, 58 percent of viewers browse the Internet while watching video programs.[19] And there is continual fragmentation between watching different TV channels in different rooms, watching the Internet and several different apps on mobile phones, and watching an electronic game on a tablet or a laptop—what Nielsen calls cross-platform.

"Divided attention affects memory encoding. It occurs when a person must attend to several things simultaneously."[20] In a number of studies, individuals allowed to give full attention to information they were asked to remember did much better in subsequent tests than those who experienced divided attention.[21] "Even our capacity to shift attention is itself limited."[22]

A question bound to arise in this context is whether it might lead to Attention Deficit Hyperactivity Disorder (ADHD). There is no evidence of it, because the cause of ADHD is still unknown. Basically, it is a neurodevelopmental psychiatric disorder which shows significant problems of lack of control of executive functions—meaning not paying attention. It causes hyperactivity. And also lack of control of the inhibitory process—or impulsiveness. It is diagnosed three times more in boys than girls, and those diagnosed in childhood continue to show symptoms as adults, of whom 2.5–5 percent suffer from ADHD. The National Survey of Children with Special Health Care Needs (2009–11) showed a much higher number of children (11 percent, or 6.4 million).

To judge from its content and characteristics, the Internet could be defined as a vehicle for deception and manipulation, even an instrument to take money from other people's pockets and put it into their own. Or as a communications vehicle to manipulate other people's lives. Nevertheless, according to Nielsen's consumer research, viewers do have power, since 67 percent switch to a different channel when commercials appear.[23]

Michael Lewis' take on the consequences is that the Internet allows the little guys to terrorize the big guys (like the hijackers who flew passenger jets into the Twin Towers in Manhattan and crashed the stock markets). But the top 1 percent is largely big guys who benefited from investing in new technologies and used their millions to speculate on the stock exchange and make billions. He admits, "It was a game people played to make money. Who cared if anything anyone said or believed was *real*?"[24]

The same applies to so-called "wealth management" companies who can't wait to get their hands on our money. But if they are so smart at multiplying assets (as they claim), how come they still spend their time scheming and finagling to get us to commit our savings to them online?

15

Selling Is a Psychological Process

A person-to-person sales pitch aimed at producing results requires continuity without distractions like the social media sinkholes on the Internet and the mindlessness of many of its advertisements or its temptations to watch erotica. And yet we frequently can't get attention when buying in a store because the salesperson is chatting, instead of closing a sale and moving on to the next customer. It is as if mindfulness and focus are in short supply and more and more people are running on automatic pilot. It was something noticed after a while with television, which was nicknamed "the idiot box," because prolonged times spent watching it caused glazed eyes and dulled wits. Gazing at the screens of computers or word processors for long periods caused other ailments, like neck cramps and back pains, and dazzled eyes that also dulled the mind. But there is no evidence from neuroscientists yet about permanent damage to brain cells.

Fortunately, there is a time-tested way to ensure a buyer listens from the moment a salesperson attracts his attention and right up to finalizing a sale. Just getting attention is not enough; it needs follow-through. Focused salespeople smile to engage with a customer. It means "I like you." Wanting to be liked makes people receptive, so they rarely turn away from someone with a contagious smile. It makes them focus, favorably. And, as we shall discover why, the smile favors saleswomen rather than men.

The age-old custom of shaking hands was originally intended to disarm people. So when we instinctively stretch out a hand for a firm handshake, we inspire trust. When selling to the trade, it always helps to say something positive and interesting about the buyer's company, his products, or his job, since it is his main preoccupation. It is what gives him his identity. His occupation is almost as dear to him as his own name. So it is not mere flattery, but recognition of his or her status and individuality.

The tried and tested way to sell was discovered by St. Elmo Lewis in 1898 by using five psychological stepping-stones, each leading to the next one, to finally result in a sale. It is described as a typical "purchase funnel." Its acronym is a woman's name, suitable for the late Victorian era—AIDA. The first "A" stands for the first step, which is to get *Attention*. "I" stands for develop *Interest* (in the product, idea, or offer). "D" stands for create a *Desire* for it. And the final "A" stands for *Ask for Action* to close the sale.

So it appeared at first that a seamless psychological flow of mindful thought and emotions along those lines would result in a satisfied customer. But it turned out not to be the case. Emotions are famously fickle and often followed by self-doubt. Failure to close some sales, and goods returned in other cases, indicated that something was missing from the psychology. Whatever it was, it made customers think or say afterward, "Why on earth did I buy that?"

Buyer remorse is fairly common after buying something too impulsively. It leads to cancellations and returns of goods. That was why a *conviction* step was found necessary to confirm that the buyer had made a wise choice. If a customer buys to fill an emotional need, it is advisable to convince her (even after having created a desire for the product) that there are also logical reasons for buying it. Then, if a buyer does falter afterward, or a spouse or friend questions why she bought it, the salesperson has already provided a good answer that should satisfy everyone. So, AIDA was transformed into AIDCA.

Even so, after convincing a buyer what a smart decision she made, a salesperson still has to finalize the sale. And inexperienced salespeople often hesitate, particularly when selling a high-ticket item. Unfortunately for the salesperson, any sign of indecision is contagious. So customers may wonder if they might have made a mistake and hastily postpone making a buying decision, probably by murmuring "I'll think about it," and moving on, after which the customer usually looks elsewhere.

Sometimes the seller's hesitation is caused by fatigue at the end of the selling process or surprise that the sale was so easy and the customer satisfied so soon. But the buyer wasn't satisfied. And yet, all it required was for the seller to ask a simple question to elicit a simple answer to close the sale, like "Visa or Master Card?" "Do you have an account or will you pay cash?" "Would you like us to deliver, or can you pick it up from our warehouse?" Or, with lower priced items, simply, "How many do you want?"

There are a multitude of reasons to justify a purchase and prevent buyer remorse. The item could be the last one in stock. Or the manufacturer may have discontinued the line. With jewelry, sunglasses, or fashionable clothes and shoes, we often hear a salesperson say admiringly, "It makes you look younger." Or "It's a fantastic bargain!" Or "Prices go up next season." Or "It coordinates with what you're wearing." There is nothing insincere or dishonest about it, since the customer has shown clear signs that she *wants* to buy it. She hesitates only because she needs reassurance and will probably look relieved when the decision is made for her. But if a salesperson lacks confidence, she will fail to convince customers and hesitate to guide a buyer's choice to purchase what she already wants to buy.

That helpful guidance is what is lacking when shopping online, so that a buyer must go to a store for that personal touch. Plenty of websites show a picture or a video of a pretty blond young woman smiling at the Internet user, as a substitute, and sometimes she is even ready to chat and reassure the buyer. It may even seduce a buyer to click in the appropriate place for their chat line on the page. Personalizing online offers is part of the art of deception. And the individual chatting to you is most likely to be sitting in a call center on the other side of the world instead of the supplier. But there are no dependable statistics as to whether the online substitute for personal service works. Logic suggests it won't work as well as personal engagement and interaction in a store. But the enormous number of online sales tends to indicate what we already suspected—that consumers in the digital society are less and less able to tell the difference between reality and fiction.

Withstanding Temporary Defeat

With more complex and time-consuming personal selling to businesses and institutions, we might consider the moral of a situation described by Napoleon Hill, who inspired and motivated millions of people.[1] He tells us how an acquaintance of his found one of the richest mines in Colorado in the gold-rush days. He set up the drills, but the vein ran out. In the end, after much disappointment and indecision, he decided to quit mining, so he unloaded the equipment to a junk man. The junk man called in an engineer to take a look at the abandoned mine. The engineer found the vein of gold actually continued only three feet away from where they had stopped digging it out. So it was the junk man who struck gold and made millions from the mine. That is why the word "persistence" keeps reappearing in just about every success story, regardless of the industry. And it is significant that many or even most historic battles (like "Waterloo" and "The Plains of Abraham") were close-run things that could have gone either way, right up to the crucial point when one side faltered and the other side won by stubborn persistence.

Failure stems from the negative mental attitude that doubt brings with it. That is why a salesperson has to think positively and single-mindedly to prevent doubts from entering the mind, from the moment he or she meets a customer, to the conclusion of a sale.

But human nature is complex, irrational, and often self-defeating. Negative memories have a habit of rising from the unconscious to distract a seller. It may be that the thought of the next mortgage installment causes hesitation or desperation. And customers are nervous about buying from a desperate seller, or one who seems to lack confidence. Anything negative can make a buyer hesitate and think "What have I missed? Maybe I need more time to think."

When a firm sale *is* concluded, the seller should immediately make a polite (but not too hasty) exit and not wait for a change of mind. Waiting may result in unintended consequences. Buying online, however, exposes all buyers to the risk of clicking on the wrong component on a website or thoughtlessly clicking to buy too soon or buying from an inferior company with a convincing and deceptive website.

Evaluating Alternatives

Being a salesperson generally means recognizing that you close some sales but not necessarily all. But it is unlikely to please those compulsive and quick-witted super-salespeople who readily assume all sorts of tactics in order to win all the time. A customer turning away instead of buying from them is interpreted as a personal insult.

When most successful salespeople lose a sale, they have two choices of what to do next. They can withdraw to analyze what went wrong and then formulate an alternative strategy to try again to sell to the same customer, using a different approach, or they can let it go from their mind and start with a new one. They will evaluate such alternative tactics every day. And, if they are fortunate to have a good sales manager who is accessible, they can discuss different options and different merchandise with him. It is what he's hired for.

Salespeople are always up against typical objections when they cold-canvass prospective buyers in different trades who are far tougher to deal with than consumers, since they spend every hour of every day examining new products from new suppliers, listening to different sales pitches, and comparing prices. They are bound to be skeptical and cynical. Four typical hurdles are flung at salespeople who cold-canvass in that quarter, time and again: (1) "I won't see you: I'm not interested!" (2) "Put it in writing." (3) "I only deal with my own supplier (or broker)." (4) "I don't know you."[2] Unprepared novices retreat in disorder. But there is always a way for experienced professionals to turn problems into opportunities.

Undeterred by the abrupt put-down of "I won't see you," an experienced salesperson may be smart enough to seize the moment by passing a message to the buyer through the receptionist: "Tell him I have an idea that will interest him but I need his advice to tailor it to his special needs." The implied flattery might give the buyer pause to reconsider what exactly his special needs are: maybe he'll even learn something to his advantage. Buyers like picking other people's brains if they can spare the time. It costs them nothing. So, curiosity may cause him to say grudgingly, "Tell him I can spare only five minutes."

If the salesman came with a well-prepared offer, headed by a USP aimed at the buyer's special needs, he will use the opportunity to introduce himself and make an impact, even if only for another time, when the buyer can't put him off by saying, "I don't know you."

"Put it in writing" is intended to deter all salespeople. But an experienced one is more likely to take it as an invitation to seize the moment, by saying, "That's exactly what I intend to do, but I need information to decide what discount or rebate I can offer your company. I'm not familiar enough with your business to know what to offer you in a letter. So, if you can spare a moment to enlighten me, I'll put my offer in writing as you suggest."

In response to "I only deal with my broker," a salesperson might say, "Of course, I understand. But I'm sure you don't do *all* your shopping from only one store. We tailor our service to your own special needs, like a specialty store. So I'm sure to offer you something to your advantage."

Instead of being deterred by "I don't know you," a professional can use the opportunity to introduce himself by pointing out that their investment vehicles are different from all others. Emphasizing an exception creates curiosity that may cause a buyer to ask *how* it differs. Perhaps there are bond issues he isn't aware of. In short, it is an opportunity to explain your seductive USP and make him a special offer.

Although those are all hypothetical responses, the situations are typical, and they exemplify what can be done to bypass the front office and reach the individual who makes decisions, then sell your service. Unlike brokerage firms that gamble with millions of dollars of other people's money, most salespeople have to be both the connector and the cold-canvasser.

Since those selling techniques are foreign to many new start-up companies, entrepreneurs are tempted to turn to selling on the Internet instead. And the total global sales figures speak for themselves. Add to them Amazon's online sales and the enormous variety of products they manage to sell, and the whole business of selling goods digitally looks highly attractive. But it requires communications experts who understand the technology, to set up a seductive entrapment system. Even so, most online sales are for regular commodities or well-respected branded goods that buyers trust. High-ticket or high-risk items like stocks, original paintings, or collectibles depend on personal selling.

Back in the peak selling period of the 1920s, Townsend wrote, "young salesmen did not need to learn salesmanship, and old salesmen forgot how to sell." That situation comes and goes in cycles of rising or falling economies and bull or bear markets. After a housing boom with buyers lining up for new homes at sales centers for six or seven years, for example, salespeople can easily forget what they knew about selling before being let go as unnecessary and replaced by clerks, who simply show buyers where to sign their name on an agreement. But when sales decline, builders need people who can sell. And new young salespeople have invariably not learned the skills, while older ones have forgotten them, just as Townsend described. It applies also to stocks and bonds and mutual funds when a bull market shows signs of roaring back. Right now, the art and craft of personal selling is largely being neglected and forgotten in favor of mass robotic online marketing, or the type of retail marketing that Walmart is famous for.

That can be an opportunity for intelligent salespeople who keep learning how to sell. Despite the overabundance of online information and all sorts of courses in community colleges and business schools, anyone who earns a living by managing sales forces knows how difficult it is to recruit salespeople who are goal oriented. Most candidates who apply have no idea how to sell. And there is a continual turnover of failures among those who are hired to sell mutual funds and other goods and services from door to door.

We may never forget how to ride a bicycle or drive an automobile, but anything requiring imaginative or analytical thinking needs constant practice to reach a stage of complete confidence with a string of successful sales. Practice starts with role-playing and overcoming obstacles under the scrutiny of a trainer or sales manager. It continues with discussions of how to overcome customer problems and choose alternatives at weekly sales meetings and rehearsing the best ways.

Selling is not for amateurs. Experts continually immerse themselves in their craft. They know the danger of fragile memories, and that getting back to work by hesitating or fumbling for words will only lead to lost sales, wasted time, and diminished earnings.

Smilers Have an Edge

We can all learn different strengths from different winners. Jack Cohen is a prime example of determination to succeed.

As a young novice in 1919, he hired a barrow and began selling fruit and vegetables in a street market in London's East End, where established traders discouraged competitors by tipping over their barrows and destroyed their goods. But young Cohen was a man of character and determination, so opposition strengthened him. He just smiled at the challenge. And he must have smiled to himself even more broadly when he opened his main store ten years later and named it after his wife Tessy.

Tesco became a private limited company in 1937. Jack Cohen floated Tesco Stores Ltd on the stock exchange ten years later. He expanded in the 1950s by buying out some of his competitors. Tesco overtook the market leader, Sainsbury's grocery chain, in 1995 to become Britain's biggest supermarket chain. Sir Jack Cohen is a lesson in character, initiative, and single-minded determination to succeed—the characteristics of a winner. Why do some people, like him, seize opportunities, when others do not?

Smiling may be the single most important ingredient in selling, because it not only transforms the smiler's outlook; it also changes other people's attitude. It portrays self-confidence. People admire that. A textbook for psychology students explains exactly what happens when you smile.[3] "We do not smile because we are happy," its authors explain; "rather we are happy because we smile." Switch on a happy smile and feel the difference! Another advantage is that happiness is contagious—it is caught by the buyer too.

"Imagine," wrote the authors, "that you and your date are enjoying a picnic in the country. Suddenly, a bull runs across the field towards you . . . Common sense tell you that you are trembling because you are afraid. But . . . emotions work in the opposite way . . . emotions occur *after* physiological reactions."

Scientific study of the smile reveals it arises first on a two- to four-month-old baby's features to mediate a social relationship by arousing a greater amount of parental love and affection.[4] Even when talking to a prospect over the phone, a smile has a way of passing through the airwaves and influencing him. So does a self-confident posture. That is because they influence *you.*

Now that we know we can control our emotions, we need never be negative or moody again. All we need to do (even when on our own) is smile. The same thing applies to assuming a self-confident posture. This technique is used by some actors to promote stage presence. By extending your body, lifting your head, and pulling back your shoulders to enlarge your chest, you can immediately create not just an appearance of confidence, but also a positive mental attitude.[5]

Focusing on a suitable target helps to stabilize one's upright posture. The target is the buyer. When a salesperson marches into his office with a smile and a firmly outstretched hand, the initiative is taken from the buyer. He will acknowledge this if he rises to take the hand that is offered to him. The salesperson will be engaging with him physically, mentally, and psychologically (and vocally with his engaging opening line to control the conversation). Not only can salespeople learn to control their own emotions by smiling, they can also learn to transform and control their attitude so that they control their environment too. It is described as charisma. Some people have it, most don't. Can its magnetism be learned? Drama instructors teach it all the time.

Wish Fulfilment

Whereas personal selling deals with the psychology of real issues, online engagement seems often to rely on fantasy-prone personalities (FFP), who may even be suffering from an identity crisis—particularly more credulous teenagers who buy, for example, numerous apps for their smartphone or search for online pornography. In more serious cases of transference, their disposition toward an overactive imagination is shown more often in violent young criminals who kill groups of innocent people for an imagined ideology knowing they will be headlined in the news media. They may represent up to 4 percent of the population who live in a continual dreamworld or are "spaced-out."[6] Celebrity tours are big in the United States in order to sell something to huge audiences, like Evangelical Christianity. More often an author's new book on dieting, exercise, or spirituality. Politicians sell themselves. President Clinton is said to demand $1 million a performance. And yet most charismatic hucksters are remarkably unconvincing when we watch them at home on a TV screen. Their falsity tends to be revealed (like reality TV or millionaire hucksters performing in business games). That they are hugely successful, at least in the United States, suggests that there are plenty of audience who simply want to engage with celebrities, hoping that some of their success will rub off on them. It is all part of the susceptibility of some people to want to transfer other people's glamorous identity to themselves with the imaginary magic of wish fulfillment.[7]

As for the impact of mindfulness, as opposed to mindlessness, or living on automatic pilot, it is even believed by some that we can change the fate of our cells by altering our thoughts and perception. And "The mind has an ability to lower illnesses."[8] Some neuroscientists believe that the mind can be trained to have positive effects, if not on one's health, which still requires more hard evidence, then certainly on one's attitude. Our perception and attitude can focus other people's attention on us in a positive way. Whether mindfulness can also cause molecular changes in the body is being studied at the University of Wisconsin-Madison and by neuroscientists elsewhere.

Assuming Leadership

There are five lessons to be learned from that: (1) Self-confidence is earned by knowledge of one's own self-worth. (2) Smiling genuinely not only immediately makes us happy, it also spreads to the buyer, so that he or she becomes receptive to engage with us because of our initiative and because it is evident that we like him/her. (3) Leadership posture not only creates self-confidence, but also engenders confidence and warmth in the buyer's perception—his mind and heart. (4) We should never underestimate what a winning smile and handshake can do–it can form a bond in which you play a leadership role. And finally, (5) you will attract a buyer's curiosity and single-minded attention by taking the leadership initiative.

Now all that is needed is a well-prepared opening remark that creates sufficient interest to establish a leadership role. That is what the

"Wolf of Wall Street" meant when he told his young stockbrokers to take control of the conversation right at the beginning.

Isaac Wolfson clearly knew how to take the initiative with people when he began business by selling clocks in the United Kingdom. He was a wise and knowledgeable Scot, of a similar cut to Andrew Carnegie in the United States. He turned the failing Great Universal Stores group into an outstanding success when he became its managing director, because he knew how to interpret the numbers on a balance sheet, and was a brilliant financier. One of his skills was recognizing how suburban family department stores lost their dedication and vigor in the next generation when sons or grandsons thought being in trade was a distraction from their profession and were embarrassed by it. It was another life-cycle opportunity. Wolfson was able to buy family stores cheap because families wanted to disembarrass themselves by selling, and he merged them into Gussies. Gussies were known as one of the safest shares to hold and recommend. He was the only person in Britain with a university named for him in his lifetime, Wolfson College in Cambridge. Dedicated to philanthropy, he established the Wolfson Foundation to share his wealth with others.

But despite carrying a perception of aiming high, salespeople are usually placed at the bottom of an organization chart in most established companies that don't depend for their success on million dollar sales. That is because most managers don't understand their volatile temperament—despite the fact that businesses need sales and no one else can provide them. Typically, a chief executive has two main vice presidents responsible to him—a creative one and an administrative one. The marketing VP is responsible for planning, marketing, advertising, and organizing sales, whereas the financial officer is responsible for payables and receivables. In a smaller company, the marketing VP may have two managers responsible to him: a sales manager and an advertising manager. Sales personnel would be directly responsible to the sales manager. The advantage of being at the bottom rung of a hierarchical ladder is that the only place to go is up.

New start-up companies are likely to differ in structure. Whereas smaller businesses may have a marketing vice president responsible for sales and advertising, some are likely to merge them with the president's responsibilities. It is often a big mistake. Sales require concentrated focus on analyzing opportunities and target markets, and planning strategies and tactics to exploit them. Those essential spheres are bound to falter with a president who has other, different tasks, distracting her.

It means she cannot focus all her attention on sales. Market forces are changing all the time and need constant watching. So do competitors' initiatives and products. It means that a new entrepreneur who is struggling to obtain finance and setting up a new company's administration and controls is likely to neglect sales, which should be the lifeblood of a company. We should never forget that 90 percent of start-ups fail before sales can provide revenues to offset the payables.

Time Can Never Be Replaced

It is not only small entrepreneurs starting up in business who have a tendency to lose track of time. Indecisive buyers often waste a salesperson's time, because they want more guidance, but then leave to shop around elsewhere. It is one reason why an experienced salesperson learns to close a sale before they leave.

Salespeople are in the opposite situation to entrepreneurs and CEOs who can jeopardize their company's future by planning only for the short term. A salesperson must seize every opportunity that presents itself and any that look likely, as if there is no tomorrow, since those opportunities may never occur again. Women (who most probably dominate the sales arena now) have an advantage that can easily turn into a disadvantage, if they are undisciplined. The female instinct to "tend and befriend" is an asset that can help them to engage with potential buyers and also make repeat sales to new-found friends. But if they forget what the acronym AIDCA means, they may find their time lost in aimless gossip instead of selling by focusing on essentials. An acronym is like a checklist to keep focused. Meandering or misdirected gossip can lose a sale.

On the other hand, ironically, it is precisely the ability to engage with people and turn them into friends that can produce future and repeat sales and referrals to new prospects. So a salesperson needs a mindfully balanced approach in order to make judgments that could affect present and future sales.

Cold-calling or canvassing is not for everyone. Most of Belfort's stockbrokers were novices in their twenties and didn't know any better than to follow a successful leader who told them exactly what to do, and avoided confusion by telling them nothing else. It restricted them to single-mindedly hunting down sales. And it worked with their top 1 percent of wealthy investors who were addicted to gambling. But sales teams that offer mutual funds door-to-door to a very different beginners market may rely on unreal statistics intended solely to motivate them—that if they make a hundred cold-canvassing calls, for example, then surely at least one must end in a sale. (Or, "throw enough mud at a wall and some of it will stick.") Wishful thinking is no substitute for common sense. And there are plenty of companies that hire young hopefuls on commission and train them to ring doorbells until hope expires. Novices repeatedly abandon selling, and those companies repeatedly hire other novices. Hiring and letting salespeople go is a continuous process for their sales managers.

Persistence is one thing, blind hope that you may just happen to call on someone who already planned to buy the service or product you offer is another. But it does happen with all sorts of products, and services like insurance and mutual funds. So, apart from frauds by dubious companies, there is a market for low-priced products sold successfully to young couples and young families in their homes, like cosmetics and toiletries, and anything else associated with sexual allure. This is where chatting up buyers may result in repeat business and referrals. But time must always be allocated wisely, with at least 80 percent focused on immediate sales and less than 20 percent on future prospects.

Since the initiative to make sales from cold canvassing depends on the character and self-motivation of salespeople, some are more like entrepreneurs. But, "There are no recipes for corporate success."[9] That is because, as Justice Oliver Wendell Holmes pointed out, our knowledge is always incomplete. So a considerable amount of trial and error continues in the marketplace of ideas. It is particularly the case with social sciences, because they involve the imperfections and irrationalities of human nature with its delusions. And fashions are always changing. Nevertheless, we can reduce the number and extent of risks of failure by intelligently analyzing the vicissitudes of greatly successful men and women who have been studied and extensively written about—described as "standing on the shoulders of giants."[10]

One of those who studied the lives and tactics of hugely successful men for clues as to why they were so successful was Napoleon Hill. He described thirteen steps to riches in his famous runaway bestseller.[11]

The Power of Great Dreams

Napoleon Hill was motivated by the extraordinary success of multimillionaire philanthropist Andrew Carnegie. Carnegie told him his "magical formula" for becoming rich. And Hill's book, entitled

Think & Grow Rich, sold seventy million copies by the time he died, making him very rich indeed. It was the sixth best-selling paperback on business in an era of high aspirations and self-development in the United States.

Hill starts off in his book by describing five characteristics that he believed could lead to riches: (1) a definite major purpose; (2) determination and persistence; (3) the opportunity that he knew from experience may appear unexpectedly through a back door; (4) it may even appear in a different form than expected—that is why it is difficult to recognize at the time; (5) don't give up at temporary defeats.

Those ingredients that Napoleon Hill considered essential for success in business and in life are compared with the views and theories of several other great motivators who follow, to identify if and where they agree on the major factors, and how they compare with Townsend, and even Belfort, when it comes not just to social acceptance or to great discoveries, but to successful selling and the acquisition of wealth.

Different times produce different buzzwords. And what Hill discovered when he analyzed the tactics of extraordinarily successful innovators was the power of great dreams to materialize if the dreamers are ambitious enough for success and riches. Among the hugely successful individuals and companies he analyzed were United States Steel Corporation, inventor Thomas Edison, Henry Ford, John Wanamaker, George Eastman, Theodore Roosevelt, King Gillette, Standard Oil's John D. Rockefeller, F. W. Woolworth, trial attorney Clarence Darrow, and inventor Alexander Graham Bell—every one of whom managed to turn wishful thinking into actual fulfillment and substantial fortunes.

What all the great motivators at that time, and later on, discovered was how to influence people by using suitable communications with key words. Perhaps motivator number one in the social stakes was Dale Carnegie (not to be confused with Andrew Carnegie) who established the most popular courses and classes aimed at achieving social acceptance. He wrote *How to Win Friends & Influence People.*[12] It sold fifteen million copies. Proof that it is the best book of its kind is that it is still in demand after eighty years.

Dale Carnegie's book is divided into four parts: (1) Fundamental techniques in handling people; (2) Six ways to make people like you; (3) How to win people to your way of thinking; (4) Be a leader: how to change people without giving offense or arousing resentment.

Each chapter ends with a one-line summary that Carnegie called his "30 principles." Some of the following principles are abbreviated:

1. Never criticize, condemn, or complain.
2. Show honest and sincere appreciation.
3. Arouse an eager want in the other person.
4. Show genuine interest in the other individual.
5. Smile.
6. Call the other person by name: it is the most important word to him.
7. Encourage others to talk about themselves and be a good listener.
8. Always talk in terms of the other person's interest.
9. Sincerely make the other person feel important.
10. Avoid arguments to avoid contradicting people.
11. Never say "You're wrong!" Show respect for their opinions.
12. If *you* are wrong, admit it openly.
13. Always open conversations in a friendly way.
14. If you can get them to agree by saying "Yes," and "Yes," they will be more likely to agree with your proposal, too.
15. Let the other do most of the talking.
16. Allow them to think the idea is theirs.
17. Remember there is always another point of view; so nod in agreement with theirs, and they will listen sympathetically to yours.
18. If you are sympathetic to their ideas and desires, they will be on your side and sympathize with your proposal.
19. Appeal to their nobler motives.
20. Dramatize your idea.
21. Throw down a positive challenge they can't refuse.
22. Start with honest appreciation and sincere praise.
23. Talk openly about your own mistakes before putting a positive spin on theirs.
24. Refer to people's mistakes only indirectly, if at all.
25. Ask questions rather than give orders.
26. Always let the other person save face.
27. Praise even the smallest improvement and be lavish in your praise.
28. Give the other person a fine reputation to live up to, and he or she will be more likely to.
29. Encourage people—show how easy any faults can be corrected.
30. Ensure the other person is happy to do what you suggest.

Those are not intended as a shortcut to Dale Carnegie, but an inducement to read his book.

Taking Control of the Conversation

The third great motivator of the time, in the self-development genre, was Norman Vincent Peale, who was one of the first to maintain that

"If you think positive, you'll *be* positive." He wrote *The Power of Positive Thinking*.[13] It sold more than five million copies and is still in demand. His philosophy is largely about how to take control of your life and be successful by having a positive outlook. The following seventeen paraphrased chapter headings illustrate what his book is about. They too are abbreviated.

1. Have faith in yourself—don't let anything defeat you.
2. A peaceful mind frees you to focus on your goals.
3. How to recharge your batteries with vigor and vitality.
4. How to release power for positive results.
5. How to choose to be happy.
6. Don't lose energy by fuming and fretting.
7. Expect the best and you'll get it.
8. Don't be defeated by imaginary obstacles—they may never appear.
9. How to stop worrying and start living.
10. Successful thinking leads to successful outcomes.
11. How faith can heal.
12. How to restore flagging vitality.
13. Invite in new creative thoughts to reshape you.
14. How to relax to release and direct power.
15. How to be appreciated and popular.
16. How to rise above grief.
17. How to draw on life-renewing powers.

Peale put life's problems into realistic proportion so that they can be overcome, instead of remaining permanent obstacles. All of it has been scientifically validated by the recent discovery that *"thoughts can change the structure and function of our brains, even in old age."*[14] Evidently all three motivators thought and expressed themselves along closely similar lines, since many of their recommendations are almost identical. They are also excellent advice for salespeople to be successful by closing sales.

The Hunt and the Kill

Sales are indispensable for any business or economy to succeed. So the founder of a new start-up company needs sales-oriented managers at the outset, to point her in the right direction and produce revenues to stay afloat, until it can break even and begin to make a profit. Urgency and focus are required. Otherwise the entrepreneur will be in constant motion but with little progress to show for it.

The advantage of an intelligent and productive salesperson being part of a new start-up is that, if it should succeed and grow, he or she may rise to management level. There is no reason why a superior salesperson should not aspire to become a multimillionaire, like Sir Jack Cohen and Sir Isaac Wolfson did—one by selling fruit and vegetables, the other from selling clocks. On a cautionary note, however, some of the best salespeople have the wrong temperament and skills for management. And, if they *are* superior, they can earn more money by selling than by managing.

Apart from the massive websites of established chain stores and department stores and big box stores, selling online frequently has a wishful thinking or desperate approach that seems to be aimed at trapping the unwary into commitments they may regret later on. And confidence in buying online depends very largely on the strength of brands that engender trust over time. Established brands have become even more important to online buyers with all the hordes of suspicious Internet entrepreneurs who seem more intent on catching the credulous in their electronic nets, rather than providing dependable products or services that consumers want or need. So buyers have to beware of the Internet.

In any case, personal selling is more flexible. It enables a seller to change her approach as a result of a buyer's reactions. It allows a seller to discover significant life-cycle factors that provide new opportunities and convey relevant information that she can *see* interests a buyer, by observing him. It provides a unique opportunity to recognize objections and instantly find ways to overcome them. For younger buyers who have not studied finance or economics, a seller can convey fascinating information on insurance, investments, real estate, mortgages, bank loans, or other specialty financial services. It also enables her to limit the information to only what a buyer needs or wants, compared with the overwhelming, desperate, often misleading, and unnecessary information on the Internet. And it enables a seller to recognize underlying reservations and bring them to the surface to counter them by providing positive solutions. Service industries in particular promise more work for dedicated salespeople who enjoy engaging with and advising other people.

Salespeople should be considered by management to be frontline troops who can prepare the market for new and future products by developing marketing relationships. Their consumer research can provide immediate feedback to marketing management about consumer response to competitors' offerings (what competitors are up to). Just as businesses have to ensure new products are developed in the pipeline, salespeople have to work on two levels: closing immediate sales and preparing new prospects for future sales. For compulsive salespeople driven by ambition, the daily challenge is almost as primal as the hunt and the kill. Analysis shows that salespeople can be usefully categorized in four ways: the *manipulative*, the *motivated*, the *unmotivated*, and *nonachievers*.

Those personality characteristics mean that about half the members of sales teams are continually being let go. In case of cold-canvassing sales, the number of failures is likely to be even greater because of lack of persistence, as well as inability to put training into practice, lack of perception, and lack of dedication. The best are likely to be born manipulators with histrionic personalities who enjoy being at the very center of the stage where the spotlights are focused. They are self-motivated. The next best are the steadily motivated.

Often the most successful salespeople are older. They relate to buyers because of their crystallized knowledge, social experience, and self-assurance. Nonachievers tend to be younger, inexperienced, naïve, and gauche.

The Top One Percent

There are three basic types of selling: *taking orders*, which means calling on the trade and asking "How many do you want?"; *sales support*, which is selling at sales centers or in stores; *getting orders*, which is what *this* chapter is about.

Selling in people's homes is known as "direct selling." businessforhome.org named 485 types of products. The average top earner in direct selling earned about $240,000 a year.[15] But to do so, they take the entrepreneurial risk of buying their products in bulk, like Amway, Organo Gold, or Nu Skin. To get close to *real* money, like Belfort did, you need to rub shoulders with the top 1 percent who are wealthy, as only Cardinals and merchant princes were in the Renaissance, or the English aristocracy in the days of empire. The question is *who are they now?* Or was Belfort just guessing or romancing?

It is difficult to put a face on who the top 1 percent in wealth really are, because wealth is the only thing they have in common. They are not only the addicted gamblers that Belfort described in his book. They are not smart speculators and philanthropic multibillionaires like Warren Buffett and Bill Gates. It is generally thought that they are either people who inherited big money, like Donald Trump, or Hollywood or TV talk show celebrities who are paid millions for their looks or wit. Or they are overpaid sportsmen who know how to hit or kick or throw a ball around so that massive audiences fill stadiums to watch them. And there are the faceless big bankers and stockbrokers, insurance moguls, and venture capitalists, whom nobody loves but everyone in a consumer society needs as moneylenders.

There are also the well-paid IT technocrats who possess a share of the action. And that's not all, according to an author who wrote a best seller named *Gold*. His book is filled with dynamic and pragmatic characters who search for gold mines and find them, from Ghana to the Congo and China. They come from South Africa and Canada, and even Britain (if you include criminals in the illegal gold industry which is bigger than the legal one). And, depending on the ups and downs of prices of other mineral resources, they don't necessarily limit themselves to gold. Diamonds have their own heroes and villains, and winners and losers, and so does oil.

"In the financial crisis of the twenty-first century, doom was in the air," writes Matthew Hart. "One theory about the super-rich saw in the growing concentration of wealth, the ultimate destruction of the class acquiring it. As they drained more and more of the available resources into their own pockets, impoverishing the other participants in the economy, they were killing the economy itself, and hence themselves. In the steady procession of awful stories through the news, there was a sense that the perpetrators of the disaster had not changed their ways. Banks engaged in criminal activities, including money laundering, interest-rate rigging, and illegal home foreclosures. As a result of the limping economy, government revenues decreased and public finances deteriorated. In this environment, gold had its best bull run in history."[16]

That was because gold (like oil and diamonds) had become the measure of fear, greed, and panic. After the collapse of Lehman Brothers—the biggest filing ever for bankruptcy in the United States—which triggered the global financial crisis in 2008, the price of gold soared: a sure sign of lack of confidence in the global economy and fear of an apocalypse. Its price more than doubled in three years from $800 an ounce to $1,900.[17] It was just one of the results of the subprime mortgage scam. Another result was the considerable increase in the number of murders in the illegal gold trade. All of those resources are stained with human blood.

Managing Sales

To be one of the few who sell high-priced goods or services successfully, it pays to learn not just how to open a sale by engaging with a prospective buyer, but by closing it. That is when most salespeople become too nervous ever to be super-salespeople in that income bracket. Recognizing *when* to close is a start. There are clear closing signals, such as when a customer reexamines the product more carefully. Or she takes possession of an item (like clips on a bracelet) takes hold of the steering wheel in the driving seat of a car, or tries out the apps. Or she may begin to read the order form. Or she nods in agreement with the salesperson's summaries. She points at samples on display. Or perhaps she remarks, "I always wanted a *more compact* printer." She might ask, "What does *this* app do?" Or "What's the difference between this and laser printing?" Nodding, "I've bought from your company *before*." Or asking, "When do you need the balance?" Or "What about a warranty?" Or "Do you sell them in *another* color?" That's the moment a salesperson says, "How soon do you want it?"

Even self-starters or big earners need advice, or a different viewpoint on a negotiation, or reviewing a client's intentions. And personal support if they develop bad habits that lose sales.

Sales managers recruit and train, plan for, organize, direct, and control a sales force, or direct individual salespeople to meet sales forecasts for a marketing organization. They ensure that salespeople know their products and consumer benefits, and a company's services. They assess how much or how little monitoring each salesperson needs. A beginner might need accompanying for a few days. Others might want personal support for bigger or complex negotiations. They also ensure sufficient advertising and promotions to provide enough leads for conversion into targeted sales.

We all make a living by selling something. Some do it better than others. All can be improved. It takes sharp focus, determination, and, yes, persistence.

Call Centers

Similar situations apply to another way of selling goods and services by phone. Call centers became a new way of life for major companies and institutions, like Sears, that chose to outsource particular departments to centers with large pools of unemployment and cheap labor. As always with low-cost labor, there are potential risks as well as benefits.

Call centers use new electronic telecommunications technologies. Working in such centers was recently described as one of the most stressful jobs in 2013. It involves long hours with an overseer standing at your shoulder to make sure you are continuously productive in taking incessant calls without stop. What used to be called "sweated labor" produces stress that results in lower productivity, absenteeism, and chronic fatigue. Not surprisingly, we don't hear of anyone claiming job satisfaction.

Here's a basic definition of a call center: "When you call, say, an airline, cable-television company, or bank, the person you deal with at the other end of the phone is a call center *agent* (or perhaps *representative, consultant,* or *associate*), and the office or department that this person works in is a *call center.* Sometimes a call center consists of just one or two people sitting beside a phone, answering customer calls. Often, it's a very large room that has a lot of people neatly organized in rows, sitting beside their phones, answering customer calls. To the customer, the call center is the voice of the company. If you're angry, you often get mad at the person at the other end of the phone. After all, you're talking to the company, right?"[18] Wrong: call centers are another example of make-believe by companies shedding responsibilities and deceiving customers by outsourcing to save money. More often than not, it involves "offshoring." And it can result in tarnishing the brand.

Hackers and Cybercrimes

All the while, persistent and shady websites are attempting to sell us something, or more likely some service that, strictly speaking, may not be on the level. Others possess deliberate criminal intent. For example, the FBI website reviewed thousands of investigations for cybercrimes during 2013, including espionage and multimillion dollar fraud schemes with their partners in law enforcement and intelligence. They involved terrorism, shoot-outs, the arrest of more than 150 pimps, and the release of 165 juveniles across seventy-six cities.

Crime has always existed, but now the Internet provides criminals with more effective, new tools that enable them to commit crimes faster and on a far larger scale across global markets. It was inevitable that computers would be used by criminal hackers and that all sorts of scams and frauds would be perpetrated on the most vulnerable victims. Internet parasites choose their own niche markets, which are little different from individuals strategically targeted by unscrupulous credit card companies and were carefully selected by financial institutions for the giant subprime mortgage scam. They are naive teenagers who love playing games online and are unaware of the dangers of interactivity with strangers. Then there are uneducated individuals and couples at the lower end of the income scale. The third target is elderly pensioners who are often confused. Many are widows or widowers living alone.

A recent scam that may be big enough to call a trend is "ransomware" that invades your computer like a virus and offers you a service to clean it of errors and problems. It portrays impressive but phony charts designed to convince you that your computer is about to crash. It is fatal to click on to their advertising to find out more about their service. Once locked on to your computer, they are like predatory wild animals that won't let go until they draw blood by demanding payment under the threat that you might lose all your information.

Whatever they claim, their main objective is identity theft. Depending on how expert they are, they may have several techniques for doing that. One is to offer their service for a small fee, like $5 to $7, to tempt you to log on to their website. Or, when it comes to pay online, instead of finding a secure payment site, like PayPal, the unwary buyer may find all her financial details stolen when she clicks on a similar but different icon. By 2015, more than half of UK users were victims of email scams. Some had all their emails hacked and scanned after phishing. The criminals trick their victims into downloading their malware.

In January 2013, "three alleged international cyber criminals were charged in New York with creating and distributing the potent Gozi virus, which infected more than a million computers worldwide and caused tens of millions of dollars in losses."

The following month, "eighteen individuals were charged for allegedly creating thousands of phony identities to steal at least $2090 million in one of the largest credit card fraud schemes ever charged by the federal government in the United States." Banks continually warn their clients not to divulge any financial details in an email. But victims get confused when they see documents that are copied from their bank, or other service companies like Bell, and tend automatically to provide fraudsters with personal details.

Since there are no national borders in the cyber world, frauds can be perpetrated from anywhere. Identity thefts and financial frauds lead the long list of different types of crimes. The most commonly known one by now involves an email that suddenly appears on the screen, purporting to be from Nigeria and asking for help. The sender states that he or she can obtain millions of dollars of unclaimed funds in a bank, which they are prepared to share with anyone who will provide the number of a bank account into which the funds can be transferred. The fraud is evidently aimed at naive couples who have some money in their bank account, and also the savings of old people struggling to live on a modest pension. Their existing savings vanish when their bank account is cleaned out. Robotics enable frauds to be carried out through emails targeted at millions of people simultaneously.

PC Security

The US Attorney's Office describes how "Nikita Kuzmin, a Russian national who created the Gozi virus was arrested in the U.S. in November 2010 and pled guilty before Judge Leonard B. Sand to various computer intrusion and fraud charges in May 2011." Two other criminals were indicted, a Latvian nicknamed "Miami," who "allegedly wrote some of the computer code that made the Gozi virus so effective," and a Romanian known as "Virus," who allegedly ran a "bulletproof hosting" service that enabled cyber criminals to distribute the Gozi virus, the Zeus trojan, and other notorious malware and to conduct other sophisticated cybercrimes."

The annual 2013 report by Norton PC Security covered twenty-four countries and 13,022 online adults aged 18–64 to determine trends in cybercrimes. They estimate there are over a million victims of consumer cybercrimes daily. Only 26 percent of smartphone users possess mobile security software with advanced protection; 57 percent are unaware it even exists; 27 percent of adults lost their mobile device or had it stolen.

The top five social media scams are (1) Hidden URLs, (2) Phishing requests, (3) Hidden charges, (4) Cash grabs, (5) Chain letters. Phishing is when sites attempt to acquire personal information, like user names, passwords, and details of credit cards, by pretending to be a trustworthy entity.

More than a third of the world's population, or over three billion people, had access to the Internet by 2015. Forty-five percent were below the age of twenty-five. The explosion in global connectivity came simultaneously with demographic transformations and rising income disparities, poor economies with tightened private sector spending, and reduced financial liquidity.

Law enforcement sees increasing levels of cybercrime, "as both individuals and organized crime groups exploit new criminal opportunities, driven by profit and personal gain." More than 80 percent was estimated to arise from organized activity, with cybercrime black markets established on a cycle of malware creation, computer information, botnet management, harvesting of personal and financial data, data sale, and 'cashing out' of financial information. Subcultures of young men engaged in computer-related financial fraud have emerged in developing countries, with nearly 14 percent being email accounts hacked, over 4 percent responding to phishing attempts, nearly 4.25 percent identity theft, nearly 4 percent online credit card fraud, 2 percent burglary, 2 percent robbery, and over 1 percent car theft.

Individual victimization "is significantly higher than for conventional crime forms." Material targeted for removal included child pornography, hate speech, content related to defamation and government criticism, "raising human rights law concerns in some cases." Nearly 24 percent of Internet traffic is estimated to infringe copyright.

The most significant cybercrime threats are child pornography (2 percent); personal harm and/or solicitation of children (4 percent); identity offenses (2 percent); breach of privacy and acts supporting terrorism offences (18 percent); fraud and forgery (8 percent); sending spam (6 percent); trademark offences and computer misuse tools (8 percent); illegal access to acquire computer data (23 percent); illegal access to computer system (19 percent); and illegal data interference or system damage (10 percent).

16

Knowing and Understanding

We rarely stop to consider how the person we are addressing is thinking, or how he or she perceives us; how much he or she really knows about what they are saying; or how much about life they understand. And most people are generally bad listeners, more comfortable with the sound of their own voice—particularly now they feel empowered by the Internet and social media.

Philosophically detached and analytical thinking is more usual in philosophers and psychologists who observe human behavior with skepticism. It requires not only a finely focused mind, but also a broad and profound worldview that enables creative ideas to rise to the surface from a reservoir of concepts waiting to be reassembled into more meaningful patterns. This chapter is about those rare types of individuals who possess those kinds of attributes, but are hard to describe because they are exceptions to the general run of people. Odd, quirky, different as they may be, they are assets the world needs in an age of anxiety that the twenty-first century brought us on a tidal wave of debris from the past.

The root of our anxiety is a growing world population and our shrinking resources that eighteenth-century economist Malthus warned us about—that populations increase faster than the food supply, forcing more people to become dependent on government welfare. But the labors of those not on welfare "will purchase a smaller quantity of provisions than before and consequently more of them must be driven to ask for support."[1] For example, the global population was approximately two billion before World War Two. It was estimated at 7.16 billion on March 26, 2014, and is expected to reach nine billion by 2046, making us victims of our own success.[2]

One of the pressures of overpopulation is a jobless society for far too many, with more and more marginalized people forced to use food-banks and more homeless people living on city streets. As pressures increase, the age-old conflict between rich and poor will quicken and harden a belief that the rich are enemies of the workers, the jobless, and the poor. It is accentuated by the ever-widening income gap between CEOs and workers in commerce and industry and the huge wealth of the top 1 percent. The only way that situation can be avoided is to use different energy resources and find new technologies or ways and means to increase food and energy supplies, as we have managed to do almost continuously until now. But Malthus's prediction is rapidly approaching reality—a possibility scheduled for somewhere before 2050. Oil supplies in particular were diminishing and the price of a barrel of oil was expected to double in the foreseeable future. Only the global recession prevented it.

No one expected the price of oil to plummet at the end of 2014, with far-reaching consequences. And, from all we know of price fluctuations of commodities, no one can predict what the price of oil will be two years from now. Nor when solar energy will replace it. What managers must recognize is not only discontinuous change but also the speed of reversals since the recent boom and bust scenarios in banks and real estate development from Ireland to Iceland and from the United States to China. It is a new kind of volatility resulting from globalization, instant worldwide digital communications, and a lust for cheaper and cheaper labor.

Despite investment advisers whose livelihood rests on their claims to predict the future, none of us can. What we *can* do is separate illusions from realities. And, with more and more illusions created by the high-tech industry, that may turn out to be the prime attribute of more intelligent and pragmatic managers. "Daddy must now reassure eyewitnesses that they didn't see what they think they saw."[3]

It is assumed by now that the sudden and unexpected plunge in oil prices was manipulated by OPEC members with the intention of forcing North American competitors out of the market by making it unprofitable for them to continue to supply oil. One of the effects of the low price was to influence the Canadian government to agree at the G7 summit meeting in June 2015 to gradually phase out all fossil fuels and replace them with other energy sources that will not pollute the atmosphere with carbon gases.

Pessimists forecast a dramatic increase also in the price of food and water, as over-fishing to feed our expanding world population has already depleted the amount of fish in the seas. The possibility of wars to obtain food and water is predicted, as the United States went to war in Iraq to control oil supplies.

Climate changes have increased the necessity for new ideas in the marketplace that are aimed at our very survival. The competition claimed by some is between automobiles and people, since more and more food is being produced for use as bio-fuel to replace oil, instead of distributing it to the poor as food. Saudi Arabia's short-term tactic of dumping is likely to change that. It may be seen by many as a battle between bio-fuel for the rich and food for the poor. It is described as a turning point for mankind that will be followed by economic turmoil. And there is the ever-present possibility of nuclear war. But whose brains can we depend on for our future survival?

Neurogenesis

A pervading theme throughout this book is that many of the dependable worthies who led us in the past were either naïve or remarkably mindless, insular, and unimaginative—hence the folly of two world wars that could have been avoided if reason had ruled, instead of the shortcomings and irrationalities embedded in human nature. It is similar to the theme running through Nietzsche's *Thus Spake Zarathustra*, when he appealed to readers to be more mindful and focused, to attempt to develop their intellects and their skills and sharpen their reasoning.

Reason was to play the major role in Nietzsche's plan for more mature supermen. It took on new significance after the brutish Nazi ideology with its mindless attitude toward the consequences of its violent and destructive antisocial actions that retarded progress during the twentieth century. What he called "supermen" would be indifferent to human obsessions with wild animal instincts, by aiming at a much higher and evolved level of development—knowledgeable instead of ignorant, rational instead of emotional and superstitious, and just. It brings us to the present cognitive revolution and the discovery of the neuroplasticity of our brain that changes itself.[4]

Now, "higher level sensibilities" and even "mental activities outside of awareness" are being discovered, almost as if Nietzsche was leading the panel launching the discourse.

No doubt that was why Dr. Norman Doidge was anxious to clear away any misconception that studies being undertaken by neuroscientists could turn us all into supermen and superwomen. Science now knows ways to improve an individual's cognition, in order to remember more clearly, to think faster and sharper, and even more rationally, as a consequence of research with fMRI machines to examine different parts of the brain. But another aspect of our age of anxiety is our aging population with all its typical ailments. So the main preoccupation of neuroscientists is reversing such medical conditions as the shrinkage of parts of the brain through aging, like the hippocampus, and inflammation which is "the cornerstone of Alzheimer's disease."[5] Neurogenesis is the capability of reversing the damage caused by our self-destructive lifestyles.

Several different panels of medical experts on the highly respected TV talk show in Toronto, named *The Agenda*, gave their opinions on how to improve cognition.[6] All agreed on the following points: (1) Memory loss is reversible, and regular physical exercise, like aerobics, is the best remedy to push back cognitive decline. Evolution developed our brains to make us better movers, and they need oxygen to make new stem cells and prolong their survival. Exercise keeps our hippocampus growing.[7] And studies showed it lowered Alzheimer's by 60 percent.[8]

(2) Retain normal weight. (3) Maintain a healthy diet.[9] (4) Don't smoke. (5) Drink only in moderation. (6) Avoid neurotoxins, since they shrink neurons. Not only nicotine, and lead and mercury from outside, but cortisol (or hydrocortisone) which our adrenal cortex produces in response to stress. Therefore also avoid stress, which releases glucocorticoids that can kill cells in the hippocampus.[10] (7) A regular sleep pattern of around eight hours a night is needed to eliminate waste products from the brain, or cognition is compromised. (8) Learn new things, experience novel environments, and be connected to small groups of people.

It takes no imaginative stretch to picture how such evolved individuals who follow all those markers would be viewed differently by a society that cannot resist eating huge amounts of junk food and is overweight or obese, drinks to excess, and probably still smokes or takes toxic drugs. That is the reality. So evolved and self-disciplined people are likely to be considered different or eccentric by the majority—most probably as smug and self-righteous spoilsports who make everyone else feel guilty about their failings. But it is precisely that difference in self-disciplined nonconformists that enables them to produce extraordinary new insights that replace outdated theories in the marketplace of ideas. They are not deluded by false ideologies, superstitions, or other fantasies. Nonconformists initiated the English Industrial Revolution because they were practical, and nonconformists fleeing religious persecution in Europe colonized North America.

Nonconforming, by definition, only means being unconventional in a conservative society. Whether they are realistic initiators who follow those eight rules for a healthy life-style, or abstract idealists who agree with Nietzsche's philosophy, they will stand out among the generality of people whose ideas are restrained or even blocked by the limitations of their knowledge, their imagination, their understanding, or self-discipline.

People who do not conform in speech or dress or daily habits have always been considered as oddballs or eccentrics that society either dismissed in the past or laughed at for their bizarre behavior. Now they are the very people we need to rethink our future. We also need to bear in mind that people who don't conform to the herd consider those who do to be strange or odd. It begs the question of what or who is "normal."

Nonconformists

Hopefully, the preceding pages will have opened readers' minds to new possibilities for self-liberation and self-development and to aspects of life, leadership, and management that they had never thought deeply about before.

Although various ways of choosing suitable personnel were commonplace in the past, one significant change since the Internet is the way jobs are advertised more prosaically online, either by digital technicians turned entrepreneurs or on social media. Such descriptions as "body-shops" versus "head-hunters" are now rarely, if ever, used online. The general impression conveyed by most popular job sites is much like an old-fashioned rural marketplace where unemployed villagers stood around on the village green to be scrutinized by prospective employers looking to hire cheap labor rather than for any other reason, bypassing other candidates with considerable experience or special skills. Bargains were one of the earliest competitive advantages on offer in the agricultural and industrial eras, and bodies cost less than mindful heads. But bargain-hunters often regret what they pay for when they fail to recognize they need value. Value, in the case of personnel, was previously equated with character. And superior education aimed at developing and enhancing it. Not so much now.

An element in this book that may have raised some eyebrows is the psychologists' classification of a type of character described as *neuroticism*, which was listed as a competitive advantage in seeking creative employees. The very word *neurotic* can ring alarm bells in the minds of people unfamiliar with psychology, as if neurotics are dangerous, when the only people they might possibly endanger is themselves. In fact, the difference between neuroticism and being a nonconforming oddball, or eccentric, is often slight. The term is frequently used loosely to describe anyone who does not conform, "unconventional and therefore strange" by definition—when diversity is exactly what we should be looking for.

For example, anyone reading about the character of the legendary Steve Jobs would surely regard him as neurotic, rather than simply quirky. He was manipulative, conflicted, contradictory, intolerant, and rude. He rebelled against authority. And, like that other genius of Menlo Park, Thomas Edison, people remarked on his lack of body hygiene, because he dismissed regular bathing as unnecessary.

In fact, people have generally become more acceptable of personal foibles in the West since the permissive society of the mid-1960s, and in particular since the threat of impeachment of President Clinton for his sexual misdemeanors at the end of the twentieth century. We no longer expect everyone to look and talk and dress and behave alike, as a previous class-conscious society did. We have become a more classless society, seeking to be recognized as individuals instead of classified by status, color, race, or gender. Steve Jobs simply took informality and individuality a step further toward oddity.

When PC designer Osborne produced the first truly portable PC on time and within budget, smugly declaring that "Adequacy is sufficient. All else is superfluous," Jobs said, "This guy doesn't get it. He's not making art, he's making shit." He was right. As English intellectual Malcolm Muggeridge admitted in old age, "What hurts most is the preference I have so often shown for what is inferior, tenth-rate, when the first-rate was there for the having." Steve Jobs understood that; he was a perfectionist who could not compromise. As far as the end product was concerned, he always aimed at first-rate value.

And yet, his biographer Walter Isaacson describes how he behaved: "As they proceeded to visit other Japanese companies, Jobs was on his worst behavior. He wore jeans and sneakers to meetings with Japanese managers in dark suits. When they formally handed him little gifts, as was the custom, he often left them behind, and he never reciprocated with gifts of his own. He would sneer when rows of engineers lined up to greet him, bow, and politely offer their products for inspection. Jobs hated both the devices and the obsequiousness. 'What are you showing me *this* for?' he snapped at one stop. 'This is a piece of crap! Anybody could build a better drive than this.'"

Global Celebrity

Jobs had become a global celebrity by then. And, since he was now a millionaire, and wealth is worshiped in the United States, he could evidently do no wrong. Social classes may be leveling out but money still establishes power. Nevertheless, it would take only one mistake for Apple's shares to crash to the ground and lose millions for investors and Steve Jobs. And it could happen from something as small as his choice of colors for one of his devices. One error and he would be reduced to tears of failure and humiliation—which was his customary reaction when he felt he'd let himself down. He walked on a razor's edge of conflicting emotions. No wonder he was given to manic depression or bipolar disorder! He dithered uncertainly. His wife declared that, by that time, "He was just completely obnoxious and thinking he could get away with anything." But appearances were deceptive—he was a tortured man.

Jobs' intensity at a meeting with NeXT's staff was described in *Esquire* magazine by Joe Nocera, who wrote, "One moment he's kneeling in his chair; the next minute he's slouching in it; the next he has leapt out of his chair entirely and is scribbling on the blackboard directly behind him. He is full of mannerisms. He bites his nails . . . His hands . . . are in constant motion."

Those could be described as symptoms of an obsessive-compulsive disorder. Now that he'd left Apple, Jobs was under considerable pressure to make a success of his new computer through innovation. And he had to show Apple's president who was the better CEO. But evidence that Steve Jobs was an obsessive-compulsive who was determined to prove his worth does not diminish his powers of innovation and invention. Nonconformity is one of the routes that often leads to creative brilliance. There are numerous examples.

It is worth elaborating on one of the most famous mathematicians at the legendary Bletchley Park, where a number of brilliant intellectuals were hired at the outbreak of World War Two in order to crack the enemy's military and naval codes. Alan Turing would become a legend for his brilliance in inventing the computer as we know it today, and also as a neurotic at a time when the English establishment was nervous about people who did not conform to their own accepted social behavior. When ill-used by the establishment because he was different, Turing famously committed suicide by injecting cyanide into an apple and eating it.

On the other hand, Mozart is an ideal example of the type of jocular manner and unreserved vocabulary and vulgarity, and a smutty sense of humor, that opens the door to new ideas. He composed about six hundred pieces of sublime music in a life span of only thirty-five years.

Studies of his mood swings, impulsive behavior, and his letters have led to the conclusion that he probably suffered from Bipolar Disorder. Wagner (who was entirely humorless but given to romantic fantasies) has been posthumously diagnosed as suffering from Borderline Personality Disorder. Both are universally admired as, perhaps, the greatest composers of classical music.

A more contemporaneous eccentric nonconformist was the brilliant modern artist Sir Stanley Spencer, whose biblical paintings grace the walls of leading art galleries and a special one devoted to his own one-man exhibition in the village of Cookham beside the Thames, where he grew up. Spencer was one of Britain's most famous twentieth-century artists. To understand the type of personality and outlook that motivated his art, it is helpful to read a twentieth-century English novel that was surely based on him.

The hero of Joyce Cary's famous 1944 novel, *The Horse's Mouth*, is an artist who decides to stop behaving conventionally as English society demands, because he finds it unnatural to conform. Alec Guinness wrote a screenplay from the novel and acted the manic role himself in a 1958 film.[11] It struck a chord in Britain, where a whole class of people rebelled against having to conform to an establishment they considered dull, boring, and incompetent. The film may have launched the permissive society of the 1960s that derided incompetent authority figures. A famous television comedy series, *Monty Python's Flying Circus*, dismissed them with laughter. And the candid BBC television journalist, James Mossman, began grilling idle and incompetent politicians in front of TV cameras to reveal how hopeless they were, and hold them to account.[12]

Giving in to Temptation

But innovation seems counterproductive to business organizations set up in the old-fashioned way with a culture intended to last forever, explains Michael E. Porter in *The Competitive Advantage of Nations*. "Past approaches become institutionalized in procedures and management controls... Personnel are trained in one mode of behavior... questioning any aspect is regarded as bordering on heresy . . . Individuals who challenge established wisdom are expelled or isolated."[13] That is what happened to Mossman, who was fired by the BBC.

It is worth repeating how Freud and Otto Rank defined neurotics in the simplest possible terms when they claimed there are only three basic types of people in the world—neurotics, psychotics, and most people who just get on with their lives however they can. Psychotics are destructive, whereas neurotics can be creative—fortunate to be able to sublimate their different thinking and vision of life into innovating, inventing, creating art, and discovering new scientific truths, alternative approaches, and new ways of doing things. And brilliant people are always eccentric, by definition, because brilliance does not conform to the behavior of the majority.

Several individuals described in these pages could not resist a temptation to undertake extraordinary achievements. On one hand, there are scientists and mathematicians driven to solve mysteries of the universe. On the other hand, there are people like Belfort's young stockbrokers with their overaggressive behavior, who could not resist the temptation to sell valueless stocks and bonds to their clients and outdo each other with increasingly bizarre behavior. And there was the eccentric Steve Jobs, who could not resist expanding the boundaries of his imagination with his "reality distortion," by designing innovative electronic devices that created pleasurable illusions. His were the temptations of rich mindfulness to think in broader terms of real creative value, compared with a mindless loss of control, resulting (in the case of the stockbrokers) in destroying other people's fortunes.

The latter personality characteristic is the impetuous and potentially dangerous one that psychiatrist Wilhelm Reich studied among vagrants and agitators in Vienna's public polyclinic, which he managed for Freud in the early part of the twentieth century. His patients were a danger to society and themselves. Reich classified them clinically as "the impulsive character." So we have to remember that there are two different sides to impulsivity, neither of which conform to society. One is tempted to contribute to society by creating, innovating, or inventing, whereas the other is antisocial and psychotic and seeks to vandalize and destroy.

A Turning Point

The idea of using the illuminated intellects of impulsive characters who are mindful and imaginative thinkers came about in 1939 with Bletchley Park, when extraordinary mathematicians were needed to decode German military intelligence to win World War Two. Even though they succeeded beyond the dreams of Prime Minister Winston Churchill and the administrators managing the group of scientists, it was not until the 1950s with the discovery of DNA that we became aware, once again, of the almost limitless capacity of the human mind to discover universal secrets.

"In every age there is a turning point," wrote Professor Bronowski, "a new way of seeing and asserting the coherence of the world."[14] Two eccentric scientists (molecular biologists James Watson and Frances Crick) stretched the boundaries of the imagination to discover the structure of the DNA molecule and became 1962 Nobel prizewinners. It was not until the turn of the twenty-first century, with the legendary Steve Jobs, that the minds of eccentric and imaginative people could be seen to have possibilities of being harnessed for commercial exploitation.

Business leaders who move with the times and know how to recognize useful talent, instead of conforming to outdated ways of doing things, know that business enterprises and government institutions usually hired safe people who look like us, but lack the imaginative spark, or are even negative influences whose single-minded worldviews discourage progress. Some may have been conscientious but were unskilled at dealing with dualities, ambiguities, and paradoxes, because of a limited worldview. And academic worthies with an encyclopedic reservoir of knowledge about one subject in their unconscious minds, who knew the latest theories from the classrooms, were often unable to put them into practice. It took school dropouts like Michael Dell, Bill Gates, and Steve Jobs to create imaginative flights of fancy, harness them, and turn them into reality. Old-thinking companies and institutions hired ordinary people when what was required were extraordinary ones. What we learnt from them and Apple is the advantages and profitable use of nonconformity.

Indifference to the Past

Since competition for resources favors individuals with characteristics that are advantageous, the marketplace of ideas needs creative people who are either bubbling over with a multitude of new ideas, one of which may survive, or a lifelong pursuit of just one brilliant idea that may change the world.

The world's present preoccupation is with global warming, new energy resources, different ways to produce more food, and toxic air pollution in major cities. The clock ticks away the hours while we watch our existing resources disappear with nothing to replace them. There is nothing new in this—previous cultures chopped down their forests for fuel. The unintended consequences were land erosion, famine, and the disappearance of civilizations. The question is how to find inventors or leaders to solve our problems before the alarm bell tells us it is too late. That is why business enterprises and research institutes require different varieties of individuals with different backgrounds and skills aimed at producing new ideas and seizing opportunities for new solutions to old and new problems.

We have been fortunate in the past that problems generally produced leading thinkers who could solve them. But sometimes it took centuries. Perhaps the two most famous examples of this are Charles Darwin and Alfred Russel Wallace, who discovered what is described as the most important single scientific innovation of the nineteenth century. Their extraordinary story has been told many times before. Both were devoted to natural history and dedicated to solving its mysteries. It was a time when most people still believed that all species are immutable. In other words, that God had created all life in its present forms that never changed from the original template. It was still considered blasphemous to claim otherwise. Then came a moment when each of them discovered that what had been commonly accepted as fact was only make-believe to cloak the embarrassment of our ignorance.

Darwin found various mocking birds during his famous voyage on the *Beagle* and brought back several specimens to show that each possessed a different shaped beak, which it used as a tool to extract food in different natural conditions. It was clear evidence (when he had the time to think about it) that species do change. In Wallace's case, he had often wondered why some species live while others die. He suddenly realized the answer after witnessing a volcano erupt in the Rio Negro and destroy thousands of species.

Our own survival depends on possessing or adopting suitably dominant and advantageous characteristics—like speed or strength, brainpower, cooperation, audacity, or deception—whichever overcomes the threat to our survival. Genetic mutation is how animals with dominant advantages, in what we might call the world of ideas, change into superior species to replace outdated ones over time. Natural Selection as the prime mechanism for evolutionary change is now absorbed into mainstream culture and is considered to be Darwin's greatest contribution to science.

So, was Steve Jobs' "reality distortion" a metaphor for genetic mutation, like deliberately breeding racehorses or domestic dogs? Possibly. Seeing things differently and doing them differently is a result of creative perception. Darwin was able to pick up clues while observing the terrain, then assembling them afterward to form an entirely different concept of the world and our position in it, than was formerly accepted for want of a better thesis in the marketplace of ideas. But there is also a darker side to the equation, since the same metaphor also accommodates the concept of artificial intelligence which may replace our individuality and sap our free will, as a consequence of a technocratic delusion that it is more useful than human brainpower, when it is evidently inferior in many ways.

The question is whether we have the most suitable learning environment for nonconforming and inventive individuals to flourish in our own time. It took Jack Welch to remark, when CEO of General Electric, that we will have to abandon everything we ever learnt in the past and think differently. It required courage to make such a claim openly, because it conflicts with established cultures that cling desperately to old ways of doing things that they have become conditioned to. Large and old-fashioned organizations and institutions are often unable to find their way out of their labyrinth without being led. He was able to lead GE. But where are our leaders now?

There is also a danger of how literally to take such a sweeping injunction. Abandon *everything*? There is now a questionable opinion expressed by the Internet generation, that since we have the whole world of information online, we don't have to learn anything anymore. Why spend years in a classroom when we can logon to find what we don't know on Wikipedia? What they are saying, without thinking it through, is that we no longer need to undertake and develop the personal experiences previously required to think, to know, and to understand before we make judgments and decisions. It presents us with a paradox, because the marketplace of new ideas cannot be ignored, and those who express that viewpoint belong to the fourteen to twenty-four age group, which is the most influential one in the twenty-first century.

Although only a theory, so far, it may discourage young people from learning history. Concern is already being expressed in thoughtful circles that most young people are disinterested in history anyway. Many commentators remark on their indifference. Some claim the only history they are interested in is their own and that nothing that happened before they were born is worth studying, since it takes only minutes to Google it.

It is ironic that their indifference to history, and their ignorance of it, comes at a time when teenagers are searching obsessively for their own identity in a narcissistic drive never encountered before. And yet they fail to understand that they can only find their identity at its source in biological, social, cultural, and political history.

A Survival Strategy

When the National Assessment of Education Progress (NAEP) released its findings on progress in mid-2013, it stated that the subject in which students performed worse was US history, with only 12 percent proficient. Evidently the development of standard-based education has devalued social studies in preference to reading and mathematics. Not only are students behindhand with history, but even the textbooks have not kept pace with what scholars now know about the subject.[15] There was no significant change in 2014. Some US schools are still afraid to upset superstitious parents by teaching their children about evolution. It suggests that public education in the United States is directed more toward a survival strategy for the poor than encouraging students to live a rich full life and contribute to science and the arts. It is part of a flattening out process toward mediocrity that democracy encourages and digital media conditions us to, in a so-called "level playing field."

Although it may be convenient to forget the violence and corruption of preceding years, America's identity is founded on the genocide of First Nations Americans, black slavery, racial prejudices and oppression, neglect of women's right, exploitation of the environment which will affect future generations, and a great deal more that we may wish to sweep under the carpet by deleting or rewriting history books. Progress requires us to remember past mistakes and understand the reasons for them, so that we can put them right and prevent them from happening again. We also need to keep in mind the evolution of ideas with the great philosophical and scientific discoveries of the past, all the social trends like the separation of church and state, and judgments and choices and battles that led to our own civil liberties and human rights, so that we can be vigilant in protecting them from encroaching governments. Otherwise we invite repetitions of past injustices.

Another irony in dismissing the past as irrelevant to the present and the future is that we now live in a global society. Only history can tell us how other societies arose and developed, and why they fell, and who took their place as well as our own history that tells us where we came from and how we managed to survive to become unique individuals and citizens in a democracy with a specific set of cultural values. And every new young generation which does not know or understand the past will have to reinvent its ideas all over again for centuries. Nevertheless, evolutionary psychologists and neuroscientists know that we see everything through the lens of the past, from which we draw our values, our strength and identity.

But a new young generation has appeared since the Internet, who are unaware that the world has always been a dangerous place. They believe, as many do, that progress always runs in a straight line, when in fact it constantly turns back on itself. Just when we thought we had reached sophisticated modernity in the twentieth century, a world war almost toppled us back into the primordial slime of Nazi Germany. History may be only the result of unintended consequences, but what it teaches us about the dysfunctions and mistakes of human nature are important lessons for our own survival. History is the only realistic yardstick we have for measuring our lives.

Nevertheless, it is doubtful if the digital generation views the world through clear and objective eyes. The technology gets in the way of the view. Instead, they are caught up in a romantic type of emotionalism borrowed from popular romances, fictional crime mysteries, and TV soap operas that transform reality into fiction. And no amount of education is likely to bring them back from imagining the cyber world is the real one.

Inertia

One of the lessons we learn from history are the centuries of sterility when one mindless establishment or another holds on to power by keeping people in ignorance and preventing progress. And our defenselessness allows other nations or cultures to become a threat. It can't happen now, because of the digital gateway that opens with a click onto the rest of the world. But what appears to be happening instead is exactly what Aldous Huxley surmised in his *Brave New World*, "the truth is being drowned in a sea of irrelevance."

"Twenty-first-century America is in a state of decline," writes literary critic Harold Bloom.[16] "It is scary to reread the final volume of Gibbon these days because the fate of the Roman Empire seems an outline that the imperial presidency of George W. Bush retraced and that continues even now. We have approached bankruptcy, fought wars we cannot pay for, and defrauded our rural and urban poor. Our troops include felons, and mercenaries of many nations are among our 'contractors,' fighting on their own rules or none at all. Dark influences from the American past congregate among us still. If we are a democracy, what are we to make of the palpable elements of plutocracy, oligarchy, and mounting theocracy that rule our state? How do we address the self-inflicted catastrophes that devastate our natural environment? So large is our malaise that no single writer can encompass it."

Social psychologist Gustave Le Bon was the first to understand why historians failed to discover the real causes of the French Revolution (and we might add the causes of World War One, which are still in doubt). They stopped short of the truth, he said, because they never analyzed the minds of the people who make history.[17]

Thinking, Knowing, and Understanding

One management specialist categorized five distinctly different types of thinking, all of which are important to an executive and everyone else. They are causative, inductive, deductive, problem solving, and the type of thinking particularized here which is creative thinking. It involves impressing a particular problem on the mind, visualizing it with great clarity, and contemplating it with the intention of formulating an idea or concept on new and different lines.[18] Neuroscientists now know it even increases the brain capacity.

Scientific thinkers, like author Arthur Koestler and mathematician Henri Poincaré, referred to an experience of "instinctual thinking," perhaps adding a sixth category. This type of thinking can be either almost instantaneous or intermittently processed over a long period of time for a particularly difficult and stubborn problem.[19] Koestler called it "thinking aside," because too much concentration can frighten the solution away. It is more often known as lateral thinking. Poincaré described the most fertile process as choosing combinations of different ideas or concepts from different domains. "Most combinations so formed would be entirely sterile; but certain among them, very rare, are the most fruitful of all."[20]

Most creative people refer to the experience simply as gut-feel. Some see it as a useful shortcut when there is no time to make more thoughtful judgments. Evidently the process works only when the thinker is well read and possesses very broad interests, from which he or she can discover new ways to exploit opportunities or solve problems. It is an ability that knowledge workers and creative people like scientists and artists possess because of their own unique encyclopedic knowledge assembled in their unconscious mind.

"For the artist with his organic, vivisectional (or living section) point of view of man and society, the natural enemy is the bureaucrat, the man with the tidy desk, the big file, the orderly mind devoid of

simultaneous modes of awareness or observation."[21] So said the prophet of the digital revolution!

Unfortunately for Britain and the United States, it was those unimaginative bureaucrats who laid the foundation for industrial failure with short-term solutions, like firing employees while distributing huge profits to shareholders and CEOs, instead of modernizing infrastructures and investing in new technologies. They failed to imagine industrial life cycles when old-fashioned docks and assembly lines would have to compete with new state-of-the-art robotics from Germany and Asia, resulting in the decline of shipbuilding on the Clyde and of automobile manufacturing in Detroit.

Britain lost its continuity by the mid-Victorian era by failing to educate and train future generations for science and engineering and industry, because it became overextended, like Rome, and had to rely on the worthies of an orderly civil service, instead of imaginative, entrepreneurial, and assertive merchant adventurers of the past. And, while Germany and Japan retained their artisan and apprenticeship traditions, the United States was even more short term in its management culture than the United Kingdom, relying more on a philosophy of "Take the money and run."

Simultaneous Awareness and Observation

Marshall McLuhan's "*Simultaneous modes of awareness and observation,*" are the very keys we have been searching for to define the criteria required of superior leaders and managers. They are the same attributes found in geniuses in the sciences, the arts, and commerce and industry. And there is a paradox here too, since they are required to deal with ambiguities, whereas artificial intelligence can handle none of it. It means that the superior individuals we need may have to be geniuses who are not likely to be lost in the illusions of cyber space.

The twenty-first century is an extraordinary era, with its boundless information on one hand and the world's desperate needs on the other. Whoever can put those two concepts together with a third one, to discover how to replace fossil fuels before they run out, or reduce environmental toxins, or find ways to provide more food for our burgeoning populations, will surely be a genius. And whether that genius turns out to be a scientist or an entrepreneur, it is the marketer who will have to lobby governments and convince users and consumers to transform their farming and eating habits, and mode of transport.

In fact, new ways of farming that are contrary to the old are being discovered. And some consumers are changing their eating habits to avoid manufactured food processes and potentially hazardous food additives that some human beings cannot tolerate. There is some likelihood, as well, of the introduction of an electric self-drive automobile.

So what is genius? And how can we acquire it? Eminent literary critic Harold Bloom, who spent most of his life searching for wisdom, wrote one book with that title which required more than eight hundred pages of explanations. He wrote others too, in numerous attempts to provide examples of literary genius alone. Genius, says Bloom, is the trait of standing both of and above its age and the gift of breathing life into what is best in every living person. In his book of geniuses, he names and profiles a hundred geniuses of language alone.[22] "There are evidences of wavering," he writes, "among those who have dismissed genius merely as an eighteenth century fetish. Groupthink is the blight of our Age of Information, and is most pernicious in our obsolete academic institutions, whose long suicide since 1967 continues. The study of mediocrity, whatever its origins, breeds mediocrity."

One of his observations on genius is particularly significant: "All genius, in my judgment, is idiosyncratic and grandly arbitrary, and ultimately stands alone."

Idiosyncrasy: "A personal peculiarity of mind, habit or behavior; quirk."[23] *Arbitrary*: "Not done according to any plan or for any particular reason."

The idea of the authority of genius, Bloom tells us, was first established by ancient Roman tradition as an alter ego, since its authority was attributed to the gods who carried past wisdom alive into the present. In their case the gods were emperors, like Augustus. But, he says, "our canonical standards for genius are now institutionalized confusions, so that all judgments as to the distinction between talent and genius are at the mercy of the media, and obey cultural politics and its vagaries." He quotes Emerson, who claimed it is all in us (but not that we all possess it). Today neuroscience confirms it. "Were you ever instructed by a wise and eloquent man? . . . Were not the words that made your blood run cold, that brought the blood to your cheeks; that made you tremble or delighted you, did they not sound to you as old as yourself? Was it not truth that you knew before?"

The octogenarian Harold Bloom belongs to a Jewish cultural tradition of lifelong search for wisdom. He found it in the mystical kabbalah which seeks the attributes of God and also of divine man seeking

261

perfection. He quotes Greek mathematician Longinus next. Longinus called literary genius the sublime which an author transfers to readers. "Touched by the true sublime your soul is naturally lifted up, she rises to a proud height, is filled with joy and vaunting, as if she had herself created this thing that she has heard." Bloom then goes on to say that "The reader learns to identify with what she or he feels is a greatness that can be joined to the self, without violating the self's integrity." To confront the extraordinary in a book is to benefit from the author's genius, which is the best path for reaching wisdom, "which I believe to be the true use of literature for life."

Of course, that is all very literary. Even so, we should have no difficulty in transforming his joy at finding sublime wisdom in literature to the excitement of discovering sublime truths in science with, for example, Einstein's elegant equation: $E = mc$ square, which explains how the mass of an object or system is a measure of its energy content. Or Ludwig Boltzmann's equation to describe his discovery that entropy occurs when energy is degraded and the atoms assume a more disorderly state. Entropy is a measure of disorder that he wrote in his now-famous formula as $S = k \log W$, which is inscribed beneath his bust on his tombstone, to represent the second law of thermodynamics. Or the eureka moment when the young Charles Darwin followed the branches of the tree of life and suddenly realized that all life-forms must be related to each other. And the instant when Alfred Russel Wallace suddenly became aware of why some life-forms survive while others die.[24]

Each discovery represents the invasion of reality by imagination. But they are bound to beg the question: "What have scientific and artistic geniuses to do with salaried marketing managers working for established market leading business enterprises, or an entrepreneur starting up her own small company?"

The answer has already been expressed in several different ways before, in attempts to achieve clarity. It is that, ever since the formation of the ancient Chinese civil service and the British administration of its Indian colony, we have relied on responsible and creative individuals to produce leadership, order, and results for us. The leadership came from government. Order was imposed by civil servants. And the results were produced by merchant adventurers motivated by profits. It was a time of limited competition and great distances that required and provided immense time for information and directions to flow across vast oceans, whereas there has never been a time of greater competition than today in the industrialized West and Japan, and with developing economies like China and India, South Korea, and Taiwan. And information now flows as instantly as a click of a key.

One result is we need dedicated and superior creative and innovative managers on whom we must depend to carry our growing populations through to the next century, by replacing our dying fossil fuel era with something more efficient, less costly, and less environmentally hazardous.

Meanwhile, a problem confronting imaginative ideas and innovations is the habit of leaders and entrepreneurs to set up a bureaucratic foundation to administer the company or institution, which is trained to follow established rules and regulations. And yet, every new genius produces some innovation which, when invented and approved, subverts the rules previously established.

The urgent need for something better than daily administrative adequacy that may satisfy bureaucrats who are not paid for imagination or initiative comes at a time when many companies have reverted to a common preference for cheap labor to cut costs, rather than develop business by addressing consumer needs with integrated marketing skills. Much of our present labor force, as a result, consists of young and inexperienced beginners who are often poorly trained. And a lack of mindfulness, knowing, and understanding can only result in further retreat into make-believe fantasies, spectacles, distortions, and delusions.

17

Facts and Figures

The following is a breakdown of global market shares of the most popular electronic communication devices ever invented.

World's Top Selling Mobile Phone Brands (Q1, 2015)	Millions of Units	Global Share (Percent)
1. Samsung	97,986	21.3
2. Apple	60,177	13.1
3. Microsoft	33,022	7.2
4. LG	19,637	4.3
5. Lenovo	19,280	4.2
6. Huawei	18,590	4.0
7. Xiaomi	14,740	3.2
8. TCL Corp	14,189	3.1
9. ZTE	12,600	2.7
10. Micromax	8,158	1.8
11. Others	161,921	64.9
Total	460.3	100

Source: Gartner, June 2, 2015.

Six Chinese phone manufacturers made their debut among the top ten mobile phone vendors in 2015. And iPhone sales in Greater China outpaced their US sales for the first time, increasing Apple's profits by a record 33 percent. "The growth rate in China is significantly higher than most parts of the world," said Apple, whose market value surged to more than $772 billion, making it the world's biggest brand.

The huge share of market of other smaller manufactures is a reminder of the situation with personal computers in 1992, when they were the most popular communication device. IBM was market leader with 12.4 percent share, Apple second with 11.9 percent, and a large number of small clone makers sharing 60.5 percent between them.

A Search for New Ideas

Which are the most innovative countries that continue to come up with new ideas and which have run out of ideas are shown by the most recently listed applications to register patents.

Number of Patent Applications (2013)

1. China	825,132	32.1%
2. United States	571,612	22.3%
3. Japan	328,436	12.8%
4. Republic of Korea	204,589	7.9%
5. Germany	63,167	2.5%
6. Russia	44,194	1.7%
7. Canada	34,741	1.3%
8. United Kingdom	22,938	0.9%
9. France	16,886	0.6%
10. Hong Kong SAR	13,916	0.5%
World total	2,567,900	100%

Note: Since the more up-to-date World Competitiveness report of 2015 informs us that Japan made the second largest number of patent applications in 2014–15, it is likely that Japan now takes precedence over the United States.

Source: WIPO, 2015.

Productivity Is Critical

"Productivity is the real critical determinant of real income growth over the long term," wrote Michael E. Porter.[1] But a transformation took place in manufacturing when countries like the United States, the United Kingdom, and some economies in the European Union failed to compete with Asia. Jobs swung into the burgeoning service industry instead, to fast-food outlets, tourism, hospitality industry, and health care. Since their wages and salaries are less than, for example, blue-collar workers in industries like automobile manufacturing at its peak, a question arises as to what percentage of labor needs to be employed in manufacturing to provide sufficient financial momentum to support an economy without deficits or debts.

There are exceptions, such as predominantly agricultural, mining, or other primary resource economies. For example, Canada's Department of Supply and Services commissioned a study by Michael Porter's Monitor Company in 1991, entitled "Canada at the Crossroads." It stated,

Percentage of Labor Force in Manufacturing

Taiwan	36.2
Iran	34.4
China	29.5
Italy	28.3
Sweden	28.2
Russia	27.8
Japan	26.2
Germany	24.6
France	24.3
S. Korea	23.6
EU	22.7
US	20.3
UK	18.2
Canada	13.0

Source: Central Intelligence Agency (CIA).

Note: Years researched vary from Canada in 2006, Iran in 2008, China in 2011, and Taiwan in 2012.

"One sign of truly competitive industry is sustained exports to many countries because this signals more robust competitive advantages," whereas 75 percent of Canada's exports went to the United States in 1989. The ratio increased to 82 percent and continued to grow to 87 percent in 2002, but decreased to 73.71 percent in 2011, because of additional export partners. But the recommendation to develop the size of its manufacturing sector was ignored by subsequent governments, so that even its infant technology sector in Kanata, Ottawa, failed to grow and foundered without government support.

Apart from lost job opportunities, failure to manufacture competitively also had a negative effect on marketing. Marketing and advertising standards were higher in the United Kingdom and the United States when they were manufacturing economies. Simultaneously, in contrast to previous decades, most families in the West experienced no gain in real after-tax income since the 1980s. The severity of the 1990–91 recession was a sign of underlying structural problems, and the global financial crisis that began a decade later demonstrates that they have not improved.

"The manufacturing-services link is becoming an important part of the argument that a nation cannot afford to ignore its international competitive position in manufacturing," Porter claimed in *The Competitive Advantage of Nations* in 1990; "a nation cannot expect its service sector to replace lost manufacturing exports." But, by now, with the continued introduction of automation, and the resultant unemployment, the entire question of labor consumption is problematic.

Global Competitiveness Report (2014–15)

National Strengths and Weaknesses

Despite the global economy moving "at a less decisive pace than it has after previous downturns, and heightened risks looming on the horizon [which] could derail the global recovery," the following survey by the World Economic Forum of the leading economies in the world reveals their considerable expertise. The report defines "competitiveness" as "the set of institutions, policies, and factors that determine the level of productivity of a country." A more competitive economy is more likely to grow faster over time. The following 20 economies, listed according to global rankings, are necessarily selective out of 144 analyzed in the report. They are our most likely business competitors, or markets for export; most of them are skilled in using the very latest technologies.

1. *Switzerland*: Placed first in the world for six consecutive years and top in innovation, for its high spending on R&D, its strong cooperation between academic and business worlds, and the sophistication of its companies that operate at the highest end of the value chain. With flexibility between employee protection and the nation's business needs, it possesses the most stable macroeconomic environment in the world. Nevertheless, it has difficulty finding qualified workers.

2. *Singapore*: Placed second for four consecutive years for outstanding stable performances across all measured criteria, it tops the goods market efficiency rating and is second in labor and market efficiency and financial market development. One of the world's best institutional frameworks (third). World-class infrastructure. A sound and dependable macroeconomic environment and fiscal management, with a budget surplus of 6.9 percent of GDP (in 2013).

3. *The United States*: Recovering from its crisis, the United States regained its third place as a consequence of improvements in its institutional framework and a more positive perception of business sophistication and innovation. Its fiscal deficit continues to narrow.

An excellent university system that collaborates with the business sector in R&D. Flexible labor markets. Largest domestic economy by far in the world, making the United States highly competitive. But its business sector is still critical of government and politicians. Its biggest weakness is its macroeconomic environment.

4. *Finland*: Possesses well-functioning and transparent institutions (first) and a high-quality infrastructure, a superior skilled workforce and training system, and high levels of technological readiness. But, due to a higher deficit and public debt (though manageable), it suffered from a slight deterioration in macroeconomic conditions.

5. *Germany*: A reliable institutional framework that collaborates with universities and research labs. Predominantly innovative medium-size companies that supply niche markets and are located close to each other. They weathered the global economic crisis well, partly because of their strengths in competitiveness, with companies spending heavily on R&D. But their education system was assessed less positively than in previous years.

6. *Japan*: Largest improvement of all top ten economies across all criteria. Continues to possess a major competitive edge in business sophistication and innovation. First for six consecutive years, second in R&D spending, third in availability of talent, world-class research institutions. Made the second largest number of patent applications per capita in the world. Its companies operate at the highest end of the value chain with high value-added goods and services. But held back by severe macroeconomic challenges. One of the lowest hirers of women in the labor force.

7. *Hong Kong SAR*: One of the most open economies in the world. Tops the infrastructure criteria with the outstanding quality of its facilities across all types of transport. Dominates the financial market criteria, due to high level of efficiency, trustworthiness, and stability of its system. Dynamic and efficient goods market (second) and labor market (third). Has a high degree of technological readiness. But needs to improve its higher education and innovation, and its limited availability of scientists and engineers.

8. *Netherlands*: A stable competitive profile of a highly productive economy. Excellent educational training system (third). Strong adoption of technology, and excellent innovation capacity with highly sophisticated business, efficient institutions, and a world-class infrastructure. Highly competitive (fifth). Hindered only by rigidities in its labor market.

269

9. *The United Kingdom*: Improved its position from lower levels of fiscal deficit and public debt. Benefits from an efficient labor market and a high level of financial development. A highly competitive and large market allows highly sophisticated and innovated businesses to spring up and develop. But effective ways are needed to raise the overall quality of the education system, particularly in maths and science. The most problematic factor to doing business here is difficulty to access loans.

10. *Sweden*: Possesses important strengths across all measured criteria, with a stable competitiveness profile, with strong, efficient, and transparent institutions. Excellent infrastructure and healthy macroeconomic conditions with low levels of fiscal deficit and public debt. Has the right conditions for innovation in a knowledge-based society. High-quality education and training provide the right skills for innovation. Problems are high taxes and labor market regulations.

NOTE on Europe and Eurasia: Portugal, Italy, Bulgaria, Romania, and Greece score relatively low among the top ten most competitive economies. It marks a European divide between a highly competitive northern Europe and a less competitive southern and eastern Europe. France and Italy show little progress in improving their rankings, whereas Greece and Portugal are implementing necessary reforms.

12. *United Arab Emirates*: Its competitiveness reflects the high quality of infrastructure (third) and its efficient goods market (third). A strong macroeconomic environment, with strong public trust in politicians and high government efficiency. But requires further investment to boost health and educational outcomes to place the economy on a more stable development path. Necessary also are a strong focus on R&D and business innovation to diversify the economy and ensure stability of economic growth.

13. *Denmark*: Favorable macroeconomic conditions. Its higher education and training system provides a workforce with needed skills to adapt rapidly to a changing environment with adoption of high levels of technology and innovation. Has one of the most efficient and flexible labor markets with strong employer relations and a large percentage of women in its labor force.

14. *Taiwan*: Stable over the past six years. Its strengths are its capacity to innovate, highly efficient goods markets, world-class infrastructure, and strong higher education. It needs to further strengthen its institutional framework which is undermined by some government inefficiency and various forms of corruption. Some inefficiencies and rigidities in its labor market need addressing. Encouraging and

assimilating more women into the workforce would help to enhance its competitiveness.

15. *Canada*: This is its lowest rankings in nine years. Canada is disadvantaged by lagging innovation. Must improve its overall competitive performance after persistent declines, to sustain its high quality of life and create opportunities for the future, or the standard of living will be at risk. Graded high in health care and primary education. But steep decline in its infrastructure, particularly the quality of roads and railroads.

17. *New Zealand*: First in institutions criteria and third in development of financial market. Excellent education system. Efficiency of its goods and labor markets is among the highest in the world.

18. *Belgium*: Improved its competitiveness level. Came third with its excellent maths and science education and second with its top-notch management schools, with a strong propensity for on-the-job training. A high level of adoption of technology and highly sophisticated and innovative businesses in a competitive market. Its environment facilitates business creation. Problematic are its government's efficiency and the regulatory burden, as well as a tax system that reduces incentives to work, and its public debt.

26. *Republic of Korea*: Stable, with excellent infrastructure. Enrolment rates at all education levels are among the highest in the world. A remarkably sound macroeconomic environment. A high degree of technological adoption and relatively strong business sophistication. But prevented from closing the competitiveness gap with the other three Asian Tigers as a consequence of its weak financial market development.

27. *Israel*: A world-class capacity for innovation (third) with innovative businesses benefiting from some of the world's best research institutions (third), government support, and a favorable financial environment for start-ups. But the educational bar needs raising because of poor math and science levels and poor primary schools which could undermine innovation in the long run.

28. *China*: Not yet an innovative powerhouse. And no longer an inexpensive location for offshoring manufacturing, it is losing manufacturing contracts to less developed economies. Problems in its financial sector with access to loans for SMEs remaining difficult. Government efficiency is improving, except for corruption and security concerns and low levels of accountability. Lack of transparency. But its public debt is among the lowest in the world, and it has a gross savings rate of

50 percent of GDP. Although trends are positive, complacency should be avoided.

29. *Estonia*: Best performing economy in eastern Europe with a solid competitiveness profile and strong and efficient institutions. A solid macroeconomic environment and high levels of education and training. A more efficient labor market than most in the region. But needs to focus on strengthening innovation and business sophistication.[2]

The Pornography Industry

Similar trends occurred with the Internet as happened previously with radio, cinema, and TV. Begun as a medium for information, art, and entertainment, it turned into a mass medium for popular entertainment, as box office takings and pay-TV shows were in demand. But whereas pornography was censored in cinemas, it became big business for pay-TV and an even bigger industry online, where more visitors access porn sites each month than search for Netflix, Amazon, and Twitter combined.[3] Porn is, perhaps, the most significant example of reality distortion, confirming that consumers choose make-believe over reality. Seventy percent of men and 30 percent of women watch pornography. And 30 percent of all Internet data are porn, according to huffingtonpost.com. Now Optenet claims 37 percent of Internet pages contain pornographic content.[4]

Research by NBCNews.com showed the largest group of viewers of Internet porn in 2004 was of age between twelve and seventeen years old. A study by Queen's University in Belfast in 2005 showed one-third of viewers admitted downloading and passing on porn. Half said they'd been exposed to sexually explicit material by coworkers while on the job. Another survey by Elle/MSNBC.com in 2006 showed that 37 percent of couples watched porn together. There were 420 million pages of pornography at the end of 2004.[5] In December 2005, there were 63.4 million unique visitors to "adult websites," reaching 37.2 percent of Internet audiences.[6] By 2010 the amount of Internet users searching for pornography reached 43 percent.[7]

Since more than half of online searches are likely to be for pornography by now, perhaps we should question the Internet's claim to be a serious, realistic, or dependable medium for research. In fact, many universities encourage students to use traditional libraries for more reliable research material. And, since it is advisable to match advertising communications to media that engenders the same reliable image as a marketer's products and services, we should also consider the suitability of the Internet for advertising.

Japan is either an exception or the forerunner of global sexual habits or addictions. "Hundreds of thousands of young men are known as *hikikomori*, shut-ins who eschew human contact and spend their days playing video games and reading comics in their parents' homes." They have withdrawn from dating. "Instead, they focus on online porn and

A. US Industry Revenues (2006)	$ Billions
Video sales and revenues	3.62
Internet	2.84
Cable/pay-per-view/in-room/ mobile/phone sex	2.19
Exotic dance clubs	2.00
Novelties	1.73
Magazines	0.95
US total	13.33
B. Worldwide Revenues (2006)	**$ Billions**
China	27.40
South Korea	25.73
Japan	19.98
United States	13.33
Australia	2.00
United Kingdom	1.97
Italy	1.40
Canada	1.00
Philippines	1.00
Taiwan	1.00
Germany	0.64
Finland	0.60
Czech Republic	0.46
Russia	0.25
Netherlands	0.20
Brazil	0.10
Others: 212 (unavailable).	97.06

Source: familysafemedia.com

games like Nintendo's Love Plus, in which players conduct a relationship with an anime girlfriend."

"The marriage rate has plummeted, and with it the birthrate . . ." By 2005, 60 percent of women and 72 percent of men had never married. With wage stagnation since the 1990s and rocketing housing prices, they cannot afford it.[8] Those are examples of how the economy shapes consumers' lives, and businesses often exploit them.

When Watsonian Behaviorist Professor Skinner designed little boxes for his experimental rats to press levers in order to be provided with food if they performed the right tricks, or punished with an electric shock if they did not, they were intended to represent human beings and discover something about motivating us by rewards and punishments. Wrote Dr. Norman Doidge about people watching pornography online, "The men at their computers looking at porn were uncannily like the rats in the cages of the NIH, pressing the bar to get a shot of dopamine or its equivalent.[*] Though they didn't know it, they had been seduced into pornographic training sessions that met all the conditions required for plastic change of brain maps. Since neurons that fire together wire together, these men got massive amounts of practice wiring these images into the pleasure centers of the brain, with the rapt attention necessary for plastic change. They imagined these images when away from their computers, or while having sex with their girlfriends, reinforcing them. Each time they felt sexual excitement and had an orgasm when they masturbated, a 'spritz of dopamine,' the reward neurotransmitter, consolidated the connections made in the brain during the sessions."[9]

The Internet draws us into an impersonal and artificial world in which we become dehumanized by technology and where reality is distorted by alienating us from the real world outside. We are becoming mindless robots, doing whatever a software program orders us to do, without discriminating, instead of using our judgment or initiative, our imagination, or our will to avoid their tunnel vision.[**]

---

[*] The National Institute of Health is one of the world's foremost medical research centers.
[**] Some claim its single-minded linear attitude (which often takes us in the wrong direction) is due to the insistence of the industry on excluding women programmers. It is reminiscent of the stereotypical male driver who stubbornly resists asking his wife or daughter for directions when lost.

18

The Law of Unintended Consequences

Apart from the selectivity and limited scope of this general summary of some of the problems and challenges of the technological disruptions in our society, no other thorough study, nor any scientific cost–benefit analysis, has so far been produced to show whether the discontinuous changes and their unintended consequences were really worth the effort, the cost, the leaks of military, personal, and industrial information, the massive unemployment and shrinkage of our consumer base, the immeasurable waste of our time, the huge loss of personal fortunes, and the frustration and discontent involved in all the distractions and fraudulent transactions. As with deindustrialization and offshoring, we might discover the costs of its disruptions outweigh the benefits.

The digital revolution began in the latter half of the previous century and continued hand in hand with the global financial crisis at the beginning of this one. By that time, a ruthless capitalist philosophy of naked greed (regardless of its consequences) had been proudly flaunted and celebrated in the financial sector, insurance, real estate development, and even educational institutions, all single-mindedly set on short-term profits, regardless of the consequences. Perhaps the best example of greed and the gambling sickness that pervades society today is shown by the rise and fall of two former technology giants, Nortel and J. D. S. Uniphase.

Nortel was a multinational telecom company, based in Canada, that couldn't seem to go wrong and was recommended almost daily as a fast-growing but safe stock that everyone should invest in—not only by most portfolio managers, but also politicians, who informed us that we would be wise to invest in the company to provide us with secure pensions in our old age. Nortel's value represented over a third of the value of all companies listed on the TSX, and employed 94,500 worldwide. Despite its failure to turn a profit, stock market

275

speculators pushed up its value. Its stock price finally rocketed to $124 (Canadian) a share, then suddenly plummeted to only 4 cents. In January 2009, Nortel initiated bankruptcy protection proceedings and ceased to operate.

The crash left individual investors and pension funds with huge financial losses, and sixty thousand former employees without jobs. The cause was considered to be market saturation, caused by the type of accelerated volumes produced by robotics and automation.

It could be argued that fund managers did what they do best—pitch investors and institutional funds to buy their recommended stocks. But they were subsequently proved to have been almost always wrong with their recommendations, year on year. It also turned out that the CEO had already sold his own stock options and made a personal gain of $135 million (Canadian) nine years earlier.

Several years later, a number of investors did what financial advisers told them to do when share prices fall—persevere for the long term and buy even more stocks to average out the losses when the stock recovers. Pensioners, and other investors who had bought millions of dollars worth of stocks, got out their laptops and bought millions more online, and lost the lot, since prices never recovered but continued to fall even further.

J. D. S. Uniphase is based in California. It designs and manufactures products for optical communications networks, test and measurement equipment, and lasers and optical solutions. It was as much a favorite of high-tech stock investors as Nortel—both often being recommended in the same breath. Its price doubled at least three times, and JDSU offered investors three stock splits around 1999–2000. It made millionaires of a number of employees who held stock options. But then came a telecom downturn. J. D. S. Uniphase announced the largest write-down of goodwill in July 2000. The price of its stock plummeted from $153 a share to less than $2. Employment was reduced from 29,000 to about 5,300. Several of its factories and other facilities were closed down when the telecommunications industry crashed. Although considerably downsized, JDSU is a survivor. Its stock currently trades at $12.78, less than 10 percent of its recommended value when it peaked.

Both technology companies were victims of greedy speculation that attracted masses of other investors in what Alan Greenspan wryly called "irrational exuberance." He was referring to the excitability of the herd instinct, which is far more influential now that the emotional plague is spread instantly and globally on the Internet.

Know Before You Go

"Know before you go" is the catchy phrase Google used to launch the major benefit of its "Street View" maps. Those four significant little words succinctly encapsulate the very opposite of the mindlessness that caused not only the disruptions from new technologies, but also the global financial crisis that followed from the banks' lack of foresight, or consideration of the consequences of lending money to low-income people who couldn't afford to repay it.

Meanwhile, business executives have been hindered from using their core skills of leadership, management, marketing, or innovation, by the introduction of the new consumer technologies, instead of viewing them simply as tools to get something or other done quicker and more cheaply. Knowing where to go is more typical of the collective responsibility of thoughtful Japanese managers who are obliged to consider the social implications in the long run, rather than America's orientation to purely short-term rewards inscribed on the bottom line of the next balance sheet.

Although the United States controls 75 percent of the new digital technologies, artificial intelligence let them down badly on 9/11, and in most subsequent military actions against rogue states in the Middle East and North Africa whom they erroneously blamed for the Manhattan tragedy. Those failings were the result of poor or nonexistent strategic planning, limited use of human intelligence on the ground, and mindless errors arising from irrational knee-jerk reactions. Then, using remote-controlled drones instead of ground troops in treacherous territories resulted in considerable civilian casualties, with lack of confidence in American military forces. So that what is now grudgingly admitted in some circles is that no technology is perfect, and it is generally more effective to use human beings.

Nevertheless, digital hardware and software makers seem to have deluded themselves that they are infallible and we must do whatever they program us to do, without question. Of course, it is in their own interest, since it means money in their banks and increases in their share values. Meanwhile, we abdicate to their demands like mindless sheep. Users who are discontented are afraid to object in case they are accused of being unable to adapt to change—even though all changes are not necessarily good.

A very large part of the problem has been the limitations imposed by the rejection of human intelligence by technologists in favor of artificial intelligence. We might call it their blind spot, or the tunnel vision of

277

the "mad scientist" syndrome. But now they have finally discovered the limitations of artificial intelligence and its obvious flaws when used on its own. The problem in finding a solution of how to blend human intelligence with artificial intelligence is recognizing the flaws in one and the exact limitations of the other. Fortunately, the recent discovery, through fMRI technology, of the implications of the mysterious plasticity of the brain has moved the conversation from the idolization of computers and robots to the potentially richer resources of the ever-changing human brain that grows as it learns.

Neuroscientists consider the brain of an infant, and even a tiny bird-brain like the gray jay's, to be superior to artificial intelligence. The jay finds and hides food in up to ten thousand different places for the winter, when its survival depends on remembering exactly where it stored each meal. The part of its brain responsible for memories (the hippocampus) visibly increases in size to accommodate all the memories. It provides a clue to the plasticity of our own brains that continually grow new cells to store our own new discoveries for future recall, comparison, analysis, and consideration, to help us solve problems. And our unconscious minds are always working a step ahead of our awareness.

Perhaps that should not surprise us when the evolutionary process of continual improvements to our brains and bodies has been going on for millions of years.[1] What jays have in common with us is they remember the past, imagine the future, and plan for it. Computers can't do that. Software programmers have to think for them, because of their limitations.[2]

Human Curators

As a result of human intervention, what we are likely to see in future are known as curator-led technologies—artificial intelligence driven or led by human minds. Curators are overseers or managers.

That practice of curation is now also being applied to "interaction with social media, including compiling digital images, web links and movie files."[3] There are now "biocurators," meaning scientists who curate, or collect and annotate, or validate biological and organism databases or information. Manufacturers who are becoming more aware of the imperfections of robotically automated goods are conscious of a necessity to use the flexibility and imagination of human curators together with artificial intelligence. That situation is not new—American automakers had problems when introducing robotics in the 1980s, before they discovered that Japanese competitors had gone a step further by mixing robotic mindlessness with the flexibility of human creative intelligence.

Similar flaws exist in cyber warfare and subversive Internet campaigns between competing nations like the United States and China, which are also fraught with technological glitches, limitations, and errors, since intelligence information networks are insecure and continually being broken into.

It certainly seems that whichever way we turn, we find failure resulting from one or other of the new digital technologies. "Disruptive" has now become a commonplace word to describe how some new electronic devices get in the way of how we traditionally tackled our flow of work, which may now, with considerable frustration, take us from about four to ten times longer than before. That is despite the instant characteristic of digital technology. Global productivity is down. The main problem is being distracted from real work in the real world by imperfect digital tools and the illusory nature of computers, social media, and the Internet.

Business executives and professional writers who have to use word processors for their work lose their sense of purpose when they are prevented from achieving best management or marketing practices, or creative and idiosyncratic content, by software that prevents them.

Software, like hardware, is still in its infancy and therefore subject to continual improvements. They often fail from design flaws, just as electric appliances do. Perhaps companies like Microsoft can be persuaded to reduce its failures by hiring more women for a more balanced view. To repeat that provocative remark made about the typing culture in the 1920s, when men typists were replaced by women, it was claimed to be because "Women are superior to men, their greater quickness of perception and motion give them obvious advantages." It was confirmed when MI6 hired thousands of code-breakers at the highly successful Bletchley Park in 1939–45: 75 percent were women. It is one of the many spheres that could benefit from their perception and natural tendencies to seek and find friendlier ways to achieve results. Microsoft began with the intention of making digital devices easier and quicker to use, and therefore more effective, instead of more and more complex. They appear to have forgotten that professional managers need ease and speed and greater accuracy to save time for more important priorities by using the type of minimalism admired by Steve Jobs.

Disruptive Transitioning

Of course, we know we are still in a transitional stage, and change brings unintended consequences. It could even be argued that the seeds of our discontent with the new technologies were sown first in the eighteenth-century English Industrial Revolution, when weavers and other artisans in cottage industries were put out of business by manufacturing plants in major industrial cities, like Manchester. It was there that the first rumblings of dissent and rebellion came from Friedrich Engels and Karl Marx with their Communist Manifesto. What caused Engels to rebel was his first-hand experience of the appalling working conditions in the Lancashire cotton mills where capitalists, like his own father, sought to make profits by hiring cheap labor—just like today. Poorly paid women and children replaced men in industry, while their unemployed husbands or partners were obliged to undertake domestic chores at home, take care of the infants, and darn their wives stockings for them.[4] The digital revolution has taken us back to the nineteenth century in that regard, since two incomes are necessary to support most households in comfort today, but robotic factories require practically no human labor to work a twenty-four-hour workday for seven days a week. As a result, we see unemployed men pushing prams today, or carrying their babies on their backs, picking up their infants from kindergartens, and taking care of the domestic chores for their partners, as others were obliged to do two centuries ago.

Overproduction was not slow to follow on the heels of the technological revolution that began to take place around 1740 and which required additional overseas markets for manufactured goods in the 1800s. That problem was solved for a time by supplying Britain's own colonies. Even so, the markets became saturated with goods by 1870, when the first major "Great Economic Depression" began, and Britain turned its capital to invest in service industries (like catering and money-lending), instead of continuing to invest in manufacturing.

Regardless of Britain's change of tactics, production became a dominant force in countries that copied the English Industrial Revolution, like Germany, America, and Japan. Britain was no longer the "workshop of the world." Instead of planned and measured marketing with forecasts and production schedules to meet specific needs in particular markets, overproduction of arms and armored vehicles in heavy industries turned into an arms race which resulted in the Russo-Japanese

War of 1904, after which Germany's industrial overproduction created a surplus or dominance of arms and armor and explosives that led to World War One, followed by the second one.

Britain is no longer a prominent manufacturer today. Nor are some other Western economies that choose to outsource and offshore manufacturing to China, India, Bangladesh, Mexico, and other areas of huge unemployment and cheap labor. One result is their once-valued brands and public image are tarnished or degraded, through appalling working conditions and poor or nonexistent quality control. We hear of and see the results of collapsing premises and fires that kill hundreds of workers, much like the similar scandal of the ill-famed Triangle Shirtwaist Factory in New York City in 1911, where 146 garment workers died in a building with no usable fire escapes; 123 were young women from the age of fourteen who fell or jumped from the eighth, ninth, or tenth floor windows to their deaths on the sidewalk below, or choked to death on the fumes. Most were recent Italian and Jewish immigrants who had been locked inside unsafe premises by their employers—just like those we hear about in countries offering cheap labor today, like Bangladesh. This is one of the ugliest faces of the drive for cheap labor today. The other is the menace of overproduction by robots that take jobs away.

That is the prospect for Mexican auto workers who are presently paid only one-tenth of what auto workers earn in North America and less than they are paid in Asia. They are well trained and their work is not inferior. And there is plenty of logic in what may appear in the news media to be their cheap labor force, since the cost of living is far lower in Mexico. So they are better off than they were before. Now they can have pride in their work as skilled labor.

But the digital technology that enabled automakers to train and use Mexican labor has its own consequences for economies like the United Kingdom, the United States, Canada, France, Italy, and even Germany. The drive to cheap labor could even rock Germany's economy and disrupt the EU.

Other Disruptions

One of the results of innovation today, when everyone aspires to an automobile or owns one, is that vehicles no longer require human minds to chart the best routes, since GPS navigation devices on the dashboard or windshield automatically show or tell us which way to go, even to avoid traffic, consider weather conditions, or take shorter cuts. But having artificial intelligence choose for us encourages the type of mind-lessness that makes us uncompetitive. And, sooner or later, Google-type self-driving cars will carry us mindlessly to our destinations, where we are destined to play passive roles to robotic devices that will tell us exactly what to do next, and leave us no choice—as computer programs do now.

That suggests that the twenty-first century may be known to future historians, not as a period of technological innovations, but as the century when individuals could no longer separate truth from illusions and the West became too soft and indolent to think for itself or even protect itself. We appear to have abdicated initiatives to algorithms.

The range of dislocations and anxieties caused by the Internet and social media is, of course, too vast to describe in just a few pages. As we already saw, with the hackers and cybercrime, hate pornography, and child solicitation, the Internet harbors a varied tangle of ever-changing lies, financial frauds, corruption, terrorist propaganda, manipulation, and mind control from every type of stalker. Among other disruptions to society, it has helped to publicize, romanticize, and even idolize the criminal activities of a great many mentally disturbed and delusional individuals. They include, for example, the psychotic Canadian homo-sexual murderer Luka Magnotta, who browsed Facebook for his victims under numerous assumed names. After luring a Chinese student to his apartment, Magnotta posted a video of himself murdering, mutilating, and dismembering his victim's body on YouTube.

Although Magnotta's psychotic acts were an exception (so far), they emphasize the uncritical use of communications technology and the seduction of narcissistic celebrity linked to it. At the same time, they typify other irrational acts that result from "malignant boredom," which many academics and psychologists have drawn our attention to since the late 1960s. It reinforces a view that the digital economy is based very largely on relieving a mental dysfunction caused by anxiety and bore-dom in the affluent and narcissistic consumer society in the West. It was first pinpointed by Professor Ludwig von Bertalanffy in his landmark lecture at Clark University in 1966 on "new forms of mental disorder diagnosed as existential disease, malignant boredom, suicidal retire-ment neurosis and the like – in fact, all symptoms of a sick society."[5] What made Silicon Valley so successful and influential was its rec-ognition of social changes as they unfolded, in that it reacted to the chronic boredom of mindless youth in a self-centered consumer society with an array of credit facilities, not only in the West, but wherever a smartphone camera or webcam is within reach for a "selfie."

Gregory Mitchell paraphrased Bertalanffy's General System Theory as a brief overview of its contribution to psychiatric theory and practice, as follows:

"World War II – a period of extreme physiological tension and psychological stress – did not produce an increase in neurotic disorders, apart from direct shock effects such as combat neurosis. In contrast, 'the affluent society' produced an unprecedented number of mentally ill. The superficial reduction of tension and the immediate gratification of instinct (living according to the Pleasure Principle unmediated by a developed Ego) gave rise to novel forms of mental disorder; for example, 'existential' neurosis. This form of mental dysfunction originates not from repressed drives, unfulfilled survival needs or from imposed stress, but from an inner conflict: the meaningless of life caused by a suppression of self-actualization. There is a suspicion that the recent increase in schizophrenia may be caused by the 'other-directedness' of Man in modern society. A new type of juvenile delinquency has appeared: crime that is committed, not for want or need, but 'for the fun of it', born from the emptiness of their lives."

That is not an isolated case. There are also the irrational and violent acts of antisocial groups who frequently make headlines in the news media as a consequence of their collective delusions. They include terrorists, and gullible and rebellious teenagers who identify with them, white supremacists, and others with misplaced identities that become lost to the Internet, where they share their imagined grievances with like-minded individuals and plan revenge on a society that excludes them.

A significant factor they nearly all share is that they are unemployed and have plenty of time to turn their delusions into reality, with the help of digital devices that provide them with timely information, funding, arms, new recruits, and global communications to spread their discontent and hatred. Of course, it could be said that the Internet merely mirrors our society. But it also reveals how fine the imperceptible line is, which separates the violent wish-fulfillment fantasies that typify electronic games from the real world.

Our Automated Future

Since mass unemployment from automation may end up by making consumers obsolete, the question that constantly hovers over us is: "Who will be able afford to buy manufactured goods, consumer durables like self-driving automobiles—or even rent them—or continue to keep our financial institutions in business?" Even the multibillionaires (who are often the cause for complaint) represent only a tiny luxury niche market of 1 percent. What will happen to the once comfortably off middle classes and the billions who aspired to reach their level of financial security?

The unintended consequences of new digital equipment became obvious as soon as Japan led the world in robotically automated factories that required few, if any, human beings in the 1980s. Massive unemployment followed, with the corollary that an even larger number of consumers would be unable to buy goods and services, because they are the jobless masses. Their families lose their buying power too. And a whole town can suffer when an entire plant is shut down.

Statistics reveal that productivity shrank in economies all over the world since the global financial crisis in 2007–08. As a result, financial policy makers search for new ways to unleash capital. But on May 13, 2015, economist Klaus Schwab pointed out that it is talent that realizes ideas which make growth possible, not capital.[6] The determining factor in an automated future is "the existence of a skilled workforce." That may seem paradoxical, particularly as he went on to say that "almost half of today's professions could be automatable by 2025."

For the past eight years we have been searching hopefully but unsuccessfully for clues to the return of normalcy, by checking the quarterly statistics on job growth and the bank rate, and wondering when pensioners could invest their savings with previous returns of 4.5 percent, even up to 8 percent interest from dividends (since about 30 percent of personal bankruptcies occur from that socioeconomic group). But there are no realistic glimpses of that return in the foreseeable future. Instead, we are stuck with a bank rate of 0.5 percent and no hope of good news. Global unemployment has already reached 212 million.[7] Another 42 million new jobs will need to be created annually for the world's economy to provide employment for the growing number of new entrants into the labor market.

Part of the paradox is that 36 percent of employers worldwide reported difficulties in finding talent in 2014 (the highest percentage in seven years). But even if those vacancies could be filled, how long would the jobs last in the face of growing automation? Although most of today's major social and political problems stem from unemployment, the root of the problem—according to Schwab—is the profound disruptions from mobiles, the Internet, cloud technology, 3D printing, advanced materials, and new energy supplies.[8]

Digital technology has opened up a Pandora's box and released an enormous variety of apparently insoluble new problems, from which hope seems to be missing.[9]

Although the use of mobiles is now more or less evenly spread across all age groups, it is teenagers who incessantly use them far more than anyone else, and that generation will influence the future. Escaping online to engage with their friends and others, and through all sorts of apps which welcome them in to fantasy lands, provides an artificial paradise which they cannot believe will ever change. The excitement of their virtual lives with its alter egos and avatars is a wonderful new discovery for them, and it comes at a time when they are searching for their own identity. But, like all new technologies, digital devices come at a cost to society. The quest for a meaningful identity has been made even more complex than before, by being drawn (with an instant click) into more options than they know what to do with, since most are unrealistic. The main problem is whether they can distinguish between illusions and reality, and get on with their *real* lives.

It has left this generation and the next ones to struggle with the discouraging job of desperately trying to cram back into the box as many of the ills that escaped from Pandora's box as they can. That dilemma results not only from the artificial fantasies conjured up by Silicon Valley but also the flaws in the impulsive and acquisitive human condition.

Robots and Human Lives

A larger and larger part of that fantasy involves the huge online pornography industry. Much of it features "hate sex" that shows women as sex objects born to be victims of violence, and other websites that applaud the sexual abuse of children under the age of fourteen and even infants. On July 29, 2015, the FBI announced on news media that "the level of pedophilia in the United States is unprecedented." It has become an epidemic. And crimes involving human sex traffic are rife.

This book is not long enough to describe all the ways that life is being cheapened by the Internet and social media or abused so that multimillion dollar industries can make bigger profits. But two other industries are featured in these final paragraphs to describe the failure of the digital revolution, which already harm society by taking away people's identities and their purpose in life through deliberate unemployment or disposing of them in other ways. One example is using robots in the auto-making industry for over three decades, which has resulted in the extinction of blue-collar workers as we knew them, when they worked their way into the middle classes and helped to create national prosperity.

The erroneous concept that robots are more perfect than human beings may have started in that industry where they have now found to their cost that robots are flawed. As a consequence, they have had to keep other robots in reserve for when the main ones break down. Meanwhile, continual recalls of millions of automobiles each year due to faulty components and accessories cost them far more than in the more skillful human engineering days of W. Edwards Deming. Deming was the total quality management expert of the 1950s and 1960s, who insisted that zero tolerance in products flowing from assembly lines was a reasonable expectation of any factory manager worth the title. Factory recalls in such huge numbers only began after robots were installed as both workers and managers of plants.

What Western manufacturers failed to understand when they slavishly copied Japanese robotics was that Japan has an entirely different economic and cultural objective that requires robots to compensate for its aging population and falling birthrate. On January 1, 2015, BBC News Online reported that Japan's 2014 birthrate fell to record lows for the fourth consecutive year. It is estimated that they will lose another thirty million newborns by 2050. That means lower potential economic growth, endangering their pension system. And the number of reproductive women is declining. Those sixty-five and over are expected to reach 40 percent of the population in 2060. In order not to dilute its culture, Japan chose a robotic labor force rather than encourage immigration as the West has done.

Robotic Keyhole Surgery

The final example is robotic keyhole surgery. On July 27, 2015, BBC News Online announced that there were 144 deaths of patients and 1,399 injuries due to robots used by the medical profession in the United States in the past fourteen years. "The events included broken instruments falling into patients' bodies, electrical sparks causing tissue burns and systems errors making surgery take longer than planned."

What attracted hospitals to robotic keyhole surgery is that it was supposed to get patients out of the hospital faster and reduce overhead costs. And the marketing feature of robotics appears to drum up more patients for the medical profession. As for the surgeon, sitting in front of a computer screen is far more comfortable than the stress of operating by hand. It begs the question of whether operations in future will be undertaken by lower-paid technicians rather than more expensive qualified surgeons—since the major attraction of artificial intelligence is cheap labor. But what about the patients?

"Is it time to curb the robot enthusiasm?" asked the Associated Press on April 10, 2013. "Some doctors say yes, concerned that the 'wow' factor and heavy marketing are behind the boost in use. They argue that there is not enough robust research showing that robotic surgery is at least as good or better than conventional surgeries." It stated that "the high-tech robot is being used in surgeries for prostates, gall bladders and wombs, but reports of problems have emerged, ranging from sliced blood vessels to patients being hit in the face." In one operation a robot "refused to let go of tissue grasped during surgery."

Keyhole surgery was stopped at both Maidstone and Tunbridge Wells hospitals in the United Kingdom in 2014 after five patients died of avoidable complications. The decision will be a permanent one said MailOnline on March 10, 2015. They were throat and stomach cancer patients. Their families are suing the local hospital trust. Dr. Martin Makary of John Hopkins authored a paper that says, "The rapid adoption of robotic surgery . . . has been done by and large without the proper evaluation."

The report that featured those cases of patients' injuries and deaths was prepared by researchers at the University of Illinois at Urbana-Champaign, the Massachusetts Institute of Technology, and Chicago's Rush University Medical Center, which took good care to reveal that, although there were 8,061 device malfunctions, they were recorded out of a total of more than 1.7 million robotic procedures carried out between January 2000 and December 2013.

Considering Deming's insistence on the reasonableness of zero failures in manufacturing consumer and industrial goods with proper quality controls, the number of human lives shrugged off by the medical profession in its pursuit for bigger profits reflects the trend in using artificial intelligence to replace the thoughts, judgments, and skills of human beings in the relentless drive to reduce costs by any means, regardless of inconvenience to society.

Acknowledgments

To authors Napoleon Hill, Norman Vincent Peale, and Dale Carnegie, and their publishers, Knopf and Simon & Schuster, for extracts from their motivational best sellers: *Steve Jobs* biography by Walter Isaacson (Simon & Schuster, New York, 2011); *Bond Salesmanship* by William W. Townsend (Henry Holt, New York, 1924); *Confessions of an Advertising Man* by David Ogilvy (Atheneum, 1963); *Reality in Advertising* by Rosser Reeves (Knopf, 1961); *How To Write Advertising That Sells* by Clyde Bedell (McGraw-Hill, New York, 1940); *On Human Nature* by Edward O. Wilson (Harvard University Press, 1978); *The Competitive Advantage of Nations* by Michael E. Porter (Free Press, New York, 1990).

About the Author

This is John Harte's second published book on leadership, management, marketing, advertising, and entrepreneurship. *Management Crisis and Business Revolution* was published in hardcover in the United States first in 1997 and in a second paperback edition in April 2014 by Transaction Publishers. Since then, electronic technologies, the Internet, social media, and mobiles have created a new make-believe world after a digital revolution, which the author addresses in this new book. But not every innovation is good, and John Harte describes how this one has failed.

The author was originally an investigative journalist in London, England, before switching his career to advertising, marketing, and management. Working with the biggest global advertising agency, J. Walter Thompson, he was responsible for servicing their major clients, the Unilever Group of Companies. Advising some of the most sophisticated marketing managers as his clients resulted in top management positions that included advising over thirty presidents of leading companies and being appointed as managing director. As an independent management consultant, he also investigated the problems of a biggest shoe conglomerate, to advise them on a restructuring program. He became marketing vice president for General Electric when it was the top global brand and was also vice president of marketing for several property developers in Canada, where he was formerly director general of the Canadian Institute of Marketing.

All of this enabled him to provide deep and practical insights in this second book, which is about why the digital revolution failed, as well as describing the major ingredients that national and global market leaders used to achieve success before the disruptions to the global economy that still plague us.

Notes

1. Introduction

1. Leonard Silk, *The Economists* (Avon Hearst, 1976).
2. H. G. Wells, *The Shape of Things to Come* (Hutchinson, 1933) Futuristic science fiction story of a modern world dictatorship that controls everyone. Wells took his story to 2016.
3. English mathematician and philosopher A. N. Whitehead, *Religion in the Making* (1926).
4. Peter Drucker, *The Practice of Management* (Harper, 1954).
5. W. Edwards Deming, *Out of the Crisis* (Cambridge, MA: MIT Press, 1986).
6. Mathematical genius John von Neumann developed the first modern computer in the late 1940s and demonstrated that machines could perform logical operations.
7. John Harte, *Management Crisis & Business Revolution* (Transaction, 1997), 391.
8. OECD report, October 2013.
9. Telegraph.co.uk, October 8, 2013.
10. *The Washington Post* referring to findings by the Organization for Economic Cooperation and Development (OECD) October 8, 2013.
11. Source: Canadian Education Association, 2008/9.
12. Marshall McLuhan, *Renaissance for a Wired World*, Vol.3 (GoogleBooks).
13. When interviewed on *The Agenda* TV talk-show, January 21, 2014.
14. Leon Lederman and Christopher Hill, *Beyond the God Particle* (Prometheus, 2013).
15. eMarketer, 2013.
16. Chris Hedges, *Empire of Illusion – The End of Literacy and the Triumph of Spectacle* (Knopf, 2009).

2. Taking Stock: A Reality Check

1. That is only part of the story for primary resource economies, like Canada for example, that have still not learnt how to add value to raw materials and market the finished product successfully. Instead, they are focused very largely on exploiting natural resources like Energy, Mining, Forests, Fishing, and Agriculture.
2. U.S. Department of State.
3. Source: Industry Canada, August 2013.
4. OECD Globalization Study, 1993.
5. Japan Small Business Research Institute.

293

6. Centre for Small and Medium-sized Enterprises, University of Warwick.
7. National rankings in the final chapter (Chapter 17) show the ratio of workers employed in the manufacturing sector of a number of different economies. It tells us a story not yet fully analyzed or explained since the start of the industrial revolution and the full effects of recent deindustrialization.
8. Management Ranking in the World Competitiveness Report.
9. Source: Nicholas Lardy. Peterson Institute, Washington, January 2014.
10. John Kay, *Why Firms Succeed* (Oxford University Press, 1995), vi.
11. By *Business Age.*

3. Untapped Potential

1. Frank Stronach, *The Magna Man* (HarperCollins, 2012).
2. *The Guardian*, London. Tuesday 15 March 2011 21.06 GMT.
3. Jibtv.com

4. Strategic Management

1. For more details read Harte, *Management Crisis*, 61. Ibid.
2. Harvard Business Review (Boston, 1960).
3. Karl Popper, *The Open Society and its Enemies* (Princeton, NJ: Princeton University Press, 1962).
4. The Global Competitiveness Report (1996).
5. William W. Townsend (Henry Holt, 1924).
6. Dale Carnegie (Simon & Schuster, 1936).
7. Napoleon Hill (Random House, 1937).
8. Norman Vincent Peale (Simon & Schuster, 1952).
9. Clyde Bedell, *How To Write Advertising that Sells* (McGraw-Hill, 1940). Rosser Reeves, *Reality in Advertising* (Knopf, 1961). David Ogilvy, *Confessions of an Advertising Man* (Atheneum, 1963).

5. Integrated Marketing and Its Enemies

1. Harte, *Management Crisis*, 63.
2. Believed to be attributed to Samuel Pepys, but not absolutely pinned down.
3. Charles St. Thomas, ed., *Modern Marketing Thought* (London: Macmillan, 1964).
4. First Canadian Edition by Nicolas Papadopoulos, William Zikmund, and Michael d'Amico (Wiley, 1988). US edition, 1984/6. Study Guide by Ray MacKinnon Cuthbert (Algonquin College, Ottawa) and Jim Grimm (Illinois State University).
5. Richard N. Foster, *Innovation: The Attacker's Advantage* (Summit, 1986).
6. James M. Utterback, *Mastering the Dynamics of Innovation* (Harvard Business School, 1994).
7. Harte, *Management Crisis*, 126.
8. Joseph A. Schumpeter, *The Theory of Economic Development* (Transaction, 1983).
9. James M. Utterback, *Mastering the Dynamic of Innovation.* Ibid., 231.
10. The Unilever Group of Companies were an example of this as late as 1968.
11. The author was awarded the Order of the British Empire for his services to literature in 1995.

12. A dramatic example of this was the disastrous crash of Britain's experimental airship R.101 in 1930, detailed by Nevil Shute, *Slide Rule* (London: Heinemann, 1954). The same people had already been responsible for the previous crash of the R.38 and "ought to have been in gaol for manslaughter," according to Shute, who worked as an engineer on the R.100. Most of them were killed in the R.101.
13. May 26, 2010.
14. Rescue Time data.
15. Panel on *The Agenda* TV talk-show January 20, 2014.
16. Jane Austin, *Pride and Prejudice* (1813): 20 million copies sold to date. Elizabeth Gaskell, *Mary Barton* (1848); *North and South* (1855).
17. The author discovered them in several warehouses on joining GE as Vice-President of Marketing in 1981.
18. Ruth Benedict, *The Chrysanthemum and the Sword* (Routledge & Kegan Paul, 1967).
19. Michael E. Porter, *The Competitive Advantage of Nations* (New York: Free Press, 1990), 237.
20. nytimes.com
21. Insurescars.com, July 2011.
22. Cairncross (1982) and Lever (1991).
23. January 19, 2013.
24. John Maynard Keynes, *The General Theory of Employment, Interest and Money* (Macmillan, Cambridge University Press, 1973).
25. Education Scotland, 2013.

6. Managing, Leadership, and Entrepreneurship

1. Those six leadership styles are elaborated on in my previous book; Harte, *Management Crisis*. Ibid.
2. Henry Mintzberg, *Mintzberg on Management* (New York: Free Press, 1989).
3. Robert McNamara.
4. Charles Hession, *John Maynard Keynes* (New York: Macmillan, 1984).
5. Mount Sinai School of Medicine. On *The Agenda*, TV talk-show, January 21, 2014.
6. Described more fully in Harte, *Management Crisis*. Ibid., 352–3.
7. Arthur Koestler, *The Sleepwalkers* (London: Hutchinson, 1959).
8. Christia Freeland, *Plutocrats* (Doubleday, 2012).
9. Jacob Bronowski, *The Ascent of Man* (Boston, MA: Little, Brown, 1975), 34–35.
10. Dr. Norman Doidge, *The Brain that Changes Itself* (Viking, 2007), 213.
11. Dr. Shelley E. Taylor and her research team. *Psychological Review, 2000.*
12. John W. Santrock and John O. Miterer, *Psychology* (McGraw-Hill, 2006).
13. *The Economist.*
14. Walter Isaacson, *Steve Jobs* (Simon & Schuster, 2011).
15. Ibid.
16. Sir Michael Perry.
17. Ross Perot.
18. Anthropologist Robin Fox. Professor at Rutgers University, NJ.
19. Quincy Wright, *A Study of War* (University of Chicago Press, 1942), 42.

20. Edwards de Bono, *Six Thinking Hats* (Little, Brown, 1985). Psychologist Edward de Bono was a business consultant for IBM, Exxon, DuPont, Prudential, Proctor & Gamble, General Foods, Shell, BP, Monsanto and Ford.
21. Robert Heller, *The Naked Manager* (London: Hodder, 1974).
22. Source: London Business School.
23. Thomas Mann's first novel, published 1901 and continually reprinted.
24. Harold Bloom, *Where Shall Wisdom be Found?* (Riverhead Books, 2005). Ibid.
25. Joseph Schumpeter's theory of creative destruction.
26. John Rothschild (Beard Books, 2000).
27. See note 76 above.

7. Advertising and Communications

1. Heller, *Naked Manager*.
2. Acquired in 2000 by Publis Group. Now based in New York with 140 branches in 76 countries and a staff of 6,500.
3. Denis Healey.
4. Advertising news and online website at campaignlive.co.uk.
5. With acknowledgments to author Cameron Chapman who wrote a more detailed and elaborate history and sixrevisions.com who published it on their website.
6. By Ray Tomlinson.
7. By Michael Hart.
8. By John Vittal at University of Southern California.
9. By Dennis Hayes & Dale Heatherington.
10. Source: Strategy Analytics.
11. Michael Lewis, *Next* (New York: Norton, 2001), 178.
12. Source: Strategy Analytics, 2015.
13. Source: Statista.com
14. Com Score, September 2013.
15. Huffpost Alberta, June 23, 2015.
16. Source: Nielsen Cross Platform Report. Q1 2014.
17. Source: Pew Research, April 2015.
18. International research company (September 13, 2013).
19. Source: *Business Insider.*
20. Source: Pew Research Center, 2015.
21. Interactive Advertising Bureau; IAB, June 2015
22. IAB, 2015.
23. Catalyst 2015.
24. Nielsen, Q3 2014.
25. Ibid.
26. *Variety*, January, 2015.
27. A concept popularised in the 20th century by American sociologist Robert K. Merton.
28. Study by Dana Beth Weinberg. PhD in Sociology from Harvard University and Assistant Professor of Sociology at Queens College. Author of numerous articles and books advertised on amazon.com. Study published online December 4, 2013.
29. Debut novel by E.L. James (Random House/Vintage, 2011). Genre: erotic romance.

30. Walter Pater. Conclusion to *The Renaissance: Studies in Art and Poetry* (1868).
31. Michaael Korda, *Another Life* (Random House, 1999).
32. Harold Bloom, *The Anatomy of Influence* (Yale University Press, 2011), 31.
33. The Codex Group, March 2014.
34. Association of American Publishers and the Book Industry Study Group.
35. International Data Corporation.
36. Walter Pater: 19th century British essayist, art and literary critic. Bloom, *Anatomy of Influence*, 21.
37. Chris Rajek, *Celebrity* (London: Reaction Books, 2001).
38. F. Scott Fitzgerald. (Scribner, April 1925).
39. Chris Hedges. Ibid.
40. Daniel J. Solove, *The Future of Reputation* (Yale University Press, 2008). Ibid., 35.
41. Frank Vosper, *Love from a Stranger* (Samuel French, 1937).
42. Solove, Future *of Reputation*. Ibid., 192.
43. Vance Packard, *The Hidden Persuaders* (Simon & Schuster, 1957).

8. How Words Sell Billions of Goods and Services

1. Unfortunately obliged to stop producing their own film commercials by the trade union.
2. Like the popular Pinterest.
3. See note 33 above.
4. Elmer Wheeler, *Tested Sentences that Sell* (1937) (Upper Saddle River, NJ: Prentice-Hall, 1947).
5. Ogilvy, *Confessions*. Ibid.
6. The Leo Burnett Agency.
7. Nielsen Media Research.
8. Ogilvy, *Confessions*.
9. Reeves, *Reality in Advertising*.

9. Pictures That Sell Goods and Services

1. CNBC, 20 December 2013.
2. McGraw-Hill, NY 1940.
3. Test undertaken by the author for Hermesetas.
4. Ogilvy, *Confessions*. Ibid.
5. Reeves, *Reality in Advertising*. Ibid.
6. Afamal was the biggest ad agency in Africa; subsequently bought out by McCann in 2012.
7. Source: eMarketer, 2014.
8. Source: Strategy Analytics, 2015.

10. The Value of Branding and Marketing

1. Source: Millward Brown BrandZ, June 2015.
2. *Printer's Ink*. First national American trade magazine for advertising. Founded 1888 by George P. Rowell. Renamed *Marketing Communications*, it ceased publication in 1972.
3. Oscar Wilde, *The Picture of Dorian Gray* (Dover, 1993).
4. Alan Greenspan, *The Map and the Territory* (Allen Lane, 2013).

5.   *Reader's Digest,* 2015.
6.   Environic Research group's methodology was validated by Professor Ken Wong (Distinguished Professor of Marketing at Queen's School of Business) and Frank Pons, Marketing Professor at Laval University in Québec.
7.   When Labour Prime Minister Lloyd George asked him how he could spread the wealth more evenly in England, Pareto told him to forget about politics and accept the economic fact that it would always return to the 80/20 formula.
8.   Sir Colin Marshall, 1995. Also Chairman of Invensys plc. and of Inchcap plc.
9.   *The Independent.*
10. World Competitiveness Report from the Economic Forum, Switzerland.
11. The author of this book was the marketing consultant hired to diagnose the problems and propose a solution for restructuring the company.
12. As described to the author of this book.
13. "Marketing would authorize production planning, phasing, and inventory control, sales, distribution, and servicing." The real situation was encountered personally by the author when making contact with GE's marketing department in Johannesburg on behalf of his clients at that time (Unilever's laundry detergent products group) when the extraordinarily talented marketing team at GE had just been fired.
14. *Library Journal,* August 1, 2013.
15. November 2014.

11. Removing Uncertainty and Ambiguity

1.   As at the end of 2012.
2.   *The Guardian,* May 20, 2015.
3.   Waitrose is owned by the John Lewis Partnership.
4.   *Boardroom* magazine, South Africa, 1991.
5.   Except for the author of this book.
6.   Quality Circles are volunteers who use systems and procedures and can provide feedback about better ways and means of doing things.
7.   Statistics for 3M, Johnson and Borden sourced from *Printers Ink.* Ibid.
8.   Doidge, *The Brain.* Ibid., 289.

12. Creative Thinking and Reasoning

1.   Thagard Paul, *The Stanford Encyclopedia of Philosophy* (2008 Edition). Edward N. Zalta (ed).
2.   Benjafield, 2004; Mills, 1998.
3.   B.F. Skinner, *The Behavior of Organisms* (1936).
4.   See note 76 above.
5.   Reed, 2004; Gardner, 1985.
6.   Solso, Macklin, and Macklin, 2005; Steinberg, 2003a; Spellman and Willingham, 2004.
7.   Santrock and Miterer, *Psychology,* 348–9. Ibid.
8.   Russell and Norvig, 2003.
9.   Hirstein and others, 2006.
10. Santrock and Miterer, *Psychology.* Ibid.
11. Goel, 2005a; Houghton, 2005.
12. Kolb, Gibb, and Robinson, 2003.
13. Wilson, 2003.

14. Blair, 2002; Greenough, 2000.
15. Kolb and Whishaw, 2005.
16. Harrington, 2006.
17. Kalat, 2004.
18. Kolb, Gibb, and Robinson, 2003; Neville, 2005.
19. Santrock and Miterer, *Psychology*. Ibid.
20. Russell and Norveg, 2003.
21. Fauconnier and Turnev, 2002.
22. Santrock and Miterer, *Psychology*. Ibid., 349.
23. Russell and Norvig, 2003; Simon, 2001.
24. Houghton, 2005; Hatzakis and Tsoukas, 2002.
25. Steve Paikin, anchor for *The Agenda*. (TVO, January 20, 2014).
26. With acknowledgment to the *Agenda* talk-show panel on January 20, 2014.
27. Two separate questions merged, from anchorman Steve Paikin on his TV program *The Agenda*.
28. A subject explored in the final chapter.
29. January 23 panel on *The Agenda* TV talk-show including Dr. David Perlmutter, and John Ratey of Harvard Medical School.
30. Woo-Kyoung and others, 2005; Askley and Maddox, 2005.
31. Medin, Profitt, and Schwartz, 2000; Burnett and others, 2005.
32. Santrock and Miterer, *Psychology*. Ibid., 352.
33. Ibid.
34. 1973; 2002.
35. Minda and Smith, 2001; Burnett and others, 2005.
36. Rogers and others, 2000.
37. Ashby and Maddox, 2005.
38. Aizenstein and others, 2000.
39. Stanovich, 1999, 2004.
40. Richard Sorrentino. University of Western Ontario, Canada.
41. Santrock and Miterer, *Psychology*. Ibid., 554–5. Lovett, 2002.
42. Neil Postman, *Amusing Ourselves to Death* (New York: Penguin, 1983).
43. Thomas Healy, *The Great Dissent* (Henry Holt, 2013).
44. Kay, *Why Firms Succeed*. Ibid., 29.
45. Lovett, 2002.
46. Starz-Fantino and Fantino, 2005; Oaksford, Roberts, and Chater, 2002.
47. Sorrentino and Roney, 2000; Hall, 2002.
48. Snook, Canter, and Bennell, 2002; Stanovich and West, 2000; Todd and Gigerenzer, 2001.
49. Bereiter, 2002.
50. Yale University Press, 1958.
51. Bronowski, *Ascent of Man*. Ibid., 432.
52. John von Neumann with Oskar Morganstern, *Theory of Games and Economic Behavior* (Princeton University, 1944).
53. *The War of the Worlds* in 1898.
54. As he informed British Prime Minister Lloyd George.

13. Motivation and Its Antithesis

1. German and Barrett, 2005.
2. Mai and others, 2004.

3. 1996 and 2004.
4. Barron and Havachiewicz, 2001.
5. Ericsson, 2005.
6. Abernethy and others, 2001; Wenke, Frensch, and Funke, 2005.
7. Kellog and others, 2005.
8. Chase and Simon, 1973; Hambrick and Oswald, 2005.
9. Ericsson, 2005.
10. HarperCollins, 1997.
11. Bruce Meyer, *The Golden Thread* (HarperCollins, 2000).
12. Miguel de Cervantes, *Don Quixote* (HarperCollins, 2003). Translation by Edith Grossman. Ch. 33–35: "The Man Who Was Recklessly Curious."
13. "What is the true object of Don Quixote's quest?" asks literary critic Harold Bloom rhetorically in his introduction. "I find that unanswerable."
14. Samuel Johnson, *Rasselas, Prince of Abyssinia.*
15. UN Labor Agency, January 2014.
16. World Economic Forum.
17. Source: The 2015 World Competitiveness Report.
18. Dan Diamond. *Forbes* magazine, May, 2013.
19. Susan Cain, *Quiet: The Power of Introverts in a World that Can't Stop Talking* (Penguin Random House, 2012).
20. "Long-winded talk with no real substance."
21. Santrock and Miterer, *Psychology.* Ibid., 359.
22. Halpern, 2002; Kamin and others, 2001.
23. Howe, 2004.
24. Santrock and Miterer, *Psychology.* Ibid.
25. Langer, Harvard University, 1989, 1997, 2000; Grant and others, 2004.
26. Malcolm Gladwell, *Blink* (Little, Brown, 2005).
27. Slife and Yanchar, 2000.
28. Hunt, 2002; Markham and Gentner, 2001.
29. Ripps, 2002.
30. Coley and others, 2005; Bisanz, Bisanz, and Karpan, 1994.
31. Johnson-Lairch, 2000.
32. Montgomery, Lipshitz, and Brehmer, 2005; Galotti; 2002.
33. Gigerenzer and Selton, 2001; Tversky and Fox, 1995.
34. Matlin, 2004.
35. Hastie and dawes, 2001.
36. Betsch and others, 2001; Fugelsang and others, 2004.
37. Kahneman and Tvesky, 1995.
38. Guilbaut and others, 2004; Bonds-Raacke and others, 2001.
39. McKelvie and Drumheller, 2001.
40. Nickerson, 2004.
41. Santrock and Miterer, *Psychology.* Ibid.
42. Cohen and Swerdlik, 2005.
43. Reed, Vernon and Johnson, 2004; Vernon, 2000.
44. In comparison there is Thurston's multiple factor theory, that intelligence consists of seven primary mental abilities; verbal comprehension, number ability, word fluency, spatial visualization, associative memory, reasoning, and perceptual speed.

45. Dr. Norman Doidge. Ibid.
46. Dr. Norman Doidge. Ibid., 288.
47. Dr. Norman Doidge quoting neuroscientist Merz. Ibid., 47.
48. Alex Pentland, *Social Physics* (Penguin, 2014), viii.
49. Goleman, Kaufman, and Ray, 1993.
50. Gardner and Tremblay, 1995; R. C. Beck, 2004.
51. Zimmerman and Campilo, 2003.
52. Schleicher and Gilbert, 2005.
53. Published by The American Psychiatric Association.
54. Santrock and Miterer, *Psychology.* Ibid., 492.
55. McGrace and Terracciano, 2005; Widiger, Costa, and McCrae, 2002.
56. Paunonen and others, 1992, 2003; Paunonen and Ashton, 1998.
57. OCEAN refers to the following attributes: *Openness* encompasses Imaginative or practical; and Interested in variety or routine; as well as Independent or conforming. *Conscientiousness* encompasses Organized or disorganized; Careful or careless; Disciplined or impulsive. *Extraversion* covers Sociable or retiring; Fun-loving or somber; Affectionate or reserved. *Agreeableness* encompasses Soft-hearted or ruthless; Trusting or suspicious; helpful or uncooperative. *Neuroticism/emotional stability* encompasses Calm or anxious; Secure or insecure; Self-satisfied or self-pitying.
58. For more on motivation; Harte, *Management Crisis* , 6; 195–218; 107; 332–4.

14. Influencing Sales and Perpetrating Frauds

1. Jordan Belfort (Random House, 2007).
2. Frank Partnoy. *F.I.A.S.C.O.* (Norton, 1997).
3. Jordan Belfort. *The Wolf of Wall Street.* Ibid., 54.
4. Ibid., 99.
5. Benjamin Graham, *The Intelligent Investor* (Harper, 1949)
6. Chris Hedges. Ibid.
7. Frank Partnoy, *F.I.A.S.C.O. Blood on the Water on Wall Street.* (Norton, 2009).
8. See note 148 above.
9. U.S. Census Bureau News, May 15, 2015.
10. eMarketer, Feb., 2014.
11. Statista, 2014.
12. Atista, 2015.
13. H. G. Wells, *The History of Mr. Polly* (CreateSpace, 2014).
14. Source: *DSM IV.*
15. Ibid.
16. Michael Lewis, *The Big Short* (New York: Norton, 2010), 254.
17. Ibid., 256.
18. Lewis, *Next*, 13–14.
19. Neilsen's 2015 Global Digital Landscape Report.
20. Santrock and Miterer, *Psychology.* Ibid., 306.
21. Pomplum, Reingold, and Shen, 2001; Cowan, 2005.
22. Karen Arnell, Brock University.
23. Nielsen 2015. Ibid.
24. Lewis, *Next. Ibid.*, 237–41.

15. Selling Is a Psychological Process

1. Napoleon Hill, *Think & Grow Rich* (Random House, 1937).
2. Townsend found exactly the same thing in the 1920s.
3. Santrock and Miterer, *Psychology.* Ibid.
4. Sociobiologist E. O. Wilson.
5. The Alexander Technique.
6. Psychologists Sheryl C. Wilson and Theodore X. Barber.
7. Remarkably, several psychological conditions are more prevalent in the U.S., like ADHD and Multiple Personality Disorder, But evidence why is hard to find.
8. Dr. Norman Doidge speaking on *The Agenda* TV talk-show when interviewed in January 2014. Author of *The Brain That Changes Itself.*
9. Professor John Kay, London Business School.
10. Quotation from John of Salisbury (1159): "Bernard of Chartres used to say that we are like dwarfs on the shoulders of giants, so that we can see more than them, and things at a greater distance . . ."
11. Hill, *Think & Grow Rich.*
12. (New York: Simon & Schuster, 1936).
13. (New York: Simon & Schuster, 1952).
14. Dr. Norman Doidge provides ample evidence in Doidge, *The Brain that Changes Itself.*
15. Source: MLM.
16. Matthew Hart, *Gold* (Toronto: Allen Lane, 2013).
17. Ibid.
18. Réal Bergevin et al., *Call Centers for Dummies* (Wiley, 2010).

16. Knowing and Understanding

1. Thomas Malthus, *An Essay on the Principle of Population* (London: J. Johnson, in St. Paul's Church-yard, 1798).
2. U.S. Census Bureau.
3. Michael Lewis, *Boomerang* (New York: Norton, 2011), 108.
4. Doidge, *The Brain .*
5. Dr. David Perlmutter, *Grain Brain* (Little, Brown, 2013).
6. January 23, 2014.
7. "Physical exercise and learning work in complimentary ways; the first to make new stem cells, the second to prolong their survival."
8. Dr. Norman Doidge.
9. "Relinquish notions that fat is detrimental to health: the brain needs fat of the right type (not hydrogenated)," Dr. David Perlmutter insisted. His book is about the dangers of wheat and carbohydrates.
10. Doidge, *The Brain.* Ibid., 248.
11. Directed by Ronald Neame.
12. Jim Mossman committed suicide while disillusioned and depressed after the political establishment pressured the BBC to fire him because of his confrontational interviewing style. It was calculated to oblige politicians to admit to their idleness and incompetence and hold them to account. They didn't like it. He was the forerunner of a candid interviewing style adopted soon after his death.

13. Porter, *The Competitive Advantage of Nations.*
14. Bronowski, *The Ascent of Man.*
15. OECD report, 2013.
16. Bloom, *Anatomy of Influence*, 4.
17. Gustave Le Bon, *The Psychology of Revolution* (Dover, 2004).
18. George W. Terry, *Principles of Management* (R. D. Irwin, 1982).
19. Harte, Man*agement Crisis.* Ibid., 351–3.
20. Dean Keith Simonton, *Scientific Genius: A Psychology of Science* (Cambridge University Press, 2009), 28.
21. Marshall McLuhan, *The Gutenberg Galaxy* (Toronto: Toronto University Press, 1960).
22. Harold Bloom, *Genius* (Warner, 2002).
23. Collins English Dictionary.
24. Alfred Russel Wallace wrote his revolutionary essay which describes his discovery of the origin of species through natural selection, after an attack of malaria stirred up memories, concepts and ideas in his brain. They developed into his famous theory, "On the Tendency of Varieties to Depart Indefinitely from the Original Type." Rebecca Stott, *Darwin's Ghosts* (Random House, 2012).

17. Facts and Figures

1. Porter, *The Competitive Advantage of Nations.* Ibid.
2. Source: Abbreviated and paraphrased from the World Economic Forum (WEF) Report, 2015.
3. The Huffington Post, April 5, 2013.
4. A SaaS provider.
5. Summit on Pornography.
6. Source: ComScore Media Matrix.
7. theweek.com
8. *The Week.com* Sarah Eberspacher. January 11, 2014.
9. Doidge, *The Brain.* Ibid.

18. The Law of Unintended Consequences

1. 2.5 million years from the beginning of the Pleistocene Age.
2. Not only Grey Jays, but also Western Scrub Jays and other birds like Ravens and Crows.
3. Digital Curation.
4. Tristram Hunt, *Marx's General* (New York: Picador, 2009).
5. www.mind-development.eu/systemps.html 2005-2015.
6. Executive Chairman of the World Economic Forum.
7. International Labor Organization, 2015.
8. Source: The World Economic Forum, 2015.
9. The Ancient Greek myth is about the unintended consequences of reckless curiosity. According to the Greek story-tellers who sought to explain why evils were scattered all over the world, Pandora was the first woman. She was given a box as a gift by the god Zeus and told not to open it. But curiosity won over caution and she had to see what was inside. When she opened the lid, all the evils escaped and entered the world. All that Zeus left in the box was an ingredient called Hope, which prevents us from giving up in despair.

Index

305